Social Media and Genre Studies

Social Media and Genre Studies

An Investigation of Facebook and Twitter Higher Education Web Pages

Thomas Kenny

LEXINGTON BOOKS
Lanham • Boulder • New York • London

Published by Lexington Books
An imprint of The Rowman & Littlefield Publishing Group, Inc.
4501 Forbes Boulevard, Suite 200, Lanham, Maryland 20706
www.rowman.com

86-90 Paul Street, London EC2A 4NE, United Kingdom

British Library Cataloguing in Publication Information Available

Library of Congress Cataloging-in-Publication Data

Names: Kenny, Thomas, 1983- author.
Title: Social media and genre studies : an investigation of Facebook and Twitter higher education web pages / Thomas Kenny. Description: Lanham, Maryland : Lexington Books, [2023] | Includes bibliographical references and index. | Summary: "This book investigates whether Facebook and Twitter have become a genre, particularly for higher education institutions. The author examines the purpose, form, and functionality of higher education's institutional web pages on these platforms through a combination of content analysis and interviews"— Provided by publisher.
Identifiers: LCCN 2023002600 (print) | LCCN 2023002601 (ebook) | ISBN 9781666907353 (cloth) | ISBN 9781666907360 (epub)
Subjects: LCSH: Social media in higher education. | Online social networks—Educational applications. | Education, Higher—Effect of technological innovations on. | Mass media genres. | Facebook (Firm) | Twitter (Firm)
Classification: LCC LB2395.7 .K46 2023 (print) | LCC LB2395.7 (ebook) | DDC 378.1/7344678—dc23/eng/20230301
LC record available at https://lccn.loc.gov/2023002600
LC ebook record available at https://lccn.loc.gov/2023002601

♾™ The paper used in this publication meets the minimum requirements of American National Standard for Information Sciences—Permanence of Paper for Printed Library Materials, ANSI/NISO Z39.48-1992.

To my wife Holly, I dedicate this book to you for all the love and patience you gave while I was writing my dissertation. Your support enabled me to accomplish such an important career goal. You always listened and your inspiring words motivated me to complete the research.

Contents

Acknowledgments

I would like to thank my Long Island University dissertation committee for their consistent guidance and feedback that always improved my research. All of you have played an important role toward publishing this book. Thank you, Dr. Greg Hunter and Dr. David Jank, for being mentors at Long Island University. Every class, conversation, and meeting with you taught me something valuable and helped formulate this study. Dr. Brian Cogan, you have been part of my academic journey from the beginning as a teacher, mentor, colleague, and more importantly, friend. I appreciate the time and support you have given me. Thank you, Dr. Jody Howard and Dr. Mandy Zhang, for your generous leadership and advice.

I would like to express gratitude and praise to Jessica Cohen and Taylor Curran for the countless hours they spent reviewing the research with me. The comments and observations you provided were necessary in helping the research evolve. You are both rising stars and I look forward to your future success. I am extraordinarily grateful to my colleagues and students at Molloy University for their support. I am particularly appreciative to Dr. Deidre Pribram, Nicole Savona, and Julia Kraemer for always listening and offering encouragement.

I am extremely thankful to my wife Holly. I appreciate the love and support you have given me to reach all my aspirations. To my sons Nathan and Zachary, I look forward to you realizing all your dreams too! Thank you to my parents, Tom and Sharon, for teaching and preparing me to accomplish any goal. Lastly, special thanks to my sister Meghan. Thank you for challenging me to apply to college. It changed my life. I can't thank you enough for taking the time to teach and demonstrate necessary skills to be successful.

Chapter 1

Introduction

Definition of Genres

Technology can influence and alter the ways in which individuals communicate, interact, and complete daily tasks. Walter Deal in an article noted that technology is a way to become informed and is necessary for people to fulfill their needs.[1] Although Deal explained technology as a tool for individual needs (entertainment, for example), he also mentioned the use of technologies within business organizations and professional industries. An industry where technology and digital media have been greatly impacted is higher education, specifically colleges and universities. Linda Mancillas and Peter Brusoe explained that colleges and universities in the United States have increased and invested in technology over the last 10 years by adding "smart classrooms, collaboratories, online courses, increasing the number and strength of WIFI connections, and creating centers integrating teaching and technology."[2] Students are bringing in a plethora of mobile devices to campuses such as laptops, tablets, and smart phones for classroom use and activities. Authors Mancillas and Brusoe believed that a big factor for increasing technology use in higher education is because most incoming and current students have always lived in a digital world using the internet, media devices, and software. Also, college students are using technology to communicate with faculty, set up academic study groups, discover scholarly resources, and to complete assignments.[3] Faculty are teaching either hybrid (half in person, half online) or fully online courses through learning management systems such as Canvas or Blackboard. Therefore, faculty, staff, and administrators of higher education institutions may have to consider ways in which they can embrace technology inside and outside of the classroom.

One form of technology frequently used by students is social media. Chris Jones and Binhui Shao stated that the "most prominent among current technologies are social networking sites."[4] Jones and Shao expressed that since students are comfortable using technology in many facets of their life, higher education must update and change the way that their employees (faculty and staff) send information and knowledge to students. Examples of social media sites include Facebook, Twitter, Instagram, Snapchat, YouTube, and TikTok. Social media sites can be described as an online community where a group of people come together in a digital environment to discuss shared interests, hobbies, information, and content. What Jones and Shao point out is that students may be using social media as their main form of communication and as learning environments, impacting coursework, recruitment, and retention. Social media platforms are being used to create digital ads that reaches young adults potentially interested in college programs. Also, social media platforms can be used as a learning community. For instance, a faculty member can create a Facebook Group for students to post articles relating to course content, and students may ask assignment questions and engage with their fellow classmates in one environment.

There have been many scholars to identify when a technology has become a genre. According to Nell Duke and Victoria Purcell-Gates, genres are important to investigate because they create and identify patterns. Duke and Purcell-Gates stated, "genres refer to patterns in the way language is used, patterns in the situation in which a text is used and patterns in the features of that text."[5] Technology is not the only format to be specified as a genre. Documents and records can be genres as well. For instance, Stephen Minot famously reviewed classical works including poetry for its characteristics of a genre. JoAnne Yates is a well-known scholar, who has researched business tools as genres including the memo for documentation of work-related and organizational tasks. There are also web or online genres for reviewing the characteristics of a website's home page. Thus, the goal for this book and study is to evaluate whether higher education social media sites are genres. Through using social media in a business setting, particularly higher education, social media platforms have never been investigated as a genre. Furthermore, I hope to bridge this gap to conclude whether social media sites and specific web pages from colleges and universities can be defined as a genre. To do so, first a definition of genre is needed.

CLASSICAL GENRES

In 2015, author Jack Anderson stated that the term "genre" is associated with several disciplines such as humanities, information studies, and social sciences. Marika Lüders, Lin Prøitz, and Terie Rasmussen explained further that a "genre is interdisciplinary, connecting all fields of study."[6] Genres can be explained as the communication between documents, technology, and humans. Genre studies scholar JoAnne Yates defined genre as "a literary term for a generic form or type of discourse."[7] Examples of classical genres are film, poetry, and dramas (theater). Films or movies have specific types that form categories. Movies are distinctly labeled in genres classified by drama, action, comedy, and western, among many others. Films identified in each of these genres follow specific patterns that are accepted by the viewing audience as plot conventions. The viewing audience will be able to watch a movie and quickly identify the genre based on similar features. For example, a horror film will have dark lighting to signify an eerie mood, suspenseful music, supernatural or mysterious elements, a protagonist (hero), antagonist (villain), scare tactics, and possible aggressive or severe imagery.

Stephen Minot detailed the genre of poetry. Minot defined poetry as a verse, "characterized by rhythmical devices, sound devices, stanza, compression of meaning, and individual reflection."[8] Characteristics that identify a poem as a genre include rhythm, which is the flow of words, sound described as listening to the relationship between words to develop figure of speech including repeating consonants and vowels, and image, which means developing similes and metaphors to apply to a poem. Additional characteristics of the genre of a poem include diction, which is in avoiding certain words such as clichés and overused expressions, and free verse, which means writing without a rhythm in mind, but through creativity, patterns, and the length of the poem.

Another classical genre to identify that was also analyzed by Stephen Minot are the attributes of a drama. Drama is defined as an art through performance such as theater that will be presented and watched by an audience. According to Minot, several characteristics of the drama genre contain conflict and action to keep an audience engaged to the story, as well as how talent physically interacts with each other on stage, character development (each scene causes characters to change based on decisions in the story), physical environments such as a set to be constructed, and costumes relating to the realism of the time period the performance is attempting to capture through what the talent is wearing. All three types of classical genres (film, poetry, and drama) describe some of the structural and linguistic elements of the work, as well as components that describe the reasons why audiences are entertained by them.

BUSINESS GENRES

Many influential scholars have written about genre relating to business. One of the leading scholars who had analyzed the business genre is JoAnne Yates. In Yates's research, the difference between classical and business genres is that business genres are "types of communication that have similar formats and purpose."[9] Yates and other genre scholars have explained that before the nineteenth century, communication was widely conducted through oral means, and was not recorded or documented. It was not until the late nineteenth century that genres came into the workplace to help with internal communications, such as recording information from a meeting or creating a manual. The incorporation of business genres was to help in the completion of tasks in an efficient manner. Additionally, business genres were introduced to control excessive amounts of information being circulated through an organization. In the early nineteenth century, businesses were flourishing and those in managerial roles needed to find ways to collect, save, and store discussions among colleagues.

A genre can document dialogue and discourse among employees and other individuals within the workplace. A genre has similar patterns, usages, and reasons for communicating or recording information. In evaluating managerial meetings as a genre, Esa Lehtinen and Pekka Palli defined genre "as ways of interacting; that is as linguistically realized activity types and ways of getting things done."[10] Lehtinen and Palli suggested that genres provide employees with an avenue to accomplish tasks and goals within an organization. John Swales recognized that "a genre comprises a class of communicative events, the members of which share some set of communicative purposes."[11] Swales explained that there are reasons for an individual using a genre, which is defined as purpose. The purpose of a genre can also be an established goal. Vijay Bhatia supported Swales's theory of genre in creating his own definition with his investigation of the topic in academic and professional environments. Bhatia defined genre as a "recognizable communicative event characterized by a set of communicative purpose(s) identified and mutually understood by the members of the professional or academic community in which it regularly occurs."[12] The definition points out that genres have an objective (purpose) for communication within the chosen community. Also, genres can have more than one purpose and are most enacted through corporate, organizational, and educational settings. Bhatia also agreed with previous scholars like Yates, Swales, and Bhatia that genre is established not only from a communicative purpose, but through form. Form is defined as linguistic, vocabulary, and grammatical structures.

Another perspective to consider with genres, specifically business genres is the goal employees utilize when using communication tools repeatedly within an organization. This is how scholars such as Yates and Swales have defined a genre as practices used time and again. Yates and Orlikowski also define business genres as "social recognized types of communicative action habitually enacted by members of a community to realize particular communicative and collaborative purposes."[13] Therefore, genres are a social act where users communicate to complete a task within their chosen community. This task happens time and time again. This is the first characteristic of a genre, which is identified as the purpose. Purpose can also be described as the goal for using a communications method. The purpose also acknowledges expectations and goals that an employee uses with the medium. For example, "the business letter is to communicate and simultaneously document business matters to a party external to the writer's organization."[14]

The second characteristic of a genre is form, which specifies noticeable features of the communication that is transpiring among a group of people. Genre scholars such as Yates and Orlikowski defined form in three components: structural features, communications medium, and language. "Structural features include text, formatting devices, lists and headings and devices for structuring interactions at meetings, such as agenda."[15] The communication medium is the location where the interaction and record are taking place such as a website, mobile device, application, software (Microsoft Word) or physical medium (notepad). Language is the vocabulary used on the communications medium, as well as the specific occupation or industry. This includes writing style, how one would articulate a message, and the design of the message.

When analyzing the genre of a new electronic communication device in a Japanese firm, Joanne Yates, Wanda Orlikowski, and Kazuo Okamura created a model for analyzing form when deciding genres. Table 1.1 describes each element with its definition.

Form includes all the physical and linguistic traits that are distinct for the specific genre and that enable communication to prosper. To provide two

Table 1.1 Elements of Form—Yates, Orlikowski, and Okamura Model[a]

Form Category	*Definition*
Greeting	Presents an introduction or welcome
Self-Introductory Greeting	Personal introduction of the individual
Embedded Message	Inclusion of all or part of a previous message
Graphics	Presence of graphical elements
Hashtags	Presence of the pound symbol
Word and Phrase Emphasis	Presence of emphasizing symbols (example: e.g.)
Unusual	Presence of the @ symbol in text
List	Presence of lists to indicate vertical options in text
Set-Apart	Separation of information from text
Ellipsis	Presence of . . . at the end of sentences
Signature	Closing remark and ending
P.S.	Additional comments at the end of a message
Emphatic Language	Strong, assertive language/words
Apologetic Language	Respectful and considerate language/words

Source: Table created by author.

[a]Joanne Yates, Wanda J. Orlikowski, and Kazuo Okamura, "Explicit and implicit structuring of genres in electronic communication: Reinforcement and change of social interaction," *Organization Science* 10, no. 1 (1999): 87.

examples of these traits, one form of a memo is that the genre requires a specific heading at the top of the page or a letter including a signature at the bottom of the document. Genre scholar JoAnne Yates demonstrated through various business practices that reports, memos, and meetings are genres because they maintain a written document, provide a record, and ensure proper operation of an employee's duties once purpose and form were established.

One of the first forms of correspondence researched to debate genre in business was the memo, which emerged in the mid-1800s. Anne Jackson worked on a study with Yates and Orlikowski when the authors stated, "the memo emerged over a 50-year period and has been maintained as a useful form of business communication for almost 90 years."[16] The purpose for the memo genre was that during this time period businesses needed to acknowledge agreements and transactions with outside companies. This enabled the memo to be viewed as a communication tool and record. Yates considered the form of a memo to use specific cordial or courteous language, as well as a specific structure decided by an organization. The structure of a memo includes the placement of the date, address, information, salutation/greeting, and complimentary close (sincerely), including the signature.

Between 1870 and 1920, the memo emerged for internal correspondence and communication. This was due to growth of employment, departments, and tasks. Additionally, the genre documented functions of employee roles. The memo became a way to document information flow and for managers to control the environment in the workplace. Yates et al. noted, "documents were preferred over oral exchanges, usually because they could be stored for future examination and reference, thereby comprising a form of organizational memory."[17] As memos entered the workplace, the genre format evolved, including the implementation of several subject lines; the shortening of the inside address and salutation; and the tweaking of language to be less formal.

In explaining genres in the business setting, Mikhail Bakhtin stated that "all the diverse areas of human activity involve the use of language and the nature and forms of this use are just as diverse as the areas of human activity."[18] Bakhtin explained that individuals communicating with one another using various genres; additional and new genres will develop over time. Also, genres already identified (such as the memo, report, or letter of recommendation) can be formatted inside a specific environment by an organization using it. Because of the influence of several employees, each genre will have different purpose and form. Genres will continually evolve, alter, and be erased as individuals interact, communicate, and collaborate with one another due to advancements in technology. As a potential new genre is established, it changes the pattern of communication and exchanges of information among individuals within a culture.

WEB AND ONLINE GENRES

Marie Williams and Kevin Crowston analyzed one thousand website homepages and developed a theoretical background for web genres. The authors discovered that individuals would engage in similar social activities (purpose) and communication style (form) through the internet, following the same traits as traditional or business genres. Important to note, the authors found that "80% of web pages included some type of hypertext link."[19] This points out that the inclusion of hyperlinks is an important aspect in the form of online genres. The authors concluded that every online platform or distinct web page could be a genre because of the different tools, structures, formats, and purposes that each offers web users. Therefore, Crowston and Williams determined that digital documents such as the homepage, email, FAQ page, online pamphlet, catalog, and brochure are web genres.

Future scholars also suggested additional digital documents as genre. In 1998, Bretan et al. added that discussion boards are an example of the web genre. In 2005, Boese and Howe declared that online calendars and contact web pages are genres. Each scholar mentioned early functions and tools when the web entered homes and businesses, otherwise known as Web 1.0. During late 1990s to early 2000s, websites were more static, with readers consuming information, as opposed to being a database that involved a high level of interactivity. For instance, visiting the web meant reading an article on a website opposed to sending audio or video files through an application such as Dropbox. While users had the ability to post comments and have conversations in chat rooms and message boards, online users were not creating media content. This is where the concept of Web 1.0 and Web 2.0 was introduced. Graham Cormode and Balachander Krishnamurthy stated that Web 1.0 is where a user consumes content, while Web 2.0 is when an online user creates and consumes content.[20] Web 2.0 can be considered participatory culture, coined by media scholar Henry Jenkins, in that individuals want to be active members of media. No longer do people simply want to watch television, but they want to record, edit, and distribute their own videos through broadcast environments such as YouTube.

Scholar Marcy Bauman defined genres on the web "as embodying many elements—including text features, the social situation in which texts are produced, and the motive or exigencies that drive their production."[21] Based on her study, Bauman believed that being on a computer network changes social and communicative ways on a personal and professional level. Bauman added, "It is not so much a matter of great numbers of people are engaging in different patterns of work and relationship activities; the part worth noticing is that the patterns and activities are structured differently from what we are used to."[22] In 1999, Michael Shepherd and Carolyn Watters stated that web and online genres have three key components: purpose, form, and functionality. Purpose and form for web genres have the same definition as business genres from authors such as JoAnne Yates, Wanda Orlikowski, and John Swales. Functionality is defined as the operation, performance, and efficiencies of the web page for users. Shepherd and Watters presumed that the main difference between web and classical genres is that when online, users have expectations about how they will interact or communicate with one another, as well as the results they will receive from the digital applications.

For example, Shepherd and Watters studied the genre of the homepage of the website. The authors explained the purpose of a homepage is to showcase the identity of an individual or company. The form of a website homepage is short snippets of information, along with links to other topics relating to the website, while the functionality of a homepage enables visitors to browse the site. An online resource, such as a library journal database, is another genre Shepherd and Watters examined. The purpose of an online resource was to locate and collect information. The form of an online resource is the links to additional journals and articles, while the functionality provides search tools and interactivity among users by browsing the database.

In 2013, Anna Tereszkiewicz researched the genre of online encyclopedias. According to Tereszkiewicz, text is the form of media most enhanced by the web because of the amount of communication exchanged through all linguistic formats online (text appears everywhere on the web). Tereszkiewicz stated that functionality is an important aspect when evaluating web genres because outside of structure, users must know how to interact with the specific tool and communication device, understand how it works, and have an expectation of its intended results. An example that Tereszkiewicz used is a search engine, which users expect to place a term or phrase into a search box and receive a list of results upon pressing enter. Tereszkiewicz discussed that business genres looked at purpose, form, and sometimes content, while web genres must include functionality to define efficiencies for the new medium or technology. Web genre scholars such as Tereszkiewicz expanded the definition to include functionality, which is important to include in the genre definition. Marina Santini argued that web pages do not fall under a single genre. For example, an online newsletter includes an interview, article, and press release, showing how genres can be mixed. Santini added, "a web page creator is virtually free to publish any kind of text in any kind of format while in the paper world constraints on genre conventions are stronger."[23] Therefore, for online platforms, multiple genres can co-exist as one.

When defining online genres, Kevin Crowston and Barbara Kwasnik pointed out that it is important to recognize "the medium for participation in a communicative act."[24] Digital technologies become genres when people and organizations place documents online and users interact with the posted information. When a digital or technological medium is released to the masses, scholars establish the various new ways communication takes place in the environment. In an online environment, this can be identified through language (form), topics discussed (purpose), media, hyperlinks, and other interactive tools that digital platforms offer. In 2005, Inger Askehave and Anne Nielsen concluded that digital genres are not documents with static forms of information, but rather interactive media with content being posted, shared, and distributed among online users. This may occur between everyday users or ones in a professional setting. Today, individuals create and participate with media content instead of only consuming it from media outlets. Therefore, users of the online platform, software or device play a pivotal role in formulating web genres.

In their study of web genres, Lüders, Prøitz, and Rasmussen stated that online genres depend on media and text. For instance, a text message is a genre because it uses media (pictures, emojis) within the message, as well as words to explain and articulate the information being communicated to one or more individuals. Lüders, Prøitz, and Rasmussen determined that web genres require the users of the message to contribute and create content that is shared with an online community. Genre scholars have noted that it takes a considerable amount of time to label something a genre because society is slow to accept new ways of production and communication. Takeshi Yoshioka, George Herman, JoAnne Yates, and Wanda Orlikowski revealed that web genres have emerged because the internet is available to all citizens. This has enabled a plethora of new communication mediums to materialize in many different capacities, such as for business reasons. In 2005, Im, Yates, and Orlikowski stated that genres, digital or not, materialize from work-related situations among employees.

Yoshioka et al. created the genre taxonomy for the web. The genre taxonomy helps understand the communicative nature of the web platform or device, while evaluating new forms of communication. Yates et al. have applied the genre taxonomy to websites and technologies in professional settings. However, it has never been applied to social media platforms in work-related environments, which I will explore (table 1.2).

DEFINITION OF GENRE

After completing the theoretical background of classical, business, and online and web genres, I will define the term genre for the following investigation of social media platforms in a professional setting. Social media have not been analyzed as a potential genre and this study looks to bridge the gap in the literature. For this study, the definition of genre is drawn from several

Table 1.2 Genre Taxonomy for Online Genres (Yoshioka, Herman, Yates, and Orlikowski, 2001)

Genre Taxonomy	*Definition*
Purpose	Topics and goals.
Content	Media used to communicate through pictures, video, audio, and text.
Participants	Users of the genre.
Location/Timing	Physical and virtual locations to send and receive information/communication using content.
Functionality	Expectations and efficiency of use.
Structure and Medium	Form: language and linguistic features; design elements.

Source: Table created by author.

scholars credited for their work in genre studies. Genre is defined as a kind of communication that has similar purpose, form, and functionality. The professional environment selected for the study (higher education) should have similar purpose, form, and functionality in the use of social media sites.

I will apply two additional characteristics toward the definition of genre. In 1993, Bhatia stated that similar purpose and form must occur in professional and academic settings. Thus, I will select the academic setting of higher education (colleges and universities) utilizing social media in the workplace. In 2011, Lehtinen and Palli concluded that genres are a way of getting things accomplished by communicating with others through various forms of language. I will be examining this through social media posts and interviews with employees in higher education. Using this definition, I consider genres to accomplish tasks and responsibilities based on the purpose, form, and functionality that social media offers in a professional environment.

Combining all the important aspects of genre together, my definition for genre is a kind of communication that has similar purpose, form, and functionality in professional and academic environments as a way for employees to interact, post content, and complete tasks and responsibilities.

NOTES

1. Walter F. Deal, "Making the connection: Technological literacy and technology assessment," *Technology and Engineering Teacher* 61, no. 7 (2002): 16.

2. Linda K. Mancillas and Peter W. Brusoe, "Born digital: Integrating media technology in the political science classroom," *Journal of Political Science Education* 12, no. 4 (2016): 375–386.

3. Mancillas and Brusoe, "Born digital," 376.

4. Chris Jones and Binhui Shao, *The Net Generation and Digital Natives: Implications for Higher Education*, 2011.

5. Nell K. Duke and Victoria Purcell-Gates, "Genres at home and at school: Bridging the known to the new," *The Reading Teacher* 57, no. 1 (2003): 30–37.

6. Marika Lüders, Lin Prøitz, and Terje Rasmussen, "Emerging personal media genres," *New Media & Society* 12, no. 6 (2010): 947–963.

7. JoAnne Yates, *Control through Communication: The Rise of System in American Management*. Vol. 6 (JHU Press, 1993), 65.

8. Stephen Minot, *Three Genres: The Writing of Fiction, Poetry, and Drama* (Englewood Cliffs, NJ: Prentice-Hall, 1965), 304.

9. Yates, *Control through Communication*, 288.

10. Esa Lehtinen and Pekka Palli, "Conversational use of genres in managerial meetings," *Scandinavian Journal of Management* 27, no. 3 (2011): 287.

11. John Swales, *Genre Analysis: English in Academic and Research Settings* (Cambridge University Press, 1990), 46.

12. Vijay Kumar Bhatia, *Analysing Genre: Use in Professional Settings* (Harlow: Longman, 1993), 3.

13. Wanda Orlikowski and JoAnne Yates, "Genre repertoire: The structuring of communicative practices in organizations," *Administrative Science Quarterly* (1994): 542.

14. Orlikowski and Yates, "Genre repertoire," 543.

15. Orlikowski and Yates, "Genre repertoire," 543.

16. JoAnne Yates, Wanda J. Orlikowski, and Anne Jackson, "The six key dimensions of understanding media," *MIT Sloan Management Review* 49, no. 2 (2008): 65.

17. Yates, Orlikowski, and Jackson, "The six key dimensions of understanding media," 66.

18. Mikhail Bakhtin, "The problem of speech genres," in *Speech Genres and Other Late Essays* (Austin, TX: University of Texas Press, 1986), 60.

19. Kevin Crowston and Marie Williams, "Reproduced and emergent genres of communication on the World Wide Web," *The Information Society* 16, no. 3 (2000): 208.

20. Graham Cormode and Balachander Krishnamurthy, "Key differences between Web 1.0 and Web 2.0," *First Monday* 13, no. 6 (2008).

21. Mary Lassota Bauman, "The evolution of Internet genres," *Computers and* Composition 16 (1999): 270.

22. Bauman, "The evolution," 272.

23. Marina Santini, "Characterizing genres of web pages: Genre hybridism and individualism," *System Sciences* (2007): 7.

24. Kevin Crowston and Barbara H. Kwasnik, "A framework for creating a faceted classification for genres: Addressing issues of multidimensionality," In *System Sciences, 2004. Proceedings of the 37th Annual Hawaii International Conference*, IEEE (2004), 1.

Chapter 2

Investigating Institutional Social Media Sites as a Genre

The definition of social media has evolved continually since its inception. Technology alters quickly with social networks having to continually create new tools for engagement with every platform, whether it's posting pictures or video, messaging, playing games, or reading news articles. Social media platforms are digital environments for people to come together online to interact and communicate with one another through content. But it's also important to look at social media sites as databases that contain user information that is then sold to advertisers in order to make a profit. Social media is an environment for users to be entertained, become informed, and continue conversations with friends in the digital realm. But they are also environments where businesses market and sell products. Thus, with the definition of social media, it is important to recognize the many layers environments offer to those who choose to use them.

In the book *Producing New and Digital Media: Your Guide to Savvy Use of the Web*, Cohen and I defined online communities as "environments found on the web such as message boards, databases, and social media sites that offer digital interaction with other online users."[1] To be an active member of an online community and engage with a group of people, users must interact with one another using content and media, such as text, pictures, video, and sound. In 2010, Andreas Kaplan and Michael Haenlien defined social media as digital technologies and environments that allow for individuals to interact and create user-generated content (UGC). UGC is media that a social media user created that you share on your own profile page or channel. User-created content (UCC) is original work that a user creates and shares with their online community, posted on their personal social media profile or channel. For example, UGC is sharing a *New York Times* article that was posted on a friend's Facebook page, now embedded on your own profile. An example of

UCC is posting a one-minute video from a concert that you attended on your personal Instagram account.

In 2008, Angelina Russo, Jerry Watkins, Lynda Kelly, and Sebastian Chan explained social media as environments and online communities with three functions: communicate, network, and collaborate. Communicate means spreading ideas and information with those who share similar interests. To network means to connect with others with the same profession, interest, or group. Collaboration refers to offering a team dynamic for creating and distributing content daily through social media. In exploring social media to create content with others, Anthony Bradley defined social media as "a set of technologies and channels targeted at forming and enabling a potentially massive community of participants to productively collaborate."[2] When social media is used within any type of organization, both employees and consumers create content individually and together. This content is seen by others in the chosen community and by spreading the message, the organization or company hopes to attract others to their information offerings. Interactivity on social media platforms is achieved when users receive feedback from messages and content from their connections (online community) within the digital environment. Scholars such as Michael Kent (2010) observed that social media is not a static environment for information and content. Rather, it is an environment and platform for constant dialogue between a user and his or her online community (friends, fans, or followers) about content posted in the chosen platform. This is particularly important for businesses that choose to use social media sites.

SOCIAL MEDIA FOR COLLABORATION IN THE WORKPLACE

In their 2005 study of a virtual start-up platform, Hyun-Gyung Im, JoAnne Yates, and Wanda Orlikowski concluded that all genres (online and business) emerge from work-related environments among employees. Harold Schroeder added, "firms now need to work at building a positive image and active presence online and to interact continuously with their customers and other internet users via social media sites."[3] Social media channels allow companies to post information to the masses, while having a back-and-forth conversation with their online community concerning their created content. By posting daily content through the interactive environments, companies are keeping their online community engaged with their product, thus building community based on what they offer to their audience. In 2018, when discussing the value of organizations using social media, Federica Fusi and Mary Feeney stated that digital environments are used constantly because they offer relationship building with customers, a professional online identity, and improved communication.

A 2012 McKinsey Global Institute report concluded that approximately 70 percent of all organizations frequently use social media sites for business practices. Research has found that businesses that incorporate social media effectively develop an identity online and reach their audience or community on an emotional level, in which individuals feel that they are involved with the product, whether it is through discussions or creating content. Several industries feel united with their online audience through strategic social media campaigns and well-produced multimedia content. As Schroeder explained, "firms also have access via social media to an unprecedented amount of data about individuals, which can be used for a range of business purposes including market research, networking and recruitment."[4] When individuals join any type of social media site, organizations can collect user interests based on how the person interacts with a post or piece of content. When collecting data over social media interaction, businesses can understand what their customers enjoy about their product and what they are satisfied or unsatisfied with. Additionally, data includes demographic information (such as gender, age, and race) and other analytics that are available in the public forum.

In 2010, Jeff Huang, Stephan Yang, Huang Yueh-Min, and Indy YT Hsaio maintained that social media provides a more positive work environment than negative one because employees can learn from one another in the digital environment. Although communication and a digital identity are valuable, social media offers a community of practice, also known as a learning community, where individuals can learn new skills to apply to their daily tasks and responsibilities. Kristopher Thomas and Mesut Akdere explained this act as collaborative media, which "enable the organization's members to interact with each other unconventionally and more rapidly, eliminating the traditional time and space restrictions."[5] When using any digital tools that offer collaborative media experiences, communication can be instantaneous outside of contracted time frames (working during "off" hours) and knowledge can spread easily offering individual and group improvements at work. Social media sites never shut down, thus business and organizational content must be always monitored.

Andrew McAfee recognized an issue for social media in the work setting. He stated that if an employee is not engaging with thc platform on a consistent basis, tasks may not be completed correctly when social media sites are used.[6] If social media is being introduced as a daily task and responsibility, there must be daily posts to learn how to use the system and garner the best reactions from the intended audience. Plus, there needs to be proper training and reinforced social media policies in the work environment to be adhered to. Matti Mäntymäki and Kai Riemer discovered a positive use of social media in the workplace, as it was a way for coworkers to resolve any issues and to develop new ideas.[7] Social media sites offer creative ways to communicate with an organization's audience and customers. In 2013, Hope Koch, Dorothy Leidner, and Ester Gonzalez stated that employees had issues implementing organizational policies for different social media platforms. For example, a document sent over an email may have to be approved by a manager first, while a social media post may not need approval and can be shared by anyone in the online community. This can also lead to problems with privacy. Issues with polices notwithstanding, Emma Forsgren and Katriina Byström concluded that social media at work increases communication and interaction. Therefore, it should be a tool used by all organizations.[8]

Elaine Bucher, Christian Fieseler, and Anne Suphan were worried that social media may cause an information overload for employees. The authors explained overload as "constant changes in work habits. Overloaded individuals perceive the changes that social media cause their daily routines and habits as a burden, and they have difficulties in adapting appropriately."[9] Some organizations do not have a separate social media manager, thus companies that implement social media platforms add it on as another task and responsibility to an existing employee's workload. Bucher, Fieseler, and Suphan found that there was a high level of uncertainty when using social media in the workplace. This is due to the many social media channels in existence, along with conversations and dialogue being different on each platform. Every social media platform may have different functionalities for communicating with an audience. In addition, by the time employees learn to use and incorporate one social media site into their daily routines, a new site may have emerged in the digital landscape. Social media users may decide to leave one platform and join another. This also may cause uncertainty because communication can take place over multiple channels. Therefore, it's recommended that when an organization adds social media to the work environment, employees become literate in each domain and channel.

SOCIAL MEDIA AND HIGHER EDUCATION

Previous studies have indicated that colleges and universities in the United States use social media to interact with current and perspective students in a variety of ways such as campus activities (events, athletics) and promoting educational programs (majors and minors). Mike Moran, Jeff Seaman, and Hester Tinti-Kane found that over 90% of faculty in higher education were using social media in the classroom and for their professional portfolio. Moran added, "two-thirds used it in class, and around one-third used it to provide students with information. Moreover, more than 40% had linked it to coursework and 20% required students to participate with online discussions."[10] This indicated that faculty were using social media in multiple teaching methods to see how the platforms worked best for their course and their students. Samantha Cooke found that while social media provided a new method of teaching and tool for engagement and assignments, there was a change in the way that students learned and acted in the classroom. Students had more responsibility in a social media environment and had the opportunity to transform discussions or learning objectives based on their posts.[11] Chris Evans said that "social media tools facilitate media and information sharing, collaboration, and participation. This makes them obvious technologies for application to higher education."[12] According to Evans, the difficulty for students is that there is a plethora of resources (articles and videos, for example) available through social media and they must figure out which sources are most applicable and significant to the course or assignment when using the technology.

Ryan Busch explained that social media is not only a technological movement; the way in which people locate news and information has evolved to be a collaborative experience.[13] This coincides with how individuals research and discover educational programs, as well as use collaborative media within their own learning. It is the transfer of both information and knowledge using modern technological environments. Raziye Nevzat, Yilmaz Amca, Cem Tanoya, and Hasan Amca (2016) disclosed that "students reported that the use of social networking tools with the university brand makes them feel more connected to their university."[14] A relationship between students and higher education institutions occurs over social media because the platforms offer interactivity. Students may have daily conversations with employees (faculty, staff, administrators, or current students) about a variety of topics. Adam Peruta and Alison Shields (2017) believed that social media is the best form of communication for an institution to reach current students, prospective students, parents, and alumni in one place.[15] This makes it easier for gathering and reaching people in one environment instead of over multiple channels where all groups can connect about their experience at the institution. In 2014, Whitney Sessa determined that one hundred percent of colleges and universities were using some form of social media site.[16] Sessa suspected that social media accounts were used strategically as databases for student engagement and for colleges and universities to interact with perspective and incoming students. As students and faculty embrace social media for everyday use, Sessa concluded that it was critical for higher education to build an online community over a digital environment to communicate with students. In a 2013 study conducted by R. A. Hesel, most prospective students used social media to research information beyond academics, as the platforms provided a glimpse of campus life, events, and what a typical day at the campus would be like.

Jean Sandlin and Edlyn Pena stated, "innovative online social media that involve student participation can provide a more dynamic and authentic depiction of the college experience."[17] By posting and sharing regularly through social media sites, students are detailing their experience with college academics and campus life from their own point of view. In doing so, students are creating free content for higher education staff to use on their institutional social media pages. A critical practice for both social media and education is engagement.

Katie Paine explained that engagement happens when a user "comments" on another person's post, "shares" content with their online community, or "likes" another individual's post.[18] There have been some studies evaluating how students' voluntary and required use of social media in the classroom builds engagement. Tehmina Kahn, Michael Kend, and Susan Robertson surveyed students majoring in accounting about their academic engagement with social media platforms. The academic activities included sharing information about the course subject with their classmates (connected social media users), course files (assignments, readings), and resources (such as online videos). It was also noted that if engagement increased on social media, it helped students enjoy the course atmosphere. Thus, it was determined that students "find social media a comfortable, team environment in which they initiate discussions at their convenience and with which they have a continuous and flexible peer access for information exchange and for academic-related discussions."[19]

Mary Culnan, Patrick McHugh, and Jesus Zubillaga suggested three strategies toward applying social media in higher education: "organizations need to make mindful decisions regarding initial adoption, organizations need to build communities and companies need to learn from the content their customers create."[20] It's asserted that while colleges can use social media platforms because they are affordable technologies and regularly used by their audience, higher education institutions should not enforce the platforms until there is a strategy in place for adoption. Additionally, colleges and universities must research the dialogue and content students are posting, which will help with the type of information shared on the databases, as well as develop a community around the name of the higher education facility. Furthermore, higher education must evaluate which social media sites they plan to implement with their social media goals and objectives in mind. There is an abundance of social media platforms to engage students, but using all may become a detriment, while others may not be necessary. For instance, if a higher education establishment does not create videos daily, it may not be reasonable to create a YouTube channel that will look bare and unoccupied. Previous research suggested to select only the platforms where content will flow daily and where students feel there is interaction with the campus community.

Social media offers communication, information, and knowledge instantaneously, combined with entertainment and media content. Using a mobile device (smart phone, tablet or laptop) these online environments are with individuals on their day-to-day routines, blending interactions and professional accomplishments at once. Therefore, students may not see issues with incorporating social media as a course method as it is already intertwined with all other aspects of their life. Huseyin Bicen and Nadire Cavus added, "students do not make a clear distinction between virtual and physical landscapes and the two seamlessly meld."[21] Therefore, according to Christine Greenhow, faculty may look to include social media within their courses because it aids and assists with learning.[22] However, it should be noted that some students, faculty, and staff may want privacy, keeping their personal and educational lives separate from each other.

It should be noted that in previous studies, social media use in the classroom has not always been successful. Charles Knight and Linda Kaye studied Twitter use by 181 students enrolled in psychology and ethics courses. Knight and Kaye discovered that the students focused more on passive information than academics, as they wanted to use the site to build community in their areas of interests. Furthermore, it was found that users read and collected information instead of posting and interacting with the course. Knight and Kaye insisted that some of the issues stem from higher education using social media for promotional purposes and students viewing the platforms as branding mechanisms instead of learning environments.[23] Joanna Dunlap and Patrick Lowenthal disagreed, as they believed Twitter can be a place for students to ask questions to a larger community and locate resources to help in completing assignments.[24] In 2014, Chris Evans found that if students already use social media, they were more likely to interact with specific courses through the online platforms. Reynol Junco, Greg Heiberger, and Eric Loken discovered that engagement increased with the influence of social media in the classroom, specifically Twitter. Thus, social media sites may be beneficial for students who become detached during the semester and keep them interested in the subject.[25] Samantha Cooke concluded that the addition of social media in coursework did not change student goals or ambitions. Cooke pointed out that "students have found the inclusion of social media useful in their learning. However, its benefit emerged from its role as a supplementary tool rather than a predominant teaching methodology."[26] This study acknowledged that social media may be effective in one's course, but not as a primary environment, practice, or assignment. Social media could be a supplemental tool to achieve course goals and objectives.

Difference among Faculty, Staff, and Administration Using Social Media

In 2013, authors Adam Peruta, William Ryan, and Robertson Engelsman asserted that higher education has been slow to adopt social media in the workplace in comparison to other profit and non-profit organizations. The lackadaisical implementation is in part due to debates between faculty and administration about best practices for social media channels, as well as differences in use. Ryan Busch noted that there is a disconnect among administrators, staff, and faculty about what to post on social media sites, as the groups disagree about the best ways to use the online platforms. Busch added, "while some information is educational and some information is promotional, information is rarely communicated for both educational and promotional use."[27] Busch identified several characteristics in social media for universities because content posted by faculty and staff is typically not simultaneously for promotional and academic use. The characteristics for higher education employees include information, content, and interaction for using a social media platform for marketing, institutional mission, and educational outcomes. Through studying several universities' use of social media, Busch theorized that faculty members were not active voices on all social media sites because the university's focal point was on the marketing and promotion areas as opposed to academics and what students were learning in the classroom.

George Veletsianos and Royce Kimmons determined that there were opposing views between faculty and staff in higher education about personal and professional social media. Social media gives faculty flexible online formats for connecting with students, while also maintaining a professional image with scholarly work. They observed that faculty found it difficult to balance professional and personal interactions when connecting with students via social media platforms. Faculty may be using a social media site for course assignments, but the same digital platform outside of campus and educational use, which has implications for personal privacy. Veletsianos and Kimmons added, "imposing particular modes of participation may conflict with faculty members' values, leading to SNS underuse or rejection."[28] SNS refers to social networking sites. The authors concluded that leaving faculty out of the process of defining social media use for classroom and branding purposes, may violate faculty governance and prevent achieving course objectives. Therefore, this may lead to faculty being less likely to use social media in higher education.

Higher Education and Genre

There have been several studies that have researched genre in the higher education environment. David Hyatt reviewed the genre of feedback on student papers. This study looked to establish the features of feedback by reviewing instructor comments to help students understand clarifications. Hyatt discovered that "23% of the students overall noted that they would have preferred much more detailed comments on their essays explaining what they ought to have done."[29] Therefore, Hyatt felt that it was important to outline the purpose and form of instructor feedback on master's level papers. Upon analysis of over six thousand papers, Hyatt pointed out categories for the genre of feedback including: phatic comments (encouragement), developmental comments (assigning additional work to help with the assignment), address a particular issue in the paper, direct comment (about the paper), structural comments (comments on the organization of the paper), and stylistic comments (language, punctuation, grammar, citations, footnotes, and other writing techniques).

Elena Afros and Catherine Schryer researched the genre of the syllabus, which is the document that highlights the course goals, objectives, assignments, and structure when the class begins. Afros and Schryer evaluated ten syllabi downloaded from the web and identified ten common features: "course title, term/semester, instructor information, course description (in four sentences), course requirements, assignments, test types/methods, late penalties, readings, and evaluation."[30]

After providing a few examples (assignment feedback and syllabus), I have identified that all genre studies in the higher education setting have focused on genres inside of the classroom. Previous studies on genres have been geared toward student learning and how faculty used documents, texts, or technological platforms/devices/software for in-class purposes. However, this leaves a gap in literature that will be bridged, as the higher education setting from the organizational and administration aspect will be used as opposed to the classroom/faculty context.

In the book *Varsity Letters: Documenting Modern Colleges and Universities* by Helen Willa Samuels, the author described how institutions of higher education were documented. To document information and content for higher education, Samuels described "seven functions that constitute modern academic institutions. These seven functions are part of every institution."[31] Samuels mentioned that traditionally, colleges and universities had three missions: "to teach, conduct research, and provide public service."[32] However, Samuels believed that this does not describe the number of activities and amount of interactivity that modern institutions offer. The following seven functions that describe activities and management of all colleges and universities will be applied in the method to research purpose and determine if institutions convey similar objectives (goals) through particular social media platforms (table 2.1).

Table 2.1 Seven Functions of Higher Education

Function	*Definition*
Confer Credentials	Describes the admission process, recruitment of students, financial aid, academic information, and graduation.
Convey Knowledge	Distribution of curriculum and the ability for students to learn.
Foster Socialization	Educational activities and events outside of class hours and lectures.
Conduct Research	Showcasing faculty, students, and alumni's research accomplishments and knowledge.
Sustain the Institution	Institutional management such as governance structure, personnel changes, budget, renovations, and additional stability of the institution.
Provide Public Service	Community service, continuing education, and helping others in the local area.
Promote Culture	Higher education institutions record and share information, art, and culture through academic facilities including libraries, archives, art galleries, performances, and other events.

Source: Created by the author.

The investigation of social media in the workplace points out ways that the sites have been used to complete tasks and responsibilities at one's place of employment, while establishing how the platforms have been utilized in the higher education realm. By examining the differences among faculty, staff, and administration, as well as previous studies of genre in higher education settings (colleges and universities), I have established a gap in the literature; where prior studies were conducted in the classroom with genres being used and communicated between faculty and staff. I will bridge the gap by focusing on staff and administration of the institution using a genre to complete professional and organizational tasks.

To investigate social media as a genre, I must identify the purpose (topics, goals, reasons), form (structure, language, vocabulary) and functionality (efficiency) of higher education social media web pages. Outside of researching purpose, form, and functionality, I discovered that another way to test for a potential genre is through use of a genre taxonomy to ask employees their thoughts on the purpose, content, participants, location, expectations, and form of social media higher education web pages. I also summarized several characteristics of social media that can describe its potential as a genre. All social media definitions stated that there must be participation from the users and online community following the social media page by having UCC and UGC. This means original posts created by the host of the social media site and borrowed content designed by a member of the online community, appearing on the same social media platform. The type of content to be posted on a social media site should include text, sound, images, and video.

Furthermore, social media sites must offer collaboration with other users, the ability to network and communicate with your connections.

The review of business and online genres indicated that both categories develop in academic and professional settings from tasks and responsibilities at work. Thus, higher education as an academic and professional environment is selected to examine social media as a genre due to its significant use at colleges and universities. When reviewing previous studies of genre in higher education, as an organization itself has not been explored. To analyze higher education, I decided to use the seven functions identified by Helen Willa Samuels: confer credentials, convey knowledge, foster socialization, conduct research, sustain the institution, provide public service, and promote culture. I will examine whether these seven functions are reflected on higher education social media pages.

Therefore, to investigate whether social media higher education web pages are a genre, I must research purpose, form, and functionality on the platforms that will represent the characteristics of genre, social media, and higher education; discuss the genre taxonomy with higher education employees who have social media responsibilities and tasks; and review the seven functions of higher education on social media platforms. One major factor discovered in both business and online genres is that to be considered a genre, purpose, form, and functionality must be similar. Therefore, I cannot study one higher education institution. The study must involve many academic institutions and if purpose, form, and functionality are similar, social media higher education pages can be considered a genre.

NOTES

1. James Cohen and Thomas Kenny, *Producing New and Digital Media: Your Guide to Savvy Use of the Web* (Routledge, 2015), 253.
2. Anthony Bradley, "Re: A new definition of social media [Web log message]," Last modified January 7, 2010. Accessed October 7, 2018. Retrieved from http://blogs.gartner.com/anthony_bradley/2010/01/07/a-new-definition-of-social-media/.
3. Harold M. Schroeder, "Social media in business strategy: The learning and development implications," *Development and Learning in Organizations: An International Journal* 28, no. 6 (2014): 12.
4. Schroeder, "Social media in business strategy," 13.
5. Kristopher J. Thomas and Mesut Akdere, "Social media as collaborative media in workplace learning," *Human Resource Development Review* 12, no. 3 (2013): 332.
6. Andrew P. McAfee, "Enterprise 2.0: The dawn of emergent collaboration," *MIT Sloan Management Review* 47, no. 3 (2006): 21.
7. Matti Mäntymäki and Kai Riemer, "Enterprise social networking: A knowledge management perspective," *International Journal of Information Management* 36, no. 6 (2016): 1042–1052.

8. Emma Forsgren and Katriina Byström, "Multiple social media in the workplace: Contradictions and congruencies," *Information Systems Journal* 28, no. 3 (2018): 442–464.

9. Eliane Bucher, Christian Fieseler, and Anne Suphan, "The stress potential of social media in the workplace," *Information, Communication & Society* 16, no. 10 (2013): 1655.

10. Mike Moran, Jeff Seaman, and Hester Tinti-Kane, "Teaching, learning, and sharing: How today's higher education faculty use social media," *Babson Survey Research Group* (2011): 3.

11. Samantha Cooke, "Social teaching: Student perspectives on the inclusion of social media in higher education," *Education and Information Technologies* 22, no. 1 (2017): 257.

12. Chris Evans, "Twitter for teaching: Can social media be used to enhance the process of learning?," *British Journal Of Educational Technology* 45 no. 5 (2014): 903.

13. Ryan Busch, "Unlocking the voice of the university: The convergence of course, content, delivery, and marketing through social media," in *Teaching Arts and Science with the New Social Media* (Emerald Group Publishing Limited, 2011), 142.

14. Raziye Nevzat, Yilmaz Amca, Cem Tanova, and Hasan Amca, "Role of social media community in strengthening trust and loyalty for a university," *Computers in Human Behavior* 65 (2016): 553.

15. Adam Peruta and Alison B. Shields, "Social media in higher education: Understanding how colleges and universities use Facebook," *Journal of Marketing for Higher Education* 27, no. 1 (2017): 131.

16. Whitney L. Sessa, "Targeting millennials social media strategies within higher education," *College and University* 90, no. 1 (2014): 3.

17. Jean Kelso Sandlin and Edlyn Vallejo Peña, "Building authenticity in social media tools to recruit postsecondary students," *Innovative Higher Education* 39, no. 4 (2014): 334.

18. Katie Delahaye Paine, *Measure What Matters: Online Tools for Understanding Customers, Social Media, Engagement, and Key Relationships* (John Wiley & Sons, 2011).

19. Tehmina Khan, Michael Kend, and Susan Robertson, "Use of social media by university accounting students and its impact on learning outcomes," *Accounting Education* 25, no. 6 (2016): 552.

20. Mary J. Culnan, Patrick J. McHugh, and Jesus I. Zubillaga, "How large US companies can use Twitter and other social media to gain business value," *MIS Quarterly Executive* 9, no. 4 (2010): 246.

21. Huseyin Bicen and Nadire Cavus, "Social network sites usage habits of undergraduate students: Case study of Facebook," *Procedia-Social and Behavioral Sciences* 28 (2011): 943.

22. Christine Greenhow, "Online social networks and learning," *On the Horizon* 19, no. 1 (2011): 4–12.

23. Charles G. Knight and Linda K. Kaye, "To tweet or not to tweet? A comparison of academics' and students' usage of Twitter in academic contexts," *Innovations in Education and Teaching International* 53, no. 2 (2016): 145–155.

24. Joanna C. Dunlap and Patrick R. Lowenthal, "Tweeting the night away: Using Twitter to enhance social presence," *Journal of Information Systems Education* 20, no. 2 (2009): 129–135.

25. Reynol Junco, Greg Heiberger, and Eric Loken, "The effect of Twitter on college student engagement and grades," *Journal of Computer Assisted Learning* 27, no. 2 (2011): 119–132.

26. Cooke, "Social teaching," 267.

27. Busch, "Unlocking the voice of the university," 143.

28. George Veletsianos and Royce Kimmons, "Scholars and faculty members' lived experiences in online social networks," *The Internet and Higher Education* 16 (2013): 49.

29. David F. Hyatt, "'Yes, a very good point!': A critical genre analysis of a corpus of feedback commentaries on Master of Education assignments," *Teaching in Higher Education* 10, no. 3 (2005): 340.

30. Elena Afros and Catherine F. Schryer, "The genre of syllabus in higher education," *Journal of English for Academic Purposes* 8, no. 3 (2009): 227.

31. Helen Willa Samuels, *Varsity Letters. Documenting Modern Colleges and Universities* (Scarecrow Press, 1998), 19.

32. Samuels, *Varsity Letters*, 20.

Chapter 3

Three Characteristics of Genre and Research Design

To discover whether higher education social media web pages are a genre, the study will use the following research questions:

- *RQ1:* Based on the seven functions of higher education, what appears to be the purpose of Facebook and Twitter institutional social media web pages?
- *RQ2:* Using the linguistic and formatting features of social media as assessment instruments, what can be said about the form of Facebook and Twitter institutional social media web pages?
- *RQ3:* Using the genre taxonomy as an assessment instrument, what is the functionality of Facebook and Twitter institutional social media web pages?
- *RQ4:* Based on the similarities of purpose, form and functionality, are higher education Facebook and Twitter institutional social media websites a genre?

There are three characteristics to test for genre: purpose, form, and functionality. Content analysis will be used to test purpose and form. I selected the first 100 institutions on the Liberal Arts and Sciences list of Best Colleges and Universities published in *U.S. News & World Report.* I collected data for the first month in the spring 2019 academic semester to classify posts (Facebook) and tweets (Twitter) based on the seven functions of all higher education institutions, which will describe the purpose of the message. Content analysis was used to analyze form and purpose of every post and tweet on Facebook and Twitter. I also investigated linguistic, structural, and grammatical form of a message publicly posted for the online community to view.

I discussed social media and genre with human subjects to evaluate the characteristic of functionality of a genre. To do so, I contacted social media employees at the selected 100 colleges and universities. Participants joined the study voluntarily after IRB approval to answer several open-ended questions based on the genre taxonomy when establishing functionality of a genre. Also, the interviewees made note of the seven functions of higher education in their responses.

JUSTIFICATION FOR METHODOLOGY

To determine whether higher education Facebook and Twitter social media web pages are a genre, the top 100 colleges and universities ranked by *U.S. News & World Report* were selected to review. As prior research noted, higher education is an ideal organization to investigate purpose, form, and functionality of Facebook and Twitter. Bhatia mentioned that genres regularly occur in professional and academic environments.[1] Also, Im, Yates, and Orlikowski revealed that genres are also developed among employees to complete tasks and work-related responsibilities.[2]

U.S. News & World Report is a fully digital online publisher (formally print) known for its yearly rankings of the best colleges, hospitals, and other industries. In addition to its yearly rankings, the publication spotlights services including, travel, health, and most importantly for this study, education. *U.S. News & World Report* was founded in 1933 by David Lawrence and has been in business for over eighty-five years. The 2019 report for best colleges, released on September 10, 2018, was used to select colleges and universities for this study because of its popularity among students researching potential higher educational institutions. Additionally, colleges and universities on the list can be expected to have an outstanding social media presence because of their reputation and academic excellence.

For this study of genre and social media, I reviewed content posted on higher education Facebook and Twitter pages to analyze for a potential genre. While there is a plethora of social media sites to evaluate besides Facebook and Twitter, only the two mentioned were used for the study since all platforms work differently. For instance, social media sites Instagram and Snapchat offer content posting only via mobile devices while Facebook and Twitter provide desktop and mobile postings. More importantly, in 2011 Nora Barnes and Ava Lescault interviewed social media managers at a large number of colleges and universities across the United States and concluded that the most widely used platforms to recruit, research, and post information to current and prospective students through social media were Facebook and Twitter.[3] While a recent report from the Pew Research Center indicated that young adults are using other social media sites such as Instagram and Snapchat more frequently than Twitter, my study is collecting data and establishing genre of higher education social media web pages.[4] Therefore, this study must use social media sites that the majority of higher education institutions incorporate and employees utilize on a consistent, daily basis.

Authors Anjali S. Bal, Dhruv Grewal, Adam Mills, and Gary Ottley stated that Facebook is the "primary social media website for adults." Additionally, when adults use more than one social media platform, the most frequently used combination is Facebook and Twitter. Research discovered that most Twitter users are Facebook users as well.[5]

Concepts and Definitions

The following section explains terms to understand the context of this study. Purpose is defined as the topics, objectives, and functions of college and university employees using institutional social media web pages through Facebook and Twitter to inform and share information among coworkers, students, and other users in their online community. To evaluate purpose, the researcher must assess the content of every message on Facebook (post) and Twitter (tweet) published by the higher education facility over the course of the selected time frame. The topics and objectives of the higher education institution that will categorize every message on Facebook and Twitter are the seven functions outlined by author Helen Willa Samuels: confer credentials, convey knowledge, foster socialization, conduct research, sustain the institution, provide public service, and promote culture.[6]

Form is defined as formatting and linguistic features of each social media post on Facebook and Twitter that communicate a public message to the online community. Form describes the structural and grammatical approach of Facebook and Twitter posts as a tool for communication and consuming information. To institute form for higher education social media web pages, the features of each post during the selected time frame will be determined through Yates, Orlikowski, and Okamura's model of formatting coding categories described in chapter 1.

Functionality is defined as the abilities, performance, and capabilities that social media platforms Facebook and Twitter offer to higher education institutions, as well as employees responsible for posting in the digital environments. To understand the functionality of Facebook and Twitter web pages, I incorporated the genre taxonomy by Yoshioka, Herman, Yates, and Orlikowski. Purpose, content, participants, location, functionality, and form were discussed with employees at higher education institutions who are tasked with posting on social media to understand how Facebook and Twitter institutional web pages are efficient.

Genre is defined as a kind of communication that has similar purpose, form, and functionality in professional and academic environments (Facebook and Twitter institutional web pages) as a way for employees to interact, post content, and complete tasks and responsibilities. If purpose, form and functionality on Facebook and Twitter are the same, then the researcher can label higher education social media web pages as a genre. If the characteristics are not similar, then higher education social media pages on each platform are not a genre or each may be its very own distinct genre.

Higher education is defined as institutions that comprise colleges and universities in the United States that offer knowledge in many areas such as humanities, social sciences, education, and business. Higher education offers undergraduate (associate's and bachelor's degrees) and graduate (master's and doctoral) degrees. Wide ranges of programs are offered in disciplines such as communications, medicine, law, nursing, political science, English, and music therapy, among others. For this study, the researcher will only analyze colleges and universities focusing on undergraduate studies.

Social media employees are defined as the population comprising of staff and administrators who are hired by colleges and universities to post regularly on the institutional Facebook and Twitter pages. When social media employees post on Facebook and Twitter, they impact the results of purpose, form, and functionality at their institutions.

Social media is defined as environments on the web that offer interaction, information, and communication with a chosen online community through content such as text, sound, video, and images. Social media is also characterized by creating a profile that represents an individual, company, or brand where interactions are public between online users. Social media platforms are resources available to higher education employees to communicate and share information to students, alumni, faculty, staff, and others about the institution. Social media are also described as environments offering user-generated content (UGC) and user-created content (UCC) that has three functions: communication, networking, and collaboration.

Facebook and Twitter are defined as online environments that colleges and universities use to communicate and interact with other digital users, as well as share information about the education facility through multimedia (text, sound, pictures, and video) content posted by the institution itself and other users in the participating community. Facebook allows for brand and company-specific "web pages" which are social media profiles for the organization. Colleges and universities adopting Twitter follow the same format as user-specific profiles where each post contains a total of 280 characters. I will review the main institutional social media websites (Facebook pages and Twitter profiles) where the purpose of the college and university may be represented, as opposed to department and office social media pages attached to the higher education facility.

Research Design

The research design will apply a content analysis to investigate two characteristics of genre: purpose and form. The research approach is also using interview methodology to understand the functionality of Facebook and Twitter higher education social media web pages from the employee perspective through the genre taxonomy.

Content analysis will be applied twice during the study to evaluate purpose and form on Facebook and Twitter higher education web pages. Through specific categories defined by the seven functions of higher education, the content analysis will enable a complete assessment of all Facebook and Twitter posts for each college and university. When investigating purpose for both Facebook and Twitter, a content analysis will be instituted to tabulate the seven functions of social media with each post. Once every post during a specific time is tabulated, the researcher will determine the role and representation of the seven functions of higher education on Facebook and Twitter, as well as evaluate the similarities of purpose among the selected colleges and universities. Similarities are critical to genre studies because as previous scholars such as Yates stated, genre is established through related or identical themes.

When investigating form, I will use a content analysis to review the structural and linguistic features of Facebook and Twitter social media higher education web pages. Outside of quantifying and tabulating the total number of every category of form, I am looking for patterns and themes that explain how Facebook and Twitter devise a message to share publicly with the online community. As stated with purpose, similarities when analyzing genre also establish form. While I am still tabulating the total number in each category, I am analyzing the characteristics that most colleges and universities make use of when designing a message to share.

Interviews allow the researcher to ask queries based on content analysis results that may be vague or need further explanation. Berger stated that interviews "find out about peoples ideas, thoughts, opinions, attitudes and what motivates them by talking to them and asking the right questions."[7] Additionally, interviews not only allow me to have direct communication with participants, but employees who will be interviewed may share important data that cannot be explained in a quantitative content analysis. Because of the limited number of higher education employees willing to take part in the interviews, the study is not generalizable based on sample selection procedures.

Framework

For the content analysis, there will be a total of four areas (and tables) representing social media sites Facebook and Twitter. This is because purpose and form will be investigated twice for each social media site. Both purpose and form content analysis will have specific categories to label a tweet (Twitter) or post (Facebook). Only public tweets from the main institution social media site for Facebook and Twitter will be collected as this is public information open and free for anyone to consume and interpret the message when visiting the website. I will gather Facebook and Twitter posts beginning with the spring 2019 academic semester, with a start date of January 15, 2019, and ending February 15, 2019. The start date is chosen as it is the mid-year point of the semester with common elements being geared toward higher education. The holiday season is over, and the beginning announcements of the semester have been completed. Thus, this gives the best opportunity for the seven functions of higher education to appear. A full month of tweets will allow me to analyze enough data to understand the purpose and form of social media sites for higher education. Every tweet and post shared on the main institution social media web page will be organized, including institutions sending information out to their online communities multiple times a day. Whether it is one tweet or five tweets a day, each message will be tabulated and evaluated in both areas of the content analysis. Outside of the time frame to collect data, no other demographic information is considered.

Helen Willa Samuels's seven functions of higher education are the identifiers used in the content analysis for purpose. Each of the seven functions will be analyzed for every Facebook and Twitter post on an institutional page. Every post on Facebook and Twitter will be placed into one or more categories to tabulate the total number in each one. I will use Yates, Orlikowski, and Okamura's model for form in the content analysis of each tweet (Twitter) and Facebook (post). Based on their model, I developed coding categories merging the identifiers of Yates, Orlikowski, and Okamura with structural and linguistic features of social media sites described in prior research. Every social media post on both platforms will be analyzed with each identifier in the message noted and transcribed into the appropriate category/classification.

Social media employees at higher education institutions will also be interviewed for the study. The interviews will discuss the third characteristic of genre: functionality. Participants will be recruited by email. Questions for the interview are based on the genre taxonomy model. With the approval of the participants, interviews will be recorded via telephone or video conference by voice application TapeACall Pro. The interview will be transcribed to make certain sufficient and reliable data have been collected. Employees responsible for posting on institutional Facebook and Twitter pages will be asked open-ended questions. I will ask questions without giving any thoughts and opinions on the subject. The interviews will last approximately thirty minutes. Once completed, I will develop themes based on the discourse and conversations. The transcripts will never appear online.

Data Collection Notes

It is also important to note that when categorizing tweets and posts for the purpose of content analysis, the indicators (categories) are exclusive and mutually exhaustive meaning that a tweet and post can only be placed in one area. According to Clare Beghtol, categories in any classification system should be exclusive. She stated, "that a certain named thing should occur in only one class and that the class in which the thing occurs should have no overlapping content within itself."[8] Beghtol also discussed "jointly exhaustive," meaning that categories only include content that makes sense and is appropriate for the study. All tweets and posts from the study period will be included, with nothing left behind. In case there are any surprising posts or unusual messages, a category for "other" is created. However, when categorizing form, tweets, and posts can have more than one way to construct a message. Thus, more than one technique will be identified.

When collecting data on higher education social media profile pages for Facebook and Twitter, *re-tweets* and *shares* will be analyzed. A retweet (Twitter) and share (Facebook) is when someone takes a message from another social media user and places it on their page (allowing their online community to see it). Retweets and shares are included because the higher education social media page is sending out a message to be reviewed by the institution's online community. They are identified by the word "retweeted" or "share" next to the institution's Twitter/Facebook handle above the content of the message.

Participants and Institutional Review Board

Since the content analysis for purpose and form is using public Facebook and Twitter social media pages, it does not require Institutional Review Board (IRB) approval. The participation of social media employees in higher education is necessary to complete the research in the area of genre studies for the functionality of a social media site. Because I am interviewing human subjects, Long Island University IRB was contacted for approval prior to beginning the study. All documents were submitted to the Long Island University IRB on February 6, 2019. The IRB approved the study on February 10, 2019, when the researcher received stamped copies of all consent forms. Documents included interview consent form, audio and video consent form, summary letter explaining the study, email recruitment letter, and Collaborative Institutional Training Initiative (CITI) certificates for working with human subjects. The interviews will include informed consent where I will explain to participants the purpose and security of the study.

Participants will be made aware that their audio (telephone) or video (Skype) interviews will be recorded. The reason for recording the sessions is to help properly transcribe the interview without missing any valuable piece of information. Only the researcher and second coder will be allowed to listen to the audio or watch the video of the interviews. If individuals contacted do not want to take part in the research, there will be no repercussions and other participants will be asked to participate in the study. Transcriptions will be written using NVivo 12 when watching video interviews or listening to audio interviews. The documents will be saved on two of the researcher's external hard drives, which are password protected. All files have been deleted upon completion of the study.

Selection of Higher Education Social Media Web Pages

To answer the research questions, I needed to select higher education (college and university) social media pages. Colleges and universities will be chosen from the 2019 Best College Rankings published on September 10, 2018, by *U.S. News & World Report*. The publication offers institutional rankings in several categories, which includes national universities, business programs, liberal arts, and regional colleges (based on location).

For this study, colleges are selected based on their ranking published in the list of National Liberal Arts Colleges, which is a category inside *U.S. News & World Report*. The National Liberal Arts Colleges rankings are chosen because the institutions on the list focus on undergraduate education with over half the degrees offered in arts and sciences. In researching the impact of social media on liberal arts, in 2012 Andrew Moore stated that the digital space and political dialogue calls for liberal arts programs to study, analyze, and research social media. Moore added, "with modes of human expression, with cultural and ideological frameworks and with power and its objects, then Facebook and other social communications technologies are suitable subjects for serious study in liberal arts classrooms."[9] The National Liberal Arts Colleges list consists of 233 schools in rank order. The first 100 colleges will be selected for this study and their institutional Facebook and Twitter web pages will be reviewed.

Table 3.1 list colleges in rank order and provide hyperlinks to their Facebook and Twitter social media pages. If for some reason an institution has no social media representation, I will select the next college/university from the National Liberal Arts Colleges Rankings after the initial list. Colleges must have both a Facebook and Twitter page to be included in the study. Any institution with only one out of the two social media pages will be excluded from the list. For example, College of the Atlantic ranked number 95, only has a Facebook account. Since the college does not use Twitter, I

Table 3.1 Colleges Eliminated and Added to the Study

Eliminated Colleges	*Added Colleges*
College of the Atlantic	St. Mary's College of Maryland
U.S. Military Academy	Austin College
U.S. Naval Academy	Hollins University
U.S. Air Force Academy	Hope College
Virginia Military Institute	Lake Forest College
	Washington & Jefferson College

Source: Created by the author.

will select another institution on the Liberal Arts rankings in ascending order after removing College of the Atlantic from the study. St. John's College appears twice on the list (ranking numbers 61 and 72) because it has two campuses (Annapolis and Santa Fe). St. John's College uses one set of social media pages for the two campuses. Therefore, I will only count St. John's once at ranking number 61 and add St. Mary's College of Maryland to the list. The College of Saint Benedict (ranked 86) and Saint John's University in Collegeville, Minnesota (ranked 95) have a partnership where students attend both campuses. Therefore, the institutions share one Facebook and Twitter page. Therefore, Austin College in Sherman, Texas was added to the study. The United States Military Academy (18), United States Naval Academy (22), United States Air Force Academy (30), and Virginia Military Institute (81) were not included in the study because they use Twitter and Facebook to discuss military matters not found at other higher education institutions. Thus, four additional colleges were added.

Recruitment Strategies

Higher education institutions will not be contacted directly for participation in the study. Their Facebook and Twitter social media pages are public with anyone permitted to view their posts, tweets, and multimedia content (pictures, video). As previously stated, institutions were selected based on the *U.S. News & World Report* of Best Colleges, specifically their ranking for Liberal Arts Colleges and Universities. By virtue of making the list, the schools are highly regarded educational institutions. My assumption is that these institutions are likely to have social media applications with a considerable amount of current and prospective student, and alumni, interest.

Social media staff and administrators were identified by visiting each institution's website and viewing their online directory. The higher education employees tasked with social media are needed for the interviews. For most institutions, social media employees are placed in the communications, public affairs, or public relations offices. Once I identified the person tasked with social media, I took note of their email address. I immediately noticed that persons tasked with social media had different job titles. There was not one consistent social media position or title. Position titles included: Director of Social Media; Social Media Strategist; Social Media Coordinator; Social Media Manager; Social Media Specialist; Social Media Producer; Director of Social Media; or simply Social Media. It is also important to recognize that some employees were tasked with social media but had a different title; social media is simply part of their daily responsibilities. When I could not locate a social media title for an employee, I read through biographies and identified the individuals hired to post on the digital platforms. Their job titles included: Communications Manager; Digital Strategist; Director of Public Relations; Editorial Director; Visual Media Producer; Director of Communications; Director of Web Initiatives; Digital Content Specialist; and Director of Interactive Media. Social media may fall under these positions because the platforms also are promotional/branding opportunities for the various communities the institution wishes to reach.

After collecting all the contact information for the social media employees, I emailed each person. I explained the study, why I was contacting them, and how I obtained their information. I informed all participants that the interview was voluntary and, while I would be recording the conversation, the file would only be used for transcription purposes. I also explained when the transcription files would be terminated. When I received confirmation from a participant willing to take part in the study, I explained their rights and attached the consent forms (audio/video recording and interview). Once I received the signed consent forms from the participants, I scheduled their interview on an agreed upon day and time.

Screening Criteria

Since some colleges and universities might have students posting on social media sites, I will require that all participants be at least 18 years of age. The study is open to all social media employees in the selected higher education institutions, whomever they may be. When a participant agrees to be interviewed, I confirm that the individual is an employee of the college by visiting the institution's website and online directory. The final screening criteria is for the liberal arts institutions selected based on the *U.S. News & World Report* of Best Colleges rankings. As mentioned, all schools that I plan to use for the content analysis must have both a Facebook and a Twitter site to be part of the study. If a college on the rankings does not have both social media sites, I will select the next college on the list.

Interviews: Functionality

Individuals employed by the colleges or universities identified that are tasked with social media daily are invited to participate. The structured interviews will begin with a few short introductory questions and with the remaining queries based on the genre taxonomy. The focus of the interview will be the functionality of Facebook and Twitter higher education institutional social media web pages viewed through the genre taxonomy. Questions will be asked on each part of the taxonomy.

Interview Questions

For all questions, please base your responses on your experiences using social media in higher education.

Genre Taxonomy Questions

1. What is the purpose (goal, topic, objective) for employees using Facebook in higher education?
2. What is the purpose (goal, topic, objective) for employees using Twitter in higher education?
3. What type of content do employees post on Facebook institutional pages?
4. What type of content do employees post on Twitter institutional pages?
5. Who are the participants posting information and content on Facebook and Twitter institutional web pages?
6. What are the roles and responsibilities of the participants posting information and content on Facebook and Twitter institutional web pages?
7. Where do employees/participants create, post, and consume content for Facebook?
8. Where do employees/participants create, post, and consume content for Twitter?
9. When do employees/participants expect to receive a response once a message is posted on Facebook?
10. When do employees/participants expect to receive a response once a message is tweeted on Twitter?
11. What are your overall expectations of using Facebook?
12. What are your overall expectations of using Twitter?
13. What is your format when constructing a post on Facebook? What are the textual and visual requirements?
14. What is your format when constructing a tweet on Twitter? What are the textual and visual requirements?
15. Do you have any formatting or linguistic requirements in your post or tweet?

Functionality Question

16. Is Facebook an efficient web page to use for higher education? Why?
17. Is Twitter an efficient web page to use for higher education? Why?

Conclusion

18. Do you have any closing comments you wish to mention before the interview ends?

According to the scholarly literature, a genre must have purpose, form, and functionality. Beyond this, there is no suggestion that a minimum number of characteristics imply validity to the genre. I am trying to document the genre of higher education social media based on the empirical evidence of this content.

After reading through each interview, I used NVivo 12 software to analyze the interview results and highlight the most common words (themes) relating to each section of the genre taxonomy. After opening the NVivo 12 software, I uploaded all ten interviews that were transcribed as Microsoft Word files. Then, I created "nodes" with the ten interviews. A node allows the researcher to organize all interview responses for each question into one document. Therefore, I created nodes for the responses for each category in the genre taxonomy including purpose, content, participants, location/timing, functionality, and structure/form. Because most of the interviewees combined responses for Facebook and Twitter, I kept all responses for purpose as a node, functionality as a node and so on. Once all nodes were created, a text search query, also known as word frequency, was conducted. The word frequency function on NVivo was used for all nodes. Once "run" was selected for word frequency, the most common words (themes) appeared. Under the heading count, the results showed how many times a particular word was used. It is important to note that the researcher created a list of stop words—terms that would not be associated with a theme for a node. Examples include: "the," "like," "and," "are," "but," "as," and "or."

Content Analysis: Purpose

A content analysis of Facebook and Twitter posts based on purpose will be conducted. There are two tables created for purpose: one for Facebook and the other for Twitter. The framework is informed by two concepts. First, the seven functions of higher education institutions from Helen Willa Samuels's book are the identifiers and categories. These functions are the

Table 3.2 2019 National Liberal Arts Colleges 1–100

College	*Ranking*	*Social Media Handles*	*Followers*
Williams College	1	https://www.facebook.com/williamscollege	23,760
Williamstown, MA		https://twitter.com/williamscollege	17,700
Amherst College	2	https://www.facebook.com/amherstcollege	18,896
Amherst, MA		https://twitter.com/amherstcollege	16,400
Swarthmore College	3	https://www.facebook.com/SwarthmoreCollege/	16,883
Swarthmore, PA		https://twitter.com/swarthmore	9,926
Wellesley College	3	https://www.facebook.com/WellesleyCollege	43,664
Wellesley, MA		https://twitter.com/wellesley	17,600
Bowdoin College	5	https://www.facebook.com/Bowdoin	22,691
Brunswick, ME		https://twitter.com/bowdoincollege	14,500
Carleton College	5	https://www.facebook.com/CarletonCollege	17,492
Northfield, MN		https://twitter.com/CarletonCollege	8,998
Middlebury College	5	https://www.facebook.com/middleburycollege/	27,058
Middlebury, VT		https://twitter.com/middlebury	13,900
Pomona College	5	https://www.facebook.com/pomonacollege/	16,180
Claremont, CA		https://twitter.com/pomonacollege	10,200
Claremont McKenna College	9	https://www.facebook.com/ClaremontMcKennaCollege	10,782
Claremont, CA		https://twitter.com/cmcnews	6,189
Davidson College	10	https://www.facebook.com/davidsoncollege.nc	23,869
Davidson, NC		https://twitter.com/DavidsonCollege	12,600
Grinnell College	11	https://www.facebook.com/grinnellcollege	11,880
Grinnell, IA		https://twitter.com/grinnellcollege	6,744
Haverford College	11	https://www.facebook.com/haverfordcollege	7,664
Haverford, PA		https://twitter.com/haverfordedu	7,861
Smith College	11	https://www.facebook.com/smithcollege	153,671
Northampton, MA		https://twitter.com/smithcollege	19,200

(*continued*)

Table 3.2 (Continued)

College	*Ranking*	*Social Media Handles*	*Followers*
Vassar College	11	https://www.facebook.com/vassarcollege/	23,183
Poughkeepsie, NY		https://twitter.com/vassar/	11,000
Washington and Lee University	11	https://www.facebook.com/washingtonandlee	16,634
Lexington, VA		https://twitter.com/wlunews	9,394
Colgate University	16	https://www.facebook.com/colgateuniversity	29,616
Hamilton, NY		https://twitter.com/colgateuniv	22,000
Hamilton College	16	https://www.facebook.com/HamiltonCollege	22,865
Clinton, NY		https://twitter.com/hamiltoncollege	12,900
Colby College	18	https://www.facebook.com/colbycollege	23,124
Waterville, ME		https://twitter.com/colbycollege	12,000
Harvey Mudd College	18	https://www.facebook.com/harveymuddcollege	11,337
Claremont, CA		https://twitter.com/harveymudd	7,235
Wesleyan University	18	https://www.facebook.com/wesleyan.university	25,505
Middletown, CT		https://twitter.com/wesleyan_u	19,900
Bates College	22	https://www.facebook.com/batescollege	19,720
Lewiston, ME		https://twitter.com/BatesCollege	13,400
Soka University of America	22	https://www.facebook.com/SokaUniversityofAmerica/	57,210
Aliso Viejo, CA		https://twitter.com/SokaUniv	6,967
Barnard College	25	https://www.facebook.com/barnardcollege	29,313
New York, NY		https://twitter.com/BarnardCollege	15,700
University of Richmond	25	https://www.facebook.com/urichmond	29,700
Richmond, VA		https://twitter.com/urichmond	23,200
Bryn Mawr College	27	https://www.facebook.com/BrynMawrCollege	15,049
Bryn Mawr, PA		https://twitter.com/BrynMawrCollege	9,588
Colorado College	27	https://www.facebook.com/coloradocollege	19,706
Colorado Springs, CO		https://twitter.com/coloradocollege	9,775
Macalester College	27	https://www.facebook.com/MacalesterCollege/	17,092
St. Paul, MN		https://twitter.com/macalester	9,627

Kenyon College	30	https://www.facebook.com/kenyoncollege	14,906
Gambier, OH		https://twitter.com/KenyonCollege	11,000
Mount Holyoke College	30	https://www.facebook.com/mountholyokecollege	25,763
South Hadley, MA		https://twitter.com/mtholyoke	14,500
Oberlin College	30	https://www.facebook.com/Ober inCollege/	23,174
Oberlin, OH		https://twitter.com/oberlincollege	7,114
Scripps College	30	https://www.facebook.com/scrippscollege	8,803
Claremont, CA		https://twitter.com/scrippscollege	5,773
College of the Holy Cross	35	https://www.facebook.com/collegeoftheholycross	20,984
Worcester, MA		https://twitter.com/holy_cross	16,200
Bucknell University	36	https://www.facebook.com/BucknellU	27,020
Lewisburg, PA		https://twitter.com/BucknellU	20,800
Franklin and Marshall College	36	https://www.facebook.com/fandm	17,242
Lancaster, PA		https://twitter.com/fandmcollege	8,611
Lafayette College	36	https://www.facebook.com/LafayetteCollege.edu	22,399
Easton, PA		https://twitter.com/LafCol	9,792
Occidental College	39	https://www.facebook.com/occidental	15,465
Los Angeles, CA		https://twitter.com/occidental	17,100
Union College	39	https://www.facebook.com/unioncollege	21,199
Schenectady, NY		https://twitter.com/unioncollege	9,185
Pitzer College	41	https://www.facebook.com/PitzerCollege	6,305
Claremont, CA		https://twitter.com/pitzercollege	6,277
Skidmore College	41	https://www.facebook.com/SkidmoreCollege	17,383
Saratoga Springs, NY		https://twitter.com/SkidmoreCollege	7,886
Denison University	43	https://www.facebook.com/denisonuniversity	23,007
Granville, OH		https://twitter.com/denisonu	10,800
Thomas Aquinas College	43	https://www.facebook.com/ThomasAquinasCollege	6,923
Santa Paula, CA		https://twitter.com/TACollege	2,530
Whitman College	43	https://www.facebook.com/whitmancollege	11,914
Walla Walla, WA		https://twitter.com/whitmancollege	3,291

(*continued*)

Table 3.2 (Continued)

College	*Ranking*	*Social Media Handles*	*Followers*
Centre College	46	https://www.facebook.com/centre	13,705
Danville, KY		https://twitter.com/centrec	7,997
Connecticut College	46	https://www.facebook.com/ConnecticutCollege	15,302
New London, CT		https://twitter.com/conncollege	12,900
Trinity College	46	https://www.facebook.com/TrinityCollege/	31,396
Hartford, CT		https://twitter.com/trinitycollege	7,948
Gettysburg College	49	https://www.facebook.com/Gburg.College	23,325
Gettysburg, PA		https://twitter.com/gettysburg	11,600
Sewanee-University of the South	49	https://www.facebook.com/sewanee	24,021
Sewanee, TN		https://twitter.com/univofthesouth	5,831
Agnes Scott College	51	https://www.facebook.com/agnesscottcollege/	10,332
Decatur, GA		https://twitter.com/agnesscott	5,611
Dickinson College	51	https://www.facebook.com/dickinsoncollege/	23,868
Carlisle, PA		https://twitter.com/dickinsoncol	9,885
Furman University	51	https://www.facebook.com/FurmanUniversity/	23,411
Greenville, SC		https://twitter.com/furmanu	12,600
Rhodes College	51	https://www.facebook.com/rhodescollege	14,477
Memphis, TN		https://twitter.com/rhodescollege	9,484
Spelman College	51	https://www.facebook.com/SpelmanCollege/	40,004
Atlanta, GA		https://twitter.com/spelmancollege	39,500
Bard College	56	https://www.facebook.com/BardCollegeNY/	20,418
Annandale on Hudson, NY		https://twitter.com/bardcollege	10,800
DePauw University	56	https://www.facebook.com/DePauwUniversity/	14,776
Greencastle, IN		https://twitter.com/depauwu	9,170
Lawrence University	56	https://www.facebook.com/lawrenceuni/	15,568
Appleton, WI		https://twitter.com/lawrenceuni	5,728
St. Lawrence University	56	https://www.facebook.com/StLawrenceU	20,610
Canton, NY		https://twitter.com/stlawrenceu	7,063

Wabash College	56	https://www.facebook.com/WabashCollegeNews/	15,671
Crawfordsville, IN		https://twitter.com/WabashCollege	5,771
Berea College	61	https://www.facebook.com/bereacollege/	34,479
Berea, KY		https://twitter.com/bereacollege	6,608
St. John's College	61	https://www.facebook.com/stjohnscollege/	10,874
Annapolis, MD/Sante Fe, NM		https://twitter.com/stjohnscollege	3,980
St. Olaf College	61	https://www.facebook.com/stolafcollege/	29,128
Northfield, MN		https://twitter.com/stolaf	9,490
Wheaton College	61	https://www.facebook.com/wheatoncollege.il/	22,976
Wheaton, IL		https://twitter.com/WheatonCollege	13,700
Kalamazoo College	65	https://www.facebook.com/KalamazooCollege/	12,121
Kalamazoo, MI		https://twitter.com/kcollege	6,704
Sarah Lawrence College	65	https://www.facebook.com/sarahlawrencecollege/	16,296
Bronxville, NY		https://twitter.com/sarahlawrence	5,204
College of Wooster	67	https://www.facebook.com/CollegeofWooster/	16,269
Wooster, OH		https://twitter.com/woosteredu	6,510
Beloit College	68	https://www.facebook.com/BeloitCollege	11,749
Beloit, WI		https://twitter.com/beloit_college	4,510
Hobart and William Smith Colleges	68	https://www.facebook.com/hwscolleges	17,115
Geneva, NY		https://twitter.com/HWSColleges	6,334
Knox College	68	https://www.facebook.com/KnoxCollege/	12,917
Galesburg, IL		https://twitter.com/knoxcollege1837	3,906
Lewis & Clark College	68	https://www.facebook.com/lewisandclarkcollege/	12,280
Portland, OR		https://twitter.com/lewisandclark	5,472
Illinois Wesleyan University	72	https://www.facebook.com/illinoiswesleyan/	13,273
Bloomington, IL		https://twitter.com/il_wesleyan	5,474
University of Puget Sound	72	https://www.facebook.com/univpugetsound/	16,268
Tacoma, WA		https://twitter.com/univpugetsound	7,143
Wofford College	72	https://www.facebook.com/woffordcollege/	14,263
Spartanburg, SC		https://twitter.com/woffordcollege	9,038

(continued)

Table 3.2 (Continued)

College	*Ranking*	*Social Media Handles*	*Followers*
Allegheny College	76	https://www.facebook.com/alleghenycollege	13,752
Meadville, PA		https://twitter.com/alleghenycol	8,566
Hendrix College	76	https://www.facebook.com/hendrixcollege	11,738
Conway, AR		https://twitter.com/hendrixcollege	5,215
Hillsdale College	76	https://www.facebook.com/hillsdalecollegemichigan	157,283
Hillsdale, MI		https://twitter.com/hillsdale	48,000
Transylvania University	76	https://www.facebook.com/transylvaniauniversity	12,024
Lexington, KY		https://twitter.com/transy	6,350
Willamette University	76	https://www.facebook.com/Willamette	14,044
Salem, OR		https://twitter.com/willamette_u	3,581
Cornell College	81	https://www.facebook.com/CornellCollege	14,748
Mount Vernon, IA		https://twitter.com/cornellcollege	4,812
Earlham College	81	https://www.facebook.com/earlhamcollege	25,119
Richmond, IN		https://twitter.com/earlham1847	3,271
Muhlenberg College	81	https://www.facebook.com/MuhlenbergCollege/	12,655
Allentown, PA		https://twitter.com/muhlenberg	7,108
Principia College	81	https://www.facebook.com/PrincipiaCollege	5,009
Elsah, IL		https://twitter.com/PrinCollege	1,300
College of St. Benedict	86	https://www.facebook.com/csbsju	24,554
St. Joseph, MN		https://twitter.com/csbsju	8,513
St. John's University			
Collegeville, MN			
Juniata College	86	https://www.facebook.com/juniata	15,658
Huntingdon, PA		https://twitter.com/juniatacollege	4,621
Wheaton College	86	https://www.facebook.com/WheatonCollege/	11,872
Norton, MA		https://twitter.com/wheaton	5,996
Luther College	89	https://www.facebook.com/luthercollege	19,804
Decorah, IA		https://twitter.com/luthercollege	7,904

Gustavus Adolphus College	90	https://www.facebook.com/gustavusadolphuscollege	17,691
St. Peter, MN		https://twitter.com/gustavus	6,849
New College of Florida	90	https://www.facebook.com/newcollegeofflorida	9,208
Sarasota, FL		https://twitter.com/newcollegeoffl	3,934
Reed College	90	https://www.facebook.com/reedcollege	14,476
Portland, OR		https://twitter.com/reed_college_	4,272
Southwestern University	90	https://www.facebook.com/SouthwesternUniversity	13,971
Georgetown, TX		https://twitter.com/southwesternu	6,521
Ursinus College	90	https://www.facebook.com/ursinuscollege	9,439
Collegeville, PA		https://twitter.com/UrsinusCollege	4,871
Augustana College	95	https://www.facebook.com/AugustanaCollege	19,271
Rock Island, IL		https://twitter.com/augustana_il	7,088
Bennington College	95	https://www.facebook.com/benningtoncollege	6,005
Bennington, VT		https://twitter.com/atbennington	2,383
Ohio Wesleyan University	95	https://www.facebook.com/OhioWesleyanUniversity	15,316
Delaware, OH		https://twitter.com/ohiowesleyan	5,932
St. Anselm College	95	https://www.facebook.com/SaintAnselm	15,124
Manchester, NH		https://twitter.com/saintanselm	12,500
St. Mary's College	95	https://www.facebook.com/saintmaryscollege	13,194
Notre Dame, IN		https://twitter.com/saintmarys	5,242
St. Mary's College of Maryland	95	https://www.facebook.com/stmarysMD/	11,415
St. Mary's City, MD		https://twitter.com/StMarysMD	3,093
Austin College	103	https://www.facebook.com/austincollege/	12,704
Sherman, Texas		https://twitter.com/austincollege	4,177
Hollins University	103	https://www.facebook.com/HollinsUniversity/	11,459
Roanoke, VA		https://twitter.com/hollinsu	2,995
Hope College	103	https://www.facebook.com/hopecollege/	21,294
Holland, MI		https://twitter.com/hopecollege	11,800
Lake Forest College	103	https://www.facebook.com/lakeforestcollege/	9,482
Lake Forest, IL		https://twitter.com/lfcollege	4,182
Washington and Jefferson College	103	https://www.facebook.com/washjeff/	8,184
Washington, PA		https://twitter.com/wjcollege	4,318

Source: Created by the author.

purposes for every Facebook and Twitter post. Additionally, I have created a final category for the content analysis titled "other," which defines purposes outside of the selected categories. Therefore, there are eight categories for purpose. Follower count is based on the time the study was conducted. Table 3.3 describes the content analysis categories that will be applied to both Facebook and Twitter.

Content Analysis: Form

A content analysis based on *form* will also be implemented. There are two tables created for form: one for Facebook and the other for Twitter. The framework uses Yates, Orlikowski, and Okamura's model to identify the formatting and linguistic features of a genre. This model will be applied in the social media setting.

Additionally, based on the definition of social media, UGC and UCC are added to decipher whether the message is an original post or shared from another social media user. There are a total of twenty-one categories for form based on the previous literature. The following descriptions will be applied to Facebook and Twitter using the same categories to gather evidence. The form descriptions below have updated definitions for the social media environment. It is important to note that the category labeled "unusual" from Yates, Orlikowski, and Okamura's model has been renamed "mentions" since the "@" symbol is a social media characteristic used regularly to communicate

Table 3.3 Content Analysis—Purpose (Facebook and Twitter)

Purpose	*Definition*
Confer Credentials	Describes the admission process, recruitment of students, financial aid, academic information, and graduation.
Convey Knowledge	Distribution of curriculum and the ability for students to learn.
Foster Socialization	Social activities and events on campus, not necessarily related to academics or coursework.
Conduct Research	Showcasing faculty, students, and alumni's research accomplishments and knowledge.
Sustain the Institution	Institutional management such as governance structure, personnel changes, budget, renovations, and additional stability of the institution.
Provide Public Service	Community service, continuing education, and helping others in the local area.
Promote Culture	Advertise and encourage the promotion of culture through art, literature, music, and other historical and creative work.
Other	Posts and tweets outside of the higher education and social media functions or identifiers.

Source: Created by the author.

Table 3.4 Content Analysis—Form (Facebook and Twitter)

Form Category	*Definition*
Greeting	Presents an introduction or welcome within every post or tweet.
Self-Introductory Greeting	The social media user (employee) introduces himself or herself at the beginning of the message.
Embedded Message	Describes a Facebook post that allows the organization to share from another user in the online community. Not only does the employee share the post on the institution profile page but adds additional comments to the message. For Twitter, the tool is described as a "retweet with comments" enabling the post from another user to appear while adding the message the institution wants to display.
Graphics	Includes any emojis or icons such as a smiley face or heart, among other graphical elements.
Hashtags	Identifying the hashtags in a post or tweet.
Word & Phrase Emphasis	Points out symbols incorporated into a message such as "e.g." and "i.e." to showcase an example. This also includes symbols that are not graphic images such as the $ sign to signify money.
Mentions	Posts and tweets that use the @ symbol to communicate with another social media user or organization.
List	Files any information alongside one another, horizontally or vertically. Also, a word, letter, number, or phrase that indexes information can identify a list.
Set-Apart	Describes two or more topics that are separated from one another within the same post or tweet.
Ellipsis	Any post or tweet that uses the symbol (. . .) to create an incomplete message.
Signature	Some existence of a closing remark or way to end the message.
P.S.	Including additional comments after the initial message has ended.
Emphatic Language	Emphasizes linguistic elements by the way of bold, assertive words as well as tone of the message.
Apologetic Language	Characterizes posts and tweets using respectful and considerate language (in tone of the message as well).
Replies	A thread of conversation adding further commentary and information to a post or tweet.
Video	Any motion pictures that are used to compliment the text within a post or tweet.
Audio	Any music, interview, or sound effects within a post or tweet.
Links	External hyperlinks allowing individuals selecting the highlighted phrase to visit another website on the internet for additional information.
Pictures	Any images that accompany a post or tweet.
User Generated Content (UGC)	Content made by other users shared to the institutional higher education Facebook or Twitter site.
User Created Content (UCC)	Content made by the employees themselves shared to the institutional higher education Facebook or Twitter site.

Source: Created by the author.

with other users. A major difference from purpose is that the form categories are not mutually exclusive, meaning that a post or tweet can appear in more than one category (table 3.4).

The similarities (purpose and form) among each institution will establish genre for social media higher education web pages. When I do my data analysis for both genre characteristics, I will be examining the extent of purpose for each category and classification. I will also be examining which forms will be typically used and embraced. The frequency distribution of each form will showcase a degree of strength in each of the characteristics. This will also explain that the results are more than just a coincidence.

NOTES

1. Bhatia, *Analysing Genre: Use in Professional Settings*, 3.
2. Yates, Orlikowski, and Okamura, "Explicit and implicit structuring of genres in electronic communication: Reinforcement and change of social interaction," *Organization Science* 10, no. 1 (1999): 87.
3. Nora Ganim Barnes and Ava M. Lescault, "Social media adoption soars as higher-ed experiments and reevaluates its use of new communications tools," *Center for Marketing Research.* University of Massachusetts Dartmouth, North Dartmouth, MA(2011): 2.
4. Monica Anderson and Jingjing Jiang, "Teen, social media, and technology," *Pew Research Center.* Available at https://www.pewresearch.org/internet/2018/05/31/teens-social-media-technology-2018/.
5. Anjali S. Bal., Dhruv Grewal, Adam Mills, and Gary Ottley, "Engaging students with social media," *Journal of Marketing Education* 37, no. 3 (2015): 194.
6. Samuels, *Varsity Letters.*
7. Arthur Asa Berger, Media and communication research methods: An introduction to qualitative and quantitative approaches, *Sage Publications* (2015): 194.
8. Clare Beghtol, "Classification theory," In *Encyclopedia of Library and Information Sciences* (2010): 959.
9. Andrew Moore, "Facebook and the liberal arts," *The Journal of General Education* 61, no. 3 (2012): 273.

Chapter 4

Purpose of Facebook and Twitter Web Pages in Higher Education

When beginning the content analysis for Facebook and Twitter, I reviewed the overall purpose of each post on Facebook or tweet on Twitter for the one hundred higher education institutions chosen from the *U.S. News & World Report* ranking of top liberal arts colleges. Purpose is defined as the goal and intention of the post.

After I coded every post, a second coder was given a glossary of terms and a hard drive with the data. Table 4.1 contains the updated definitions (still based on Samuels's research) that were given to the second coder. The glossary for purpose definitions is important for the second coder to understand how the researcher placed posts and tweets into specific categories. The coder labeled every post or tweet by its purpose. The second coder has a master's degree in communications from New York Institute of Technology and agreed to participate in the study when contacted by the researcher. Upon being provided the hard drive with data, the second coder took several months to analyze the posts and tweets. After the second coder completed the analysis, the researcher reviewed their notes.

Since Samuels's work was published in 1998, there were slight modifications made to the seven functions. This was done to make certain each function reflected contemporary higher education institutions. The category titled "other," was created for any messages that did not fit into the seven functions for higher education. The posts or tweets may be associated with higher education, but not fall within the seven functions. I also added two additional categories based on the characteristics of social media. Communicate was added to define any interactions that take place between the institution and the online community. Collaborate was included to explain when a user in the online community partners with the institution. Table 4.1 helps to understand how each post and tweet was classified.

Table 4.1 Glossary of Coding Definitions for Second Coder (Purpose)

Purpose	*Definition*
Confer Credentials (Administrative)	Describes the administrative offices and academic services provided to students. Examples include admissions, food services, registrar/registration, financial aid, and commencement information.
Convey Knowledge (majors/minors)	Promote academics including department majors and minors. Additional topics include study abroad programs, lectures, workshops, and internships. Anything on the platform to learn.
Foster Socialization (campus life—activities)	Opportunities for engagement. Campus activities that include upcoming athletic games, talks, and events for students to interact with the campus community.
Conduct Research (Showcasing work—papers, presentations, etc.)	Showcasing faculty, students, and alumni research accomplishments. Achievements also include awards, media outreach, and scholarly presentations.
Sustain the Institution (upgrades to facility)	Upgrades and renovations to campus facilities/buildings. Also, employee changes or new hires for departments. Includes any announcements pertaining to the college or department budget.
Provide Public Service (community service)	Community outreach and relations helping others in the local area where the institution is based.
Promote Culture (promoting values, social issues, and events)	Any office or service at the institution, such as the library, art gallery, or museum that advertises and sponsor's culture. This may include events, exhibits, social issues and movements, theater, music, and art. Includes historical references to the institution to archive information.
Communicate	Facebook posts and Twitter tweets that offer the ability to interact with other users on the platform. This category was added based off the definition of social media.
Collaborate	Facebook posts and Twitter tweets that offer an opportunity to showcase teamwork and create content together. This category was added from the definition of social media.
Other	Posts and tweets outside of the higher education system. Also includes information and content occurring in the higher education setting, but does not fall under the nine other categories, which includes individual sport accomplishments, holiday wishes, motivational quotes, first day of class announcements, weather cancellations, and other topics.

Source: Created by the author.

FREQUENCY EVIDENCE OF GENRE MANIFESTATION: TWITTER PURPOSE RESULTS

Table 4.2 displays the results for purpose, relating to Twitter posts. In total, there were 7,607 tweets from the 100 higher education institutions in the one-month time frame (January 15, 2019 to February 15, 2019). Since the second coder agreed with the classification of the purpose of tweets, there were no changes to the original categorization.

The results for Twitter purpose start with the highest number (most used purpose) and end with the lowest number (least utilized purpose). There was no category that received zero tweets, as each function was a purpose at some point in the month. However, based on the ten categories, the researcher identified five categories that are top priorities for Twitter, while the last five are lower priorities for social media employees using Twitter.

The five categories of purpose that are the focus for social media employees using Twitter are: foster socialization, other; promote culture; convey knowledge; and conduct research. The main purpose for Twitter in the entire month's data for all 100 institutions was to foster socialization. In total, there were 1,507 tweets categorized for on- and off-campus events and activities. Many tweets were focused on social gatherings and places for students to interact with one another outside of the classroom setting. This indicates that on Twitter, the primary purpose is to foster socialization by promoting activities for campus life, attracting students to cheer on their sporting teams, and encouraging them to get involved on campus (figure 4.1).

The category of tweets outside of the seven functions is titled other and earned the second highest number, 1,480 tweets. Many tweets included weather announcements, with snow causing campus closures and class cancellations. Tweets also promoted student athletes but did not promote a game

Table 4.2 Twitter Purpose Results

Purpose Category	*Twitter Purpose—Total Amount of Tweets*
Foster Socialization	1,507
Other	1,480
Promote Culture	1,019
Convey Knowledge	1,012
Conduct Research	918
Confer Credentials	458
Communicate	361
Sustain the Institution	318
Provide Public Service	232
Collaborate	76

Source: Created by the author.

Figure 4.1 Foster Socialization (Twitter Purpose). *Source*: @Occidental on Twitter, screenshot captured by author.

for students to attend in a social environment. This result indicates that many higher education institutions are creating tweets outside of the seven functions of higher education (figure 4.2).

In total, 1,019 tweets promoted culture: upcoming art exhibits, new additions to the library, a film screening, or performances such as ballet and the orchestra. Also, several tweets promoted the arts, such as off-campus museums in the local community where the institutions were located. Twitter became a vehicle for promoting the arts to the online community. Thus, promoting culture is a primary purpose for colleges and universities to use Twitter (figure 4.3).

Conveying knowledge earned 1,012 tweets for the month. There were many tweets describing academics, such as majors or minors offered through various departments. Whether it was a new major, or highlighting a department for recruitment purposes, the institution promoted ways to attain knowledge. Another aspect of conveying knowledge is to promote learning opportunities, which included guest speakers, lectures, and workshops for students to attend. Because of the large number of tweets in this category, conveying knowledge is a primary purpose for using Twitter in higher education. Conducting research was identified 918 times in the analysis of purpose. Tweets in this category recognized faculty and student research. Faculty tweets focused on publications such as textbooks or journal articles, while student research highlighted research projects, conferences, and senior papers. Although not identified as frequently as other categories, conducting

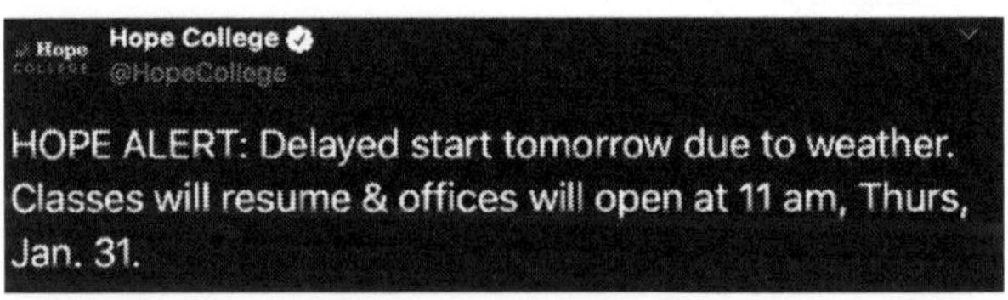

Figure 4.2 Other (Twitter Purpose). *Source*: @HopeCollege on Twitter, screenshot captured by author.

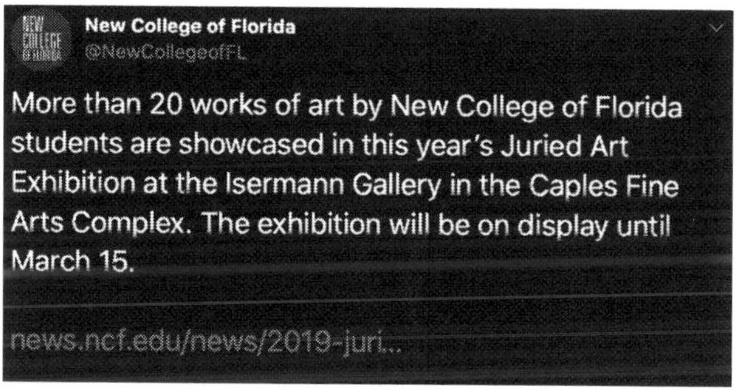

Figure 4.3 Promoting Culture (Twitter Purpose). *Source*: @NewCollegeofFL on Twitter, screenshot captured by author.

research is still a priority for social media employees when creating messages and content for Twitter (figure 4.4).

The next five categories of purpose for tweets (confer credentials, communicate, sustain the institution, provide public service, and collaborate) were not used as frequently by social media employees. Confer credentials was classified 458 times when analyzing the tweets. Most of the tweets focused

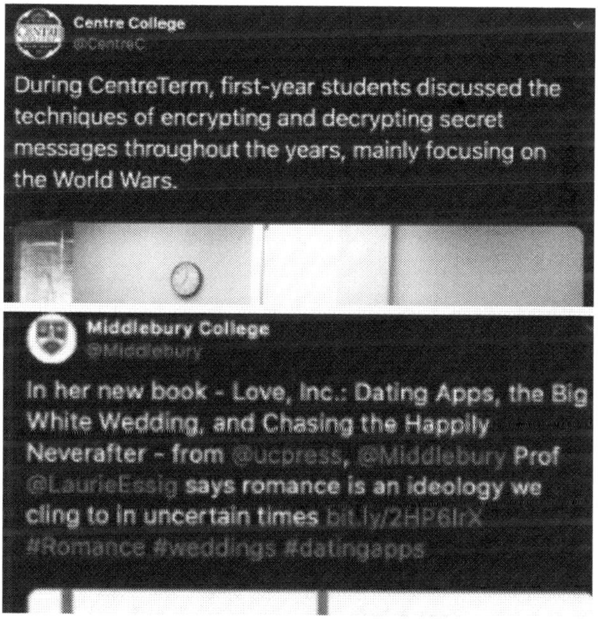

Figure 4.4 Above Is a Convey Knowledge (Twitter Purpose) and Below Is a Conducting Research Example (Twitter Purpose). *Source*: @CentreC (top) and @Middlebury (bottom) on Twitter, screenshot captured by author.

on graduation information and deadlines for students. Also, there was information about scholarships as well as when to apply to the institution. There also were several tweets about offices and services, whether it was the writing center or campus cafeteria menu choices. Tweets that were labeled communicate were discovered 361 times in the analysis of Twitter. Although not one of the seven functions of higher education, there were a fair number of tweets simply used to have conversations with members of the online community and those who follow the institution on the social media platform. Thus, some tweets were meant to communicate, interact, or respond to community members via Twitter. Tweets classified in this category were noted as a reply to another Twitter user. All the replies used text only, without any media. All tweets were meant to start a discussion and focus on a conversation, as well as answer questions from specific users (figures 4.5 and 4.6).

Sustaining the institution only had 318 tweets for the month. This only seems to be utilized by social media employees if there was an announcement to be made regarding facilities, improvements to classrooms, or partnerships. Many tweets for sustaining the institution announced college presidents, athletic coaches, new faculty, or new staff members. Providing public service had 232 tweets for the month, the lowest category of the seven functions of higher education. These tweets centered on students helping non-profit organizations and conducting activities for elementary and middle schools near the institutions. There also were several community service announcements because of the timing of the content collection near Martin Luther King Jr. Day. Based on the analysis of the tweets, while social media employees may

Figure 4.5 Confer Credentials (Twitter Purpose). *Source*: @lewisandclark on Twitter, screenshot captured by author.

Figure 4.6 Communicate (Twitter Purpose). *Source*: @Hillsdale on Twitter, screenshot captured by author.

use sustaining the institution or providing public service to publicize information to their online community, both categories are not a main purpose of using Twitter in higher education (figure 4.7).

The lowest category was "collaborate," which was reflected in 76 tweets for the month and is not a main purpose for using Twitter. Very few tweets discussed working together or showcasing teamwork in any fashion. When collaborating on Twitter, social media employees asked for content, such as pictures from their followers. This is not a necessary category for social media employees using Twitter (figure 4.8).

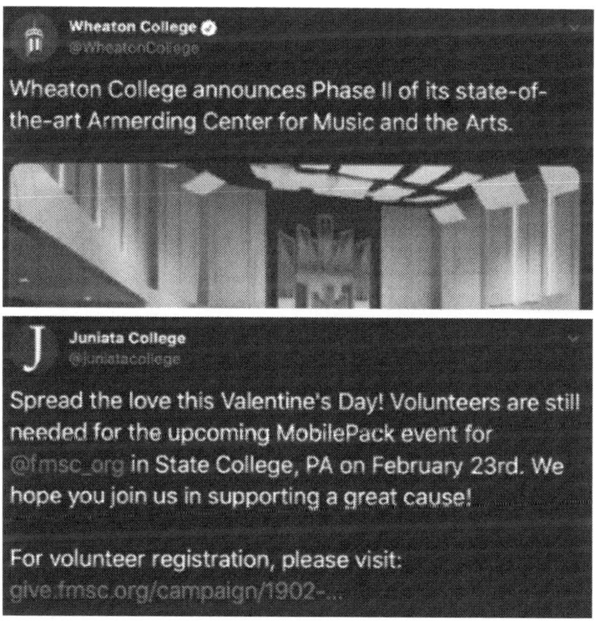

Figure 4.7 Above Is an Example of Sustaining the Institution (Twitter Purpose). Below Is an Example of Providing Public Service (Twitter Purpose). *Source*: @WheatonCollege (top) and @juniatacollege (bottom) on Twitter, screenshot captured by author.

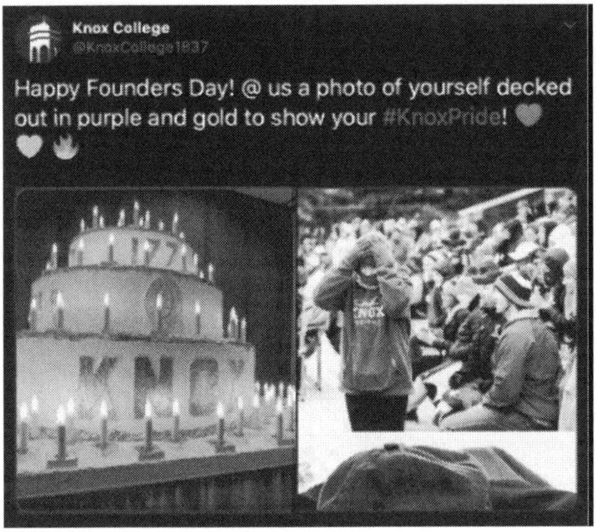

Figure 4.8 Collaborate (Twitter Purpose). *Source*: @KnoxCollege1837 on Twitter, screenshot captured by author.

FREQUENCY EVIDENCE OF GENRE MANIFESTATION: FACEBOOK PURPOSE RESULTS

Table 4.3 displays the results for the purpose of Facebook posts. In total, there were 2,969 Facebook posts combined for all 100 higher education institutions in the month time frame (January 15, 2019 to February 15, 2019). During the coding process, eight Facebook posts were labeled as "N/A" (not available). This is because the college or university deleted the post before I began the coding process. Therefore, 2,961 Facebook posts were analyzed.

Table 4.3 Facebook Purpose Results

Purpose Category	*Facebook Purpose—Total Amount of Posts*
Promote Culture	550
Other	535
Convey Knowledge	469
Foster Socialization	451
Conduct Research	385
Confer Credentials	206
Sustain the Institution	188
Provide Public Service	141
Collaborate	24
Communicate	12

Source: Created by the author.

Based on the second coder's classification of purpose, there was very little to be discussed, or any changes to classifications. The only alterations needed pertained to the labeling of communicate and collaborate. There was some confusion about how to differentiate the topics from one another. After further discussion with the second coder, it was agreed that collaborate would be any Facebook post which requested the online community to produce content associated with the initial post created by the higher education institution. An example would be posting a picture or video in response to the initial message. Communicate, on the other hand, is any Facebook post to which a user in the online community responds or leaves a comment. An example would be if a Facebook post asks a question and a social media user responds, thus leaving a comment underneath the college or university query.

The analysis of Facebook purpose includes the seven functions of higher education and three additional categories (other, collaborate, and communicate). Table 4.3 presents the results from highest (most used purpose) to lowest (less utilized purpose). There was no category that received zero Facebook posts, as each function was a purpose at some point in the month.

The main purpose of Facebook for the entire month for the 100 colleges and universities was promoting culture. Many posts (550) promoted the arts, such as upcoming theater or music performances on campus. Also, many Facebook posts promoted museums in the local area, new paintings in campus art galleries, or new collections in the library (figure 4.9).

Not too far behind, the category of other was the second highest (535). There was a substantial number of Facebook posts discussing the weather forecast for the week or cancellations due to snow. Also, many Facebook posts promoted students who were athletes, but did not promote a game for socialization. This indicates that many colleges and institutions use Facebook outside of the seven functions of higher education, thus indicating that potential new themes or additional categories should be created for analyzing Facebook (figure 4.10).

The third highest category for purpose was to convey knowledge, which received a total of 469 Facebook posts. While a good number of Facebook

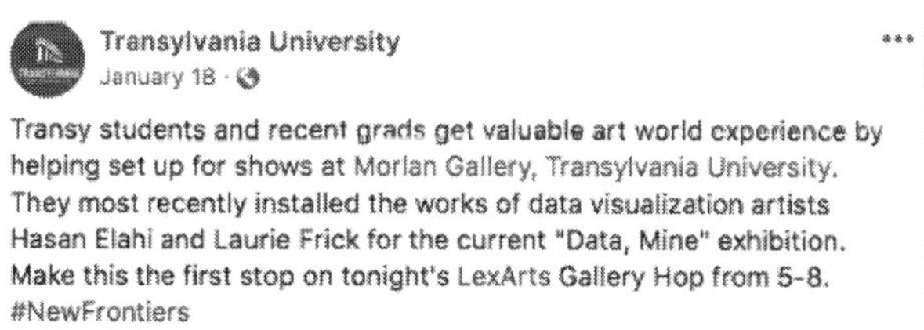

Figure 4.9 Promoting Culture (Facebook Purpose). *Source*: Transylvania University on Facebook, screenshot captured by author.

Figure 4.10 Other (Facebook Purpose). *Source*: Mount Holyoke College on Facebook, screenshot captured by author.

posts discussed majors or minors on campus, it also was used to promote learning on campus. Many Facebook posts helped educate the online community about various topics and disciplines offered at the college or university. Many Facebook posts discussed guest lectures or workshops. Also, Facebook was used as a form of digital classroom to highlight the knowledge of the campus faculty. Although conveying knowledge was not the category receiving the highest number of Facebook posts, a primary purpose of colleges and institutions using Facebook is to promote academic programs and educational opportunities for students and the local community. The fourth purpose category for Facebook posts for higher education institutions is to foster socialization. In total, there were 451 Facebook posts in this category. The largest number of posts in this category were to promote upcoming athletic events, such as a basketball game. There were many Facebook posts geared toward campus events, such as a bake sale gathering for students to interact with one another. This indicates that a primary purpose on Facebook is to foster socialization by promoting campus activities for students to attend and by building a fan base for their sports teams. While not the highest category, fostering socialization still received a fair number of posts, which makes this still a primary purpose for colleges and universities using Facebook (figure 4.11).

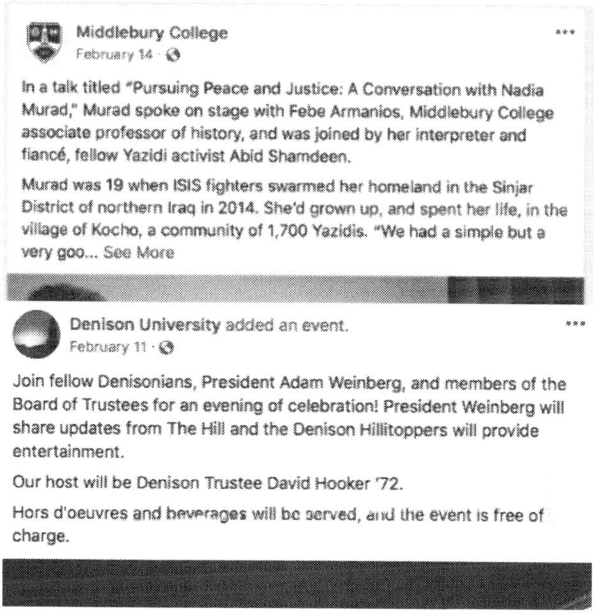

Figure 4.11 Above Is an Example of Conveying Knowledge (Facebook Purpose) and Below Is an Example of Fostering Socialization (Facebook Purpose). *Source*: Middlebury College (top) and Denison University (bottom) on Facebook, screenshot captured by author.

The fifth category is to conduct research. In total, there were 385 Facebook posts labeled as research. The 385 Facebook posts in this section described both student and faculty research. There were a fair number of Facebook posts for each. Student research was primarily about conferences they attended to present their research, as well as promoting studies they conducted. Faculty research included publicizing upcoming or recently released books or journal articles. Also, research represented any faculty, student, or alumni appearing in the media (radio, television) discussing their work. Although not a top priority for the purpose of Facebook, social media managers invest a fair amount of time highlighting the work, research, and background of their faculty, students, and alumni, which is a benefit for the college or university. The sixth most utilized purpose of Facebook is to confer credentials. There were 206 Facebook posts identified in this category. Most posts had to do with graduation information, whether it was announcing commencement speakers or information on when students had to apply for graduation. A regularly used Facebook post in this category was also for interested students who planned on applying to a particular college and university. These students were notified about deadlines on Facebook. Lastly, another example of credentials included information on campus services: the financial aid office for any payment queries, menu options for campus cafeterias, or shuttle service times for students who are traveling. Although 205 Facebook posts are much less than the category for culture, conferring credentials was still posted fairly frequently on the social media platform (figure 4.12).

The seventh category in descending order is to sustain the institution. This category received 188 Facebook posts. The vast majority focused on three areas: (1) budget or grant announcements, generating income into the institution; (2) upgrades to campus buildings including new classrooms, enhancements to the infrastructure and technology, and announcements of new facilities; and (3) hiring of new faculty and staff for academic departments and college offices that benefit students and imply a commitment to learning. Sustaining the institution was not a primary post for most colleges and universities, but it was used quite regularly when there were announcements to be made to the community on social media. Providing public service is the last of the seven functions of higher education evaluated. In total, 141 Facebook posts were determined to be providing public service in their message. The posts in this category highlighted volunteer work or community

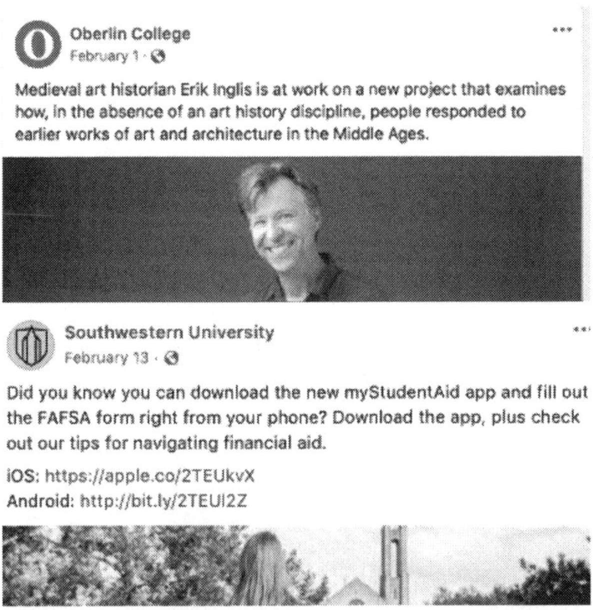

Figure 4.12 Above Is an Example of Conducting Research (Facebook Purpose) and Below Is an Example of Conferring Credentials (Facebook Purpose). *Source*: Oberlin College (top) and Southwestern University (bottom) on Facebook, screenshot captured by author.

service (helping an organization or cause raise money or awareness on campus or within the local community). Clearly, the results indicated that social media employees in higher education do not use the social media platform daily to post about community service but will do so when there is information to share with the public. A total of 185 Facebook posts for a month is still a fair amount of content, messages, and information about public service (figure 4.13).

The ninth and tenth categories regarding purpose on Facebook institutional social media pages are the two identifiers not associated with the seven functions of higher education. Both defined the term social media and its organizational use to complete tasks and responsibilities. However, neither category turned out to be a major purpose for social media employees using Facebook at the one hundred institutions selected. "Collaborate" received 24 posts and "communicate" was associated with 12 posts. This result clarifies that Facebook's main purpose is not to communicate and interact with an online community. Users may communicate, comment, and interact with one another based on the other categories, but if a post is specifically to collaborate with the online audience to produce content or have a continuous conversation on the platform, it does not occur. Therefore, Facebook is mostly used as a website to present information to the public (figure 4.14).

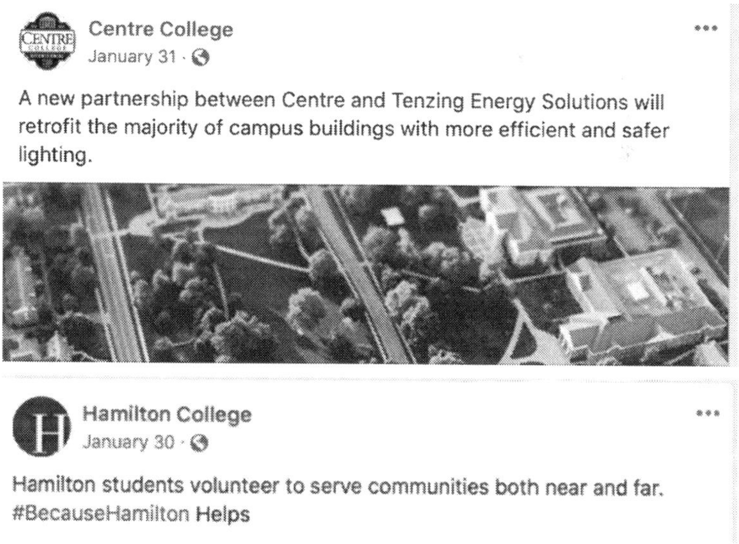

Figure 4.13 Above Is an Example of Sustaining the Institution (Facebook Purpose) and Below Is an Example of Providing Public Service (Facebook Purpose). *Source*: Centre College (top) and Hamilton College (bottom) on Facebook, screenshot captured by author.

Figure 4.14 Collaborate and Communicate (Facebook Purpose). *Source*: Haverford College on Facebook, screenshot captured by author.

THEMES: SIMILARITIES AND DIFFERENCES OF PURPOSE BETWEEN TWITTER AND FACEBOOK

The results for purpose indicate many similarities between Facebook and Twitter. The first six categories for Facebook and Twitter were the same. Even though there are slight differences in the order, the same functions of higher education appeared: promote culture, foster socialization, other, convey knowledge, conduct research, and confer credentials all appeared as a purpose of using Facebook and Twitter in higher education. "Confer credentials" had 206 posts on Facebook and 458 tweets on Twitter. This result is the sixth purpose for both platforms and can be considered a purpose for both Facebook and Twitter. Social media managers infrequently posted information on both platforms about offices, services, tuition, application deadlines, and other institutional deadlines. However, based on the top results of both Facebook and Twitter, both are used to convey knowledge, conduct research, foster socialization, and promote culture in their messages to their online communities when relaying information on both platforms.

For both Facebook and Twitter, the category "other," which is information outside of the seven functions of higher education, was the second highest purpose. Based on this result, institutions are posting information on Facebook and Twitter outside of the characteristics of higher education. Thus, new categories should be considered in future research that may include weather, sports, and additional topics that came up regularly in this study. The final four functions of higher education were the same for both Facebook and Twitter, meaning that sustain the institution, provide public service, communicate, and collaborate are not a major purpose for colleges and universities posting information on Facebook and Twitter (table 4.4).

The first difference to note is that what appeared on Facebook would usually also appear on Twitter, but this did not work in reverse. If a message appeared on Twitter, it would not necessarily appear on Facebook. This is because of the different number of posts on the respective platforms, as well as Twitter being used more as a conversational tool. One of the biggest differences is that Twitter is used more frequently than Facebook. In total, there were 7,607 tweets on Twitter, while Facebook had 2,969 posts for the month. There is a clear difference in how social media employees are attempting to communicate information to their audience via the social media platforms in that Twitter is the preferred social media environment out of the two.

It is very clear from the results that Facebook and Twitter have different first purposes. The first result for Facebook is to promote culture: music, art, libraries, and museums for example. Twitter, on the other hand is used primarily to announce and promote upcoming campus events for social activities outside of the classroom, such as meet-ups to dinner, student clubs, or attending a sports game.

Twitter has a clearly defined purpose. In looking at the top five results for Twitter: foster socialization, other, promote culture, convey knowledge, and conduct research are all purposes for using Twitter. The last five categories

Table 4.4 Facebook and Twitter Similarities and Differences: *Purpose*

Facebook Purpose	*Total Posts*	*Twitter Purpose*	*Total Tweets*
Promote Culture	550	Foster Socialization	1,507
Other	535	Other	1,480
Convey Knowledge	469	Promote Culture	1,019
Foster Socialization	451	Convey Knowledge	1,012
Conduct Research	385	Conduct Research	918
Confer Credentials	206	Confer Credentials	458
Sustain the Institution	188	Communicate	361
Provide Public Service	141	Sustain the Institution	318
Collaborate	24	Provide Public Service	232
Communicate	12	Collaborate	76

Source: Created by the author.

(confer credentials, communicate, sustain the institution, provide public service, and collaborate) are not a major purpose for Twitter. However, on Facebook all categories can be used in some way by a social media employee. For example, the highest category of "promoting culture" had 550 posts for the month and the seventh category, "sustaining the institution" had 188 posts in the month. While there was a difference for each function, there was not a significant difference in the total (362 posts). Therefore, Twitter primarily uses their top five functions of purpose and uses the other categories less frequently, whereas Facebook uses all functions of higher education and categories regularly within the month.

Although the final four categories are the same regarding purpose, they are in a different order on Facebook and Twitter. For Facebook, the last four include the following: sustain the institution (188), provide public service (141), collaborate (24), and communicate (12). On Twitter, the last four are as follows: communicate (361), sustain the institution (318), provide public service (232), and collaborate (76). As for the functions of higher education, neither platform is used regularly for announcements regarding community service or upgrades to the campus facilities or faculty. The difference in order mostly refers to communicate and collaborate. For Facebook, the additional categories are not sufficient to identify as a purpose for the platform. Both received very few posts on the platform. However, on Twitter, although low and not a clear purpose, "communicate" earned 361 tweets. This was because the institution replied much more frequently to their followers and online community on Twitter, which rarely happened on Facebook.

Chapter 5

Form of Facebook and Twitter Web Pages in Higher Education

After establishing purpose for Facebook and Twitter, I analyzed the overall form of each post on Facebook or tweet on Twitter for the same 100 higher education institutions chosen from the *U.S. News & World Report* list of top liberal arts colleges. Form includes the tools used to construct and communicate a message. Table 5.1 defines the categories of form based on Yates, Orlikowski, and Okamura's research about the elements of a genre.[1] When I analyzed form on Facebook and Twitter, all 21 characteristics can be labeled as many times as they appear in the message.

After form was coded in every tweet and post, a second coder was given the glossary of terms and a hard drive with the data. The second coder reviewed the researcher's classifications. Upon completion of analysis, the researcher reviewed the notes of the second coder. Based on their understanding of the meanings of each characteristic, there were some modifications to the glossary. The form element self-introductory greeting was defined as using names in the beginning of a message. Since most posts are kept relatively short, it was agreed that if an individual's first and last name was used in a message, it can be identified as a self-introductory greeting. During the coding process, the researcher left off several words that could be identified as emphatic language. After discussion with the second coder, we agreed on whether a word is emphatic. For the form element known as mention, the researcher and second coder agreed that links count as a form of mention on Facebook, meaning it does not have to use the @ symbol. If you see a Facebook user's first and last name highlighted as a hyperlink, this also means that the user has been notified and mentioned on the platform.

The second coder and researcher also discussed the meaning of a hashtag (#). The hashtag identifier is only used for the code (when something is classified and turned into a hyperlink on Facebook), opposed to using the symbol in front

Table 5.1 Twitter Form Results

Form Category	*Twitter Form—Total Number of Tweets*
Picture	4,932
UCC	4,627
Link	4,457
Hashtags	3,176
Mention	3,140
UGC	2,707
P.S.	2,642
Self-Introductory Greeting	2,263
Greeting	2,242
Embedded Message	1,923
Signature	1,764
Word/Phrase Emphasis	1,348
Emphatic Message	1,140
Graphics	1,018
Ellipsis	946
Set Apart	794
Video	563
Replies	412
List	90
Apologetic Message	25
Audio	22

Source: Created by the author.

of a number. Thus, this would turn the hashtag into word/phrase emphasis. For example, #40 is not classified in the hashtag category because it is referring to a number. However, #MovieNight represents a phrase to research a message or content, thus is labeled as a hashtag. In further discussion about word/phrase emphasis, the second coder and I agreed that abbreviated months (Jan., Feb.,) and time notations (a.m. or p.m.) count as a phrase. Lastly, there were a few pictures identified as user-created content (UCC). However, after further analysis, they were changed to user-generated content (UGC) because a person within the online community was the author and creator of the photograph, not the college itself. In the message, the creator of the photo was given credit for the image. Aside from the changes to the glossary, most changes from the second coder related to the researcher missing a characteristic of form in a post or tweet.

FREQUENCY EVIDENCE OF GENRE MANIFESTATION: TWITTER FORM RESULTS

In total, there were 40,141 characteristics of form in the tweets collected from the 100 higher education institutions in the one-month time frame (January

15, 2019 to February 15, 2019). Table 5.1 presents Twitter form results for the 21 characteristics of formatting a message when defining a genre, from the highest number (most utilized form) to the lowest number (least utilized form).

The highest category of form to construct a tweet was picture. In total, there were 4,932 tweets with a picture in it. Although not all tweets had a picture in them, as there were many with text only, there is still a significant number of tweets that utilized visuals to construct a message. Thus, the results define picture as a required format for creating a tweet on Twitter (figure 5.1).

Although UCC received the second highest result at 4,627 appearances in a tweet, it was not a characteristic necessary to the format of a message. UGC and UCC were added to see if a tweet was original information or if it was borrowed from other users on the social media platform. On Twitter, the results show that social media employees are creating their own content. However, the results do not mean that tweets are distinctively UCC as 2,707 tweets were identified as UGC. UGC came in as the sixth most frequent format on Twitter. This result highlights that UCC is the preferred method for creating original tweets. However, most institutions also post information created by other Twitter users to share with the online community that follows the college or university. On Twitter, it was very easy to identify UGC.

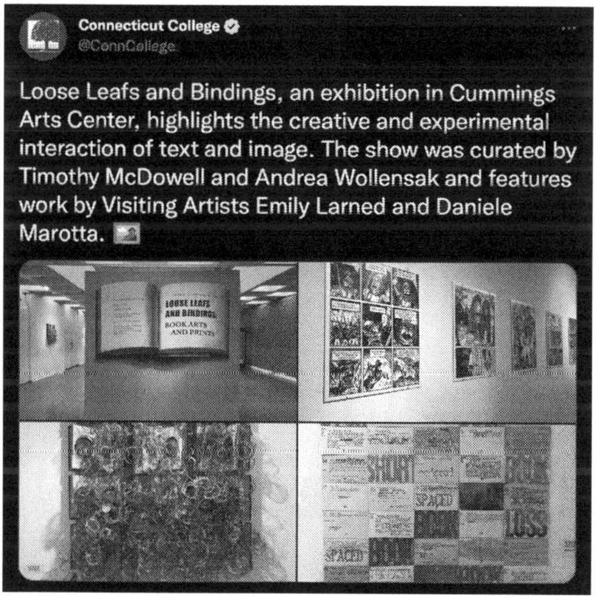

Figure 5.1 Picture: Twitter. *Source*: @ConnCollege on Twitter, screenshot captured by author.

A tweet will be labeled re-tweet on top of the message, signifying that the tweet was shared from another account (figure 5.2).

Above is an example of UCC on Twitter from Dickinson College. The tweet is an original message posted on the Twitter institutional social media page with the employee writing the text and posting the image. Below is an example of UGC from Dickinson College. This is labeled as UGC due to the phrase "retweeted" appearing on top of the message. Also, the post was from a different account instead of the main institutional channel on Twitter. Additionally, the acronym "RT" stands for retweet.

Hyperlinks, also known as links, were counted 4,457 times within the tweets collected, as a major requirement for tweets. Most of the time a link would appear at the very end of a tweet. The text would appear first with mentions and hashtags mixed in, and the blue hyperlink last, giving the user the indication that they can click it. The link will bring the Twitter user to

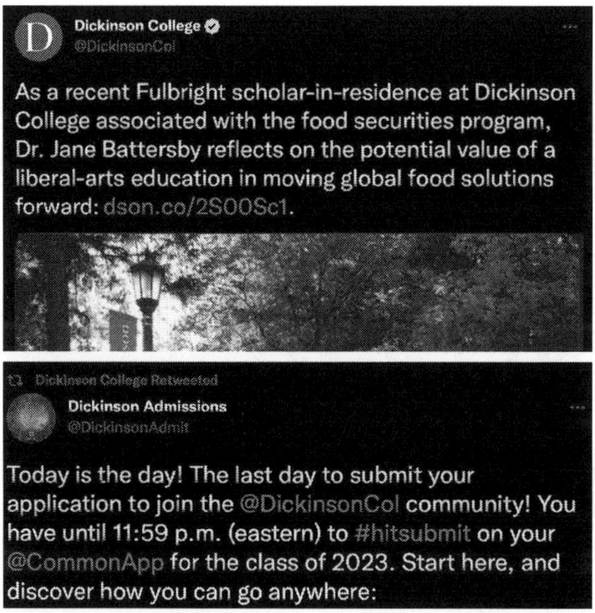

Figure 5.2 The Tweet Is an Original Message Posted on the Twitter Institutional Social Media Page with the Employee Writing the Text and Posting the Image. Below is an example of user-generated content (UGC) from Dickinson College. This is labeled as UGC due to the phrase "retweeted" appearing on top of the message. Also, the post was from a different account (@DickinsonAdmit) instead of the main institutional channel (@DickinsonCol) on Twitter. Additionally, the acronym "RT" stands for Retweet. *Source*: @DickinsonCol (top) on Twitter and @DickinsonAdmit (bottom), screenshot captured by author.

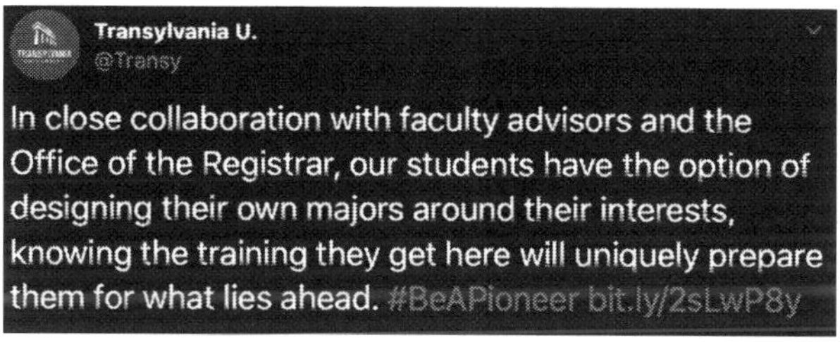

Figure 5.3 Link: Twitter—The Hyperlink Appears at the End of the Message for Transylvania University. Due to the character length, many employees would create a bit.ly link, meaning it will shorten the URL on Twitter. *Source*: @Transy on Twitter, screenshot captured by author.

another web page. Based on the results, links should be considered a required format for a tweet (figure 5.3).

Overall, there were 3,176 hashtags. There were a significant number of tweets placing a hashtag within a message. This was utilized by the social media employees to categorize their tweets in the Twitter search engine or for creativity purposes. Hashtags would be placed in the beginning, middle, or end of a tweet. Because of the results, hashtags are a required format for Twitter. There would also be occasions when an employee would use a hashtag more than once in a tweet. Thus, hashtags are an important aspect of grammar on the platform (figure 5.4).

Mentions was a format counted 3,140 times within the collected tweets. Mentions is established as a required format on Twitter because of the high results, but also because of the many social media employees using the characteristic to identify people or Twitter users on the social media site. Many

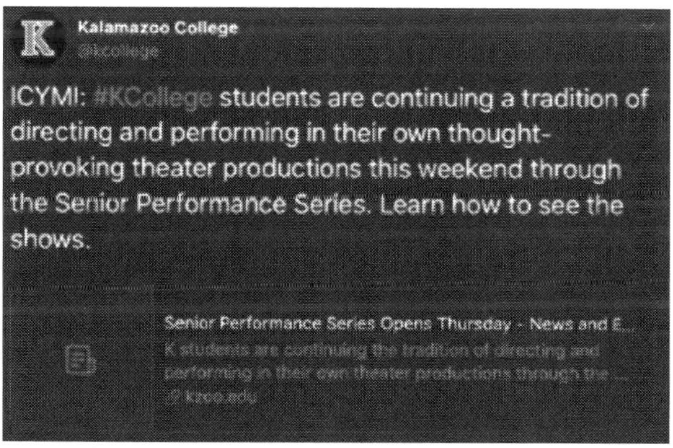

Figure 5.4 Hashtag: Twitter. *Source*: @kcollege on Twitter, screenshot captured by author.

institutions would use the "@" to identify the person or the college itself they are discussing in the tweet. The mention used within a sentence is established as part of the grammar on Twitter (figure 5.5).

At 2,642, P.S. was the next most frequent format among the tweets. If P.S. occurred, the tweet was about more than one item for discussion. Usually, there was no space between the two topics, as the sentence continued in the tweet. Based on the results, it appears social media employees regularly tweet about more than one topic within the required 280-character limit (figure 5.6).

Self-Introductory Greeting was represented in a significant number of tweets, earning 2,263 in total to be considered a required format. For Twitter, not all users had a handle (mention). Thus, social media employees would use their first and last name in the post. At times, more than one name appeared. Although names were mentioned in the beginning of a tweet, there were times the researcher would find a name at the end of a tweet. Because of the high number of tweets using Self-Introductory Greeting, social media employees should consider this format in the structure of a tweet (figure 5.7).

Greeting was discovered 2,242 times in the content analysis of tweets. Many social media employees would write a welcome message before the

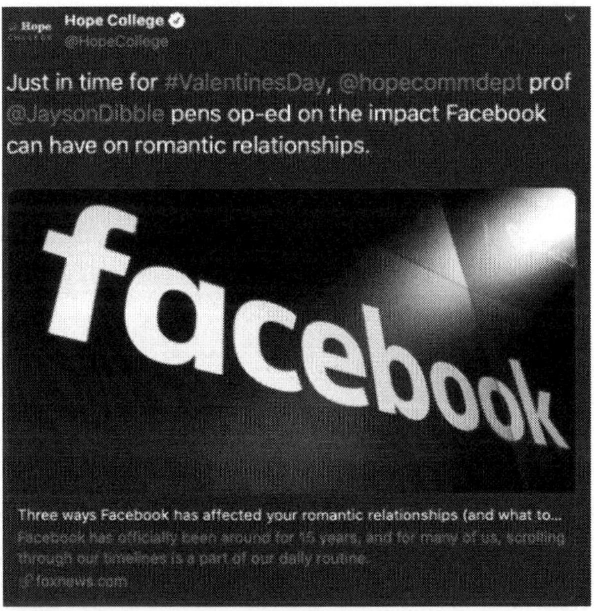

Figure 5.5 Mention: Twitter—An Example of Using Mentions on Twitter as the Tweet Is Recognizing the Communications Department at Hope College, as well as the Professor's Twitter Account. *Source*: @HopeCollege on Twitter, screenshot captured by author.

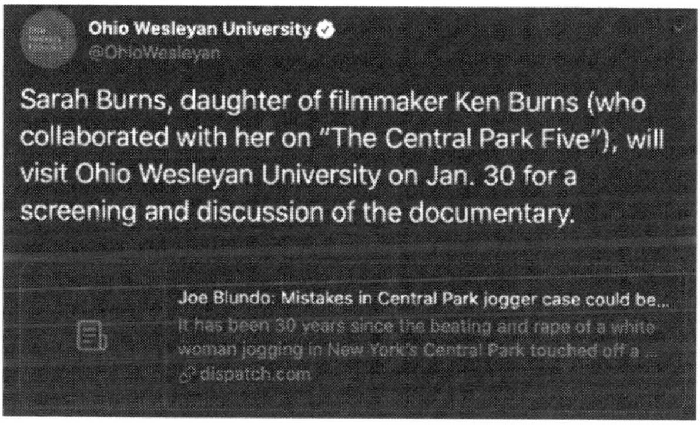

Figure 5.6 P.S.: Twitter—The Above Tweet Is an Example of P.S. The message is about Sarah Burns having a screening on campus, but in parenthesis the tweet mentions her father and a project they previously worked on, which is supplemental to the original post. *Source*: @OhioWesleyan on Twitter, screenshot captured by author.

Figure 5.7 Self-Introductory Greeting: Twitter—Furman University Utilizing Self-Introductory Greeting for the Following Tweet Using the Full Name of the Author Visiting Campus. *Source*: @Furman University on Twitter, screenshot captured by author.

remainder of the tweet. An opening greeting would include a phrase such as "Hello." Questions to the audience also were counted as a greeting to begin a conversation. Because of the results, greeting is a form on Twitter that social media employees should consider when writing a tweet (figure 5.8).

The next five formats received lower totals then the previous ones but were used frequently enough for a social media employee to consider them in the structure of a tweet. This may come down to the purpose and reason behind the tweet. Embedded Message appeared 1,923 times for the month. This is when information is shared from another Twitter user, but with an original message on top of what is embedded underneath. An individual viewing the tweet can see both messages on the Twitter profile page. There was never a tweet with just an embedded message; all institutions created an original message on top of what was shared from the other Twitter account. The institution is giving credit to the original post, creating a form of citation on Twitter. The results imply that social media managers may embed tweets in a post, but not as often as other formats. Another format for social media employees to consider, but which may not be required for all tweets, is signature. In total, signature was noted 1,764 times for the entire month of collected tweets. A signature included a call to action to visit the institution website or read more information about an event. There were a few times when a social media employee would have a closing statement as part of a tweet, but for the most part, it was asking the online community to take some sort of action (figure 5.9).

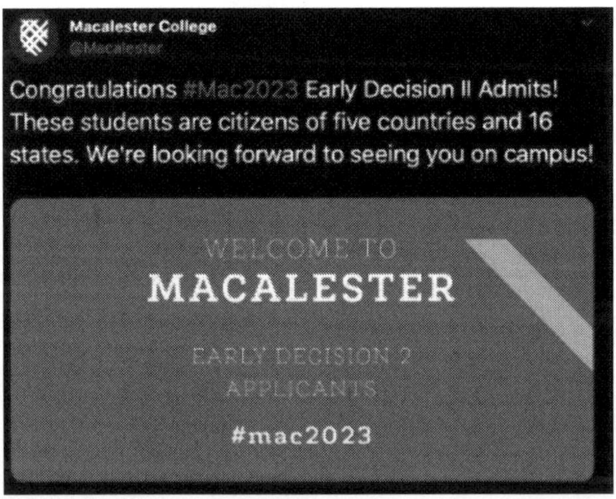

Figure 5.8 Greeting: Twitter—Macalester College Is Using the Form Greeting by Using the Word "Congratulations" at the Beginning of the Tweet. *Source*: @Macalester on Twitter, screenshot captured by author.

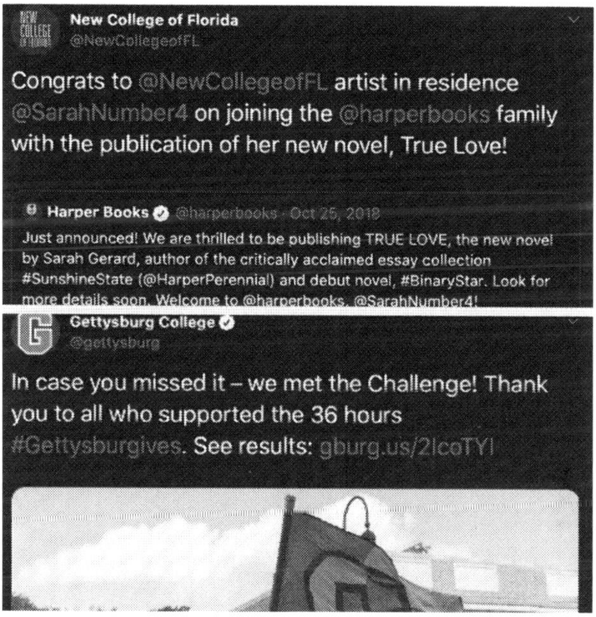

Figure 5.9 Above Is an Embedded Message on Twitter. The following is an example of an embedded message from New College of Florida as the institution is sharing a message from Harper Books but adding an original comment and information above. **Below is a Signature on Twitter.** *Source*: @NewCollegeofFL (top) and @gettysburg (bottom) on Twitter, screenshot captured by author.

Word/Phrase Emphasis was discovered 1,348 times during the month of data collection. This was used to shorten words to create an acronym or recognized phrase for online users. This was used often as social media employees have a strict 280-character limit. Word/Phrase Emphasis used symbols or shorten titles such as Mr. or Mrs. The result indicates that Word/Phrase Emphasis is not utilized for all tweets, but social media managers may use it if necessary for their messages (figure 5.10).

Several of the social media employees in higher education used Emphatic Language to express information and thoughts to their online audience. In total, Emphatic Language was identified 1,140 times for the month. Using assertive, powerful language was somewhat frequent on Twitter for the month, but not a required feature by many of the institutions. This was much different than the other type of language I was analyzing, which is Apologetic Language. There were only 25 tweets in total using Apologetic Language as a format and structure to a tweet. Thus, this is not a format for the genre of Twitter. On the other hand, Emphatic Language can be considered as a format for social media employees in higher education (figures 5.11 and 5.12).

Figure 5.10 Word/Phrase Emphasis: Twitter—Haverford College Is Using Word/Phrase Emphasis in Their Tweet to Shorten the Word "and" to Use the & Symbol. This helps shorten the character limit on Twitter. *Source*: @harverfordedu on Twitter, screenshot captured by author.

The last format on Twitter for social media employees to consider is Graphics, using emojis and animated symbols such as a clock to describe the time, or any additional digital art. Based on the results, graphics were used somewhat frequently with 1,018 in total. Many tweets did not have them, but they were used, if necessary, in the post. It also depended on if a word had a graphic to match it, such as basketball, for example. However, the results show that text, hashtags, pictures, and other tools are more important to the structure of a tweet than graphics (figure 5.13).

The formats for Ellipsis (946), Set Apart (704), Video (563), and Replies (412) were not utilized often in a tweet. These four characteristics of form were sparingly used. Ellipsis was mostly found when a hyperlink had three periods within the URL. Otherwise, it was not used to continue dialogue, but as part of the continuation of the link itself. Set Apart was used occasionally by the social media employees to place a space between two paragraphs of information. However, most social media employees kept the information within one paragraph. Although pictures were used quite often as a visual element, video was rarely used on Twitter. During the month of collecting tweets, social media employees preferred to post static, still pictures opposed

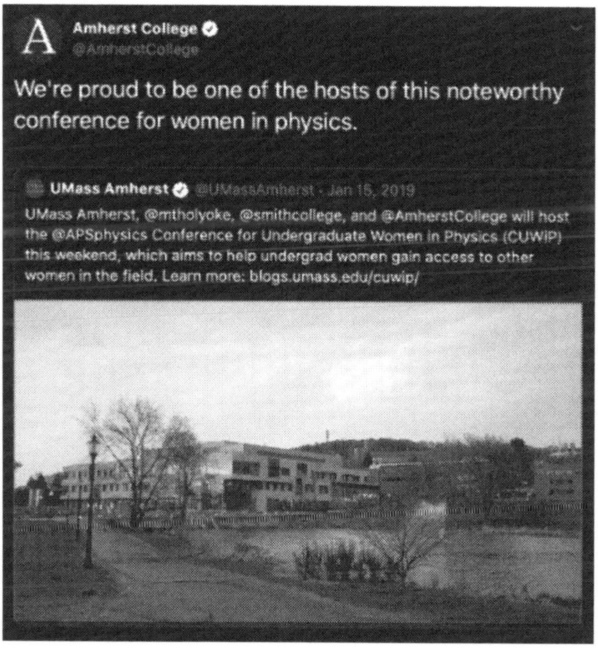

Figure 5.11 Emphatic Language: Twitter—Amherst College Is Using Emphatic Language in Their Tweet Stating that the Institution Is Proud to Host a Conference for Women in Physics. The word proud is identified as emphatic language. *Source*: @AmherstCollege on Twitter, screenshot captured by author.

to videos. Even though Twitter is a platform for conversations, there were not many replies collected in the month. Therefore, even though Twitter is used for conversations, the platform is being used for UCC and daily information, as opposed to consistently responding to the institution's online audience (figure 5.14 and figure 5.15).

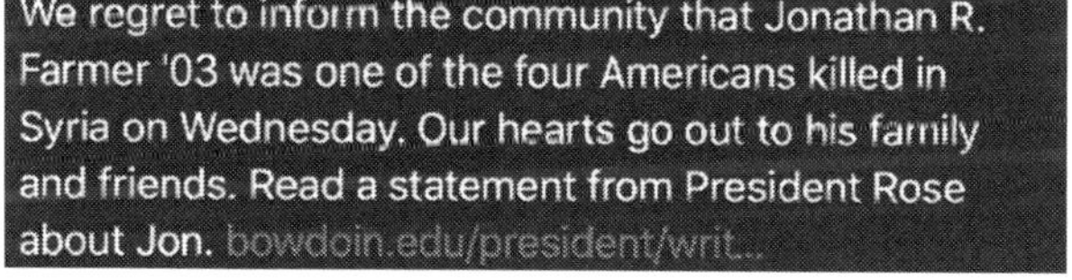

Figure 5.12 Apologetic Language: Twitter—The Following Tweet Is an Example of Apologetic Language as Bowdoin Institution Is Using the Word "Regret" to Apologize to the Community and Send Sympathy to the Family for the Loss of an Alumni. *Source*: @Bowdoin College on twitter, screenshot captured by author.

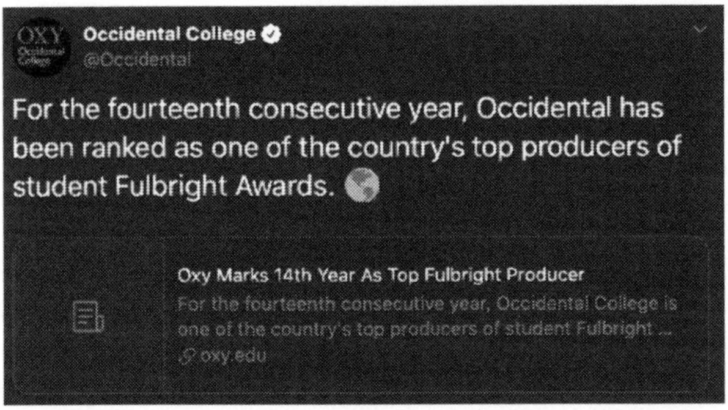

Figure 5.13 Graphics: Twitter—Occidental College Is Using a Graphic, Also Known as an Emoji of the World or Globe to Describe Their Ranking in the United States. *Source*: @Occidental on Twitter, screenshot captured by author.

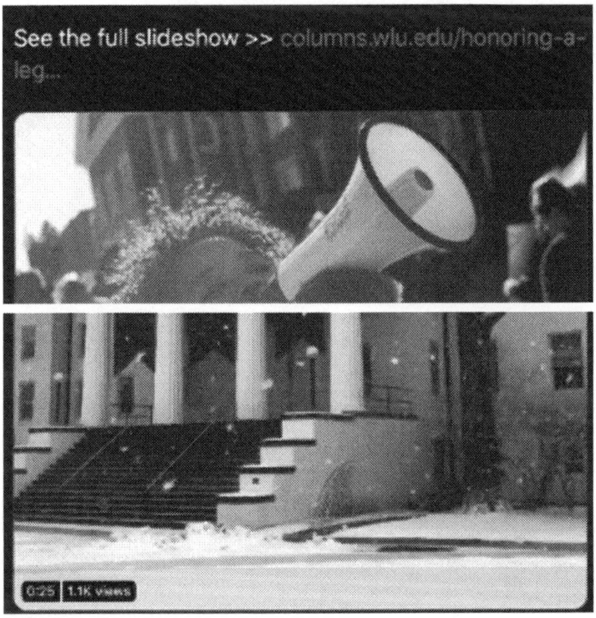

Figure 5.14 Above Is Ellipsis and Set Apart: Twitter. Washington and Lee uses set apart to separate the opening paragraph and the signature to view the slide show. Also, ellipsis is found within the hyperlink at the very end indicating additional characters in the URL. **Below is Video: Twitter.** Gettysburg College is using video to showcase snow on campus. On the bottom left, Twitter users can see the video with the duration playing on the bottom of the screen. Also, a video will automatically play when hovering the mouse over the tweet. *Source*: @Washington and Lee College (top) and (bottom) @Gettysburg College on Twitter. Screenshot captured by author.

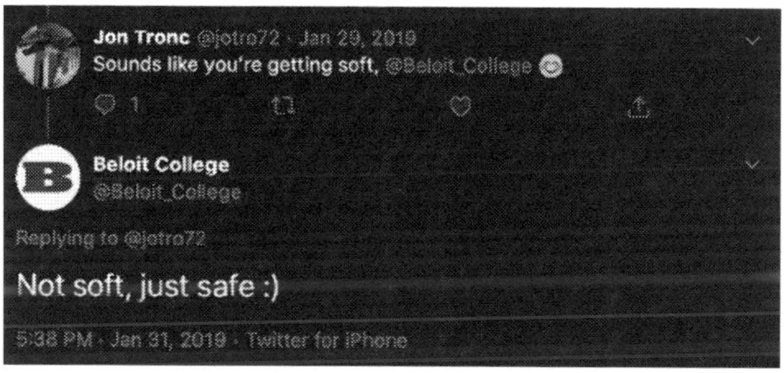

Figure 5.15 Reply: Twitter—Beloit College Is Responding to One of Their Followers on Twitter Concerning Snow on Campus. *Source*: @jotro72 and @Beloit_College on Twitter. Screenshot captured by author.

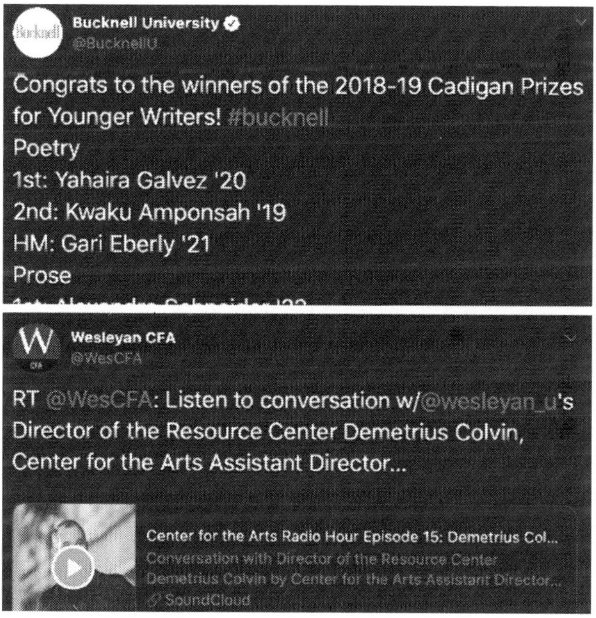

Figure 5.16 Above Is a List: Twitter—Bucknell University Is Displaying the Poetry Winners Vertically, Using the Structure of a List. Below is Audio: Twitter—Wesleyan University is promoting an interview for their radio show that is posted on SoundCloud. SoundCloud is a platform that contains audio files. *Source*: @BucknellU and @WesCFA on Twitter. Screenshot captured by author.

Along with Apologetic Language, two other characteristics of form that were not utilized very often and therefore are not a requirement for tweets are*:* List and Audio. List was identified 90 times during the month, while

Audio was counted 22 times. Most social media employees post information in one paragraph, not a list. If there was Audio in a tweet, it was mostly combined with video. But this format was looking for audio files only, such as music, a podcast or radio show. Overwhelmingly, most institutions were not sharing or posting audio files for their online audience (figure 5.16).

FREQUENCY EVIDENCE OF GENRE MANIFESTATION: FACEBOOK FORM RESULTS

In total, there were 17,147 characteristics of form within the Facebook posts for the 100 higher education institutions in the one-month time frame (January 15, 2019, to February 15, 2019). The results for Facebook form are presented by the 21 characteristics of formatting a message when defining a genre, ranked from the highest number (most utilized format) to the lowest number (least utilized format). There was no category that received zero Facebook posts, as each characteristic of form was discovered.

UGC received the highest number for any category. However, this is not necessarily a trait to devise and construct a message. UGC and UCC were added to the definition of form as they relate to either a social media employee posting original content or borrowing content from someone else. Overwhelmingly on Facebook, the results indicate that social media employees create their own content (pictures, video, text) without borrowing from other Facebook users or businesses. 2,909 Facebook posts are categorized as UCC while only 84 posts are considered UGC. In total, there were 2,993 Facebook posts for the entire month, which highlights that social media employees in higher education are expected to produce and create original content daily, outside of constructing a message on Facebook (figure 5.17).

Based on the results for form, there are many characteristics that are clearly important for higher education institutions to use when designing a message for their online community. Additionally, there are three levels that I believe represent the form of a Facebook message: required characteristics, possible characteristics, and unlikely characteristics.

Beginning with the required characteristics of form established from the results of the content analysis, out of the 2,993 Facebook posts for the month, 2,552 of them contained a picture. It was very rare to find a Facebook post that did not include a picture. All the photos incorporated with a post were user created, taken by the institution and social media employees. The image matched the text in the message (academics, events, or other purposes) to share with the online community surrounding the institution. Therefore, the results indicate that pictures are a required format when constructing a

Figure 5.17 The Above Facebook Post Represents UCC as the Social Media Employee Created the Message and Picture Without Giving Credit to Another User. UCG Below Represents the Social Media Employee at Hamilton College Crediting a Student on Campus for Creating the Picture. The social media employee did not create the image and is borrowing the picture for their message. Additionally, the camera emoji identifies giving credit to the students who created the image. *Source*: Colby College (top) and Hamilton College (bottom) on Facebook. Screenshot captured by author.

message for Facebook; they should be original photographs, as opposed to borrowing photographs from other users (figure 5.18).

Another required characteristic for form is the use of hyperlinks, or links, within the message of a Facebook post. For the most part, links were discovered at the very end of a message. Usually, the text for a Facebook post would appear first, communicating information to the online community, followed by the hyperlink. Every hyperlink on Facebook is blue. When a user clicks on the link, it brings them to another website. In total, 2,144 links were categorized within the Facebook posts for the month. This result indicates that a social media employee should include a link when designing a message on Facebook, as users may expect to visit a website that corresponds with the

Figure 5.18 Picture: Facebook. *Source*: Macalester College on Facebook. Screenshot captured by author.

information being provided. P.S. is used to include additional or supplementary information regarding the initial message. Within the same Facebook post, a social media employee would include a second message. Once the first topic would end in one or more sentences, a second topic or additional information would follow inside the same paragraph. I discovered that including additional information and more than one message (or topic) to discuss with an online community is regularly required when formatting a Facebook post. It seems social media employees do not worry how long a post may be and add as much information on a topic as possible within a Facebook post: P.S. was identified 1,666 times in the one-month analysis (figure 5.19).

I consider Self-Introductory Greeting as a required element when creating a Facebook post for social media employees in higher education. In total, Self-Introductory Greeting appeared 1,360 times in the month of Facebook posts collected from the colleges and universities analyzed. For Facebook, Self-Introductory Greeting was noticed many times as the social media employee constructing the message regularly included the first and last name of the person the message is about. For various posts, more than one name is included. As agreed, with the second coder, the first and last names of the people the message describes can appear in the beginning, middle, or end of the post. Because of the massive number of times Self-Introductory Greeting

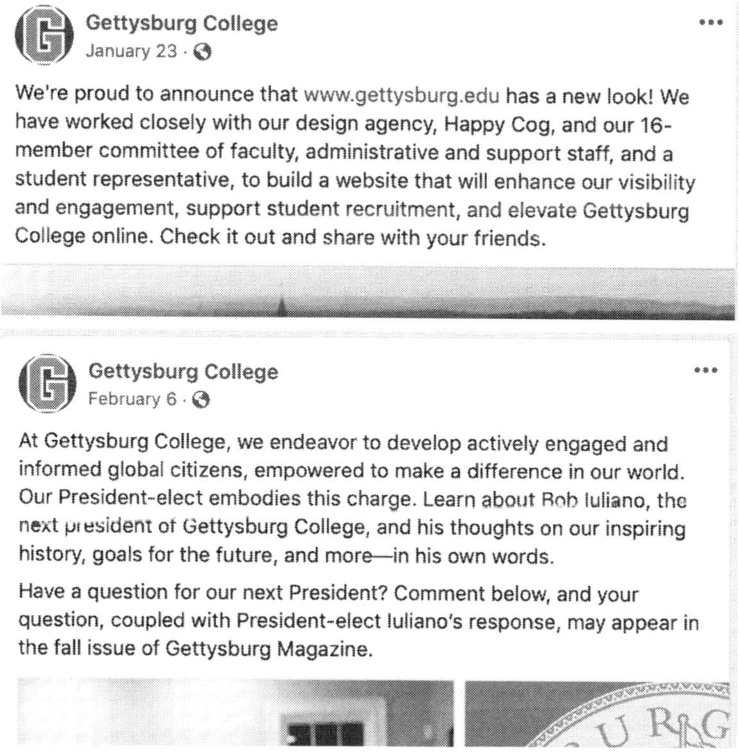

Figure 5.19 The Images from Gettysburg College Presents the Format of P.S. Due to Adding a Sentence to the Facebook Post after the Initial Goal. The first message is sharing the mission statement of the new president, and the second message is requesting the online community to ask a question in the comment section, creating a second, distinct topic. *Source*: Gettysburg College on Facebook. Screenshot captured by author.

appeared, Facebook posts within a higher education institution should include the individual's name (first and last name), if applicable for the post (figure 5.20).

Based on the results, one final required format for designing a message on Facebook is that a signature should appear at the very end of the post. In total, Signature was counted 1,128 times from all the Facebook posts for the 100 colleges and universities for the month. A Signature is a closing statement at the end of a message. For example, on Facebook, one would close a post, mentioning "For more information" or "visit our website." Therefore, because of the many times a Signature was used, I believe this is a required format when constructing a post for Facebook. I describe possible formats for Facebook as characteristics that were observed between 500 and 1,000 times on institutional profiles. These formats may appear on a Facebook post but

Figure 5.20 Self-Introductory Greeting: Facebook—Lawrence University Uses Self-Introductory Greeting for This Post Using the First and Last Name of the Individual the Message Is About. *Source*: Lawrence University on Facebook. Screenshot captured by author.

not on a regular basis. A social media employee may use the format depending on the message and how they decide to communicate with their followers and audience. An Embedded Message appeared 825 times for the one month of Facebook posts of colleges and universities. An Embedded Message for Facebook occurs when the social media employee shares on the college and university page a message posted by another Facebook user, business, or institution. The higher education Facebook page normally added an original message above the embedded message. There were a few rare posts that only included the embedded message. Embedded Messages can be a valuable resource for institutions wishing to share information from other accounts while giving credit to the originator of the message or content (figure 5.21).

A bit less frequently used was a Greeting. Some institutions or social media employees would post an opening message before informing their audience of the specific topic. An opening greeting would include such phrase as "Welcome" or a question to begin the dialogue among the online community before explaining the topic of the message. There were 771 Greetings identified through all the Facebook posts. Greetings are a form for Facebook that is used by some social media employees and can be considered by higher education institutions to begin

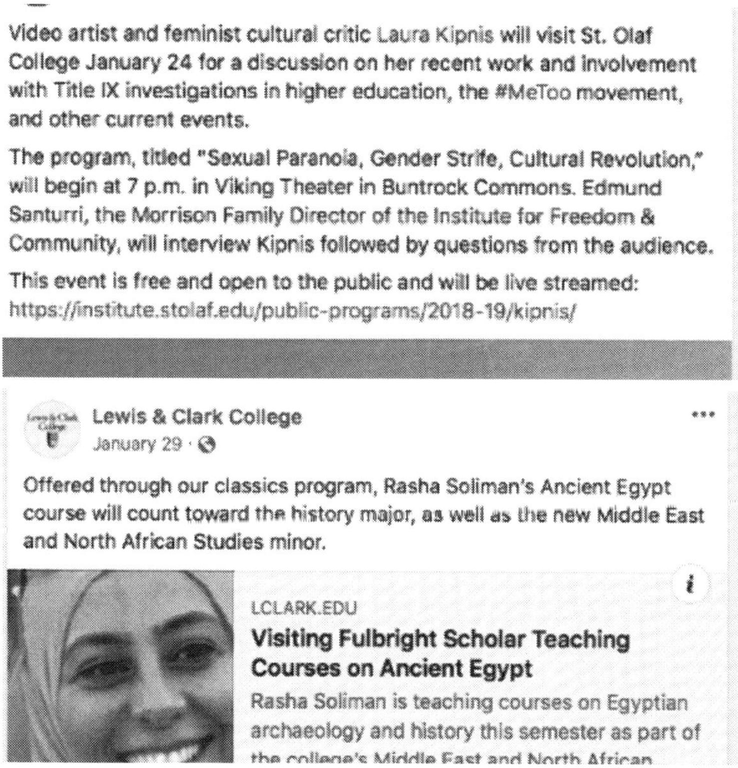

Figure 5.21 Above Is Signature: Facebook. The Facebook post from St. Olaf College serves as an example of Signature that could be found from many of the colleges and universities evaluated. The closing statement used gives the online community "something to do" or call to action, in this case visiting the web page to watch the event online. Also, many signatures told the online community if they wished to attend that the event is free and open to the public. **Below is Embedded Message: Facebook.** The following Facebook post presents a second way an Embedded Message can be used. When adding a hyperlink, Facebook creates a message from text on the page, as well as the title of the article. Also, you will find a picture included in the Embedded Message. *Source*: Lewis & Clark College on Facebook. Screenshot captured by author.

a conversation, dialogue, and message on Facebook, if the format is needed. Set Apart was utilized for many Facebook posts, particularly when associated with P.S. As stated in the definitions of form, Set Apart is separating the content into more than one paragraph. While not the priority for a social media employee to use, the researcher discovered that Set Apart was a form of constructing a message 713 times on Facebook. Coinciding with the format of a greeting, Set Apart is used when there is more than one topic within the post and additional information needs to be provided to the online community (figure 5.22).

Figure 5.22 Above Is Greeting: Facebook. Hendrix College Is Using the Form "Greeting" in This Facebook Post. Many colleges and universities analyzed using this format did so to start the message with a congratulatory statement. **Below is Set Apart: Facebook.** Wheaton College Massachusetts is a prime example of the use of Set Apart as all three paragraphs in the Facebook posts are separated by a space. *Source*: Hendrix College on Facebook. Screenshot captured by author.

Word/Phrase Emphasis was used sparingly on Facebook to shorten words into smaller phrases, such as initials for a university: Professor (Prof.) or states (N.Y.), among others. For the most part, the 100 institutions analyzed for Facebook all shortened similar words into phrases or acronyms, the most common being a.m. and p.m. When designing a message, the researcher discovered that Facebook did not frequently utilize the form of Word/Phrase Emphasis but did so on words that are commonly shortened when writing information to others. In total, Word/Phrase Emphasis was classified 690 times on Facebook (figure 5.23).

Hashtags are not commonly used on Facebook for social media employees in higher education. The results indicated that in all the posts from the 100 colleges and universities for the month, hashtags appeared 667 times. This is

Figure 5.23 Word/Phrase Emphasis: Facebook—Aside from Reed College Using P.M. for the Time Again as Word/Phrase Emphasis, the Institution Also Shortens the Words Question and Answer by Using the Phrase Q&A. *Source*: Reed College on Facebook. Screenshot captured by author.

a major difference from Twitter. On Facebook, it seems that higher education institutions use hashtags for posts less frequently and do not look to use them as a search mechanism to locate information later. Hashtags were only used if there was some sort of promotion or campaign involved or if the institution has previously created a hashtag associated with its brand. Thus, it appears that hashtags are used as a form on Facebook when needed for a particular purpose, as opposed to regularly logging every post using Facebook as a library or database of information. Emphatic Language is one of the two ways of expressing information to an online community. Although Emphatic Language was used much more frequently than Apologetic Language, the strong, bold, forceful, and definitive language was not implied too regularly on Facebook as the posts were more conversational, as opposed to coming across too strongly. It seemed that social media employees in higher education would use Emphatic Language, counted 556 times for the month, only when posting important information that the institution was announcing or making sure that an idea, subject, or topic was clearly understood by the online community. Therefore, Emphatic Language as a form is only used, when necessary, based on the post, as social media employees on Facebook seemed to want to be more conversational (figure 5.24).

Three formats that are rarely used when creating a message on Facebook as discovered during the content analysis were Ellipsis (413), Graphics (316), and Video (263). Ellipsis used three or more periods within a message, continuing the conversation or if there was a follow-up message. However, this only appeared on Facebook at the very end of a hyperlink, very similarly to Twitter. This implied that there was more text associated with the hyperlink, but it was not needed on the message as the user was able to still click on it and visit the associated web page. Ellipsis on Facebook means that the format is used for hyperlinks when designing a message, but not for text.

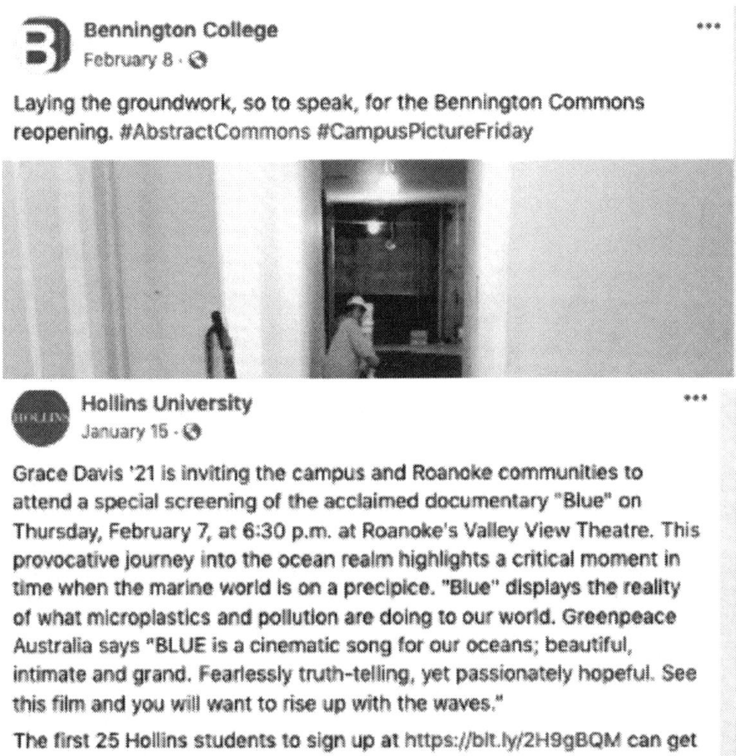

Figure 5.24 Above Is an Example of Using Hashtags on Facebook. Below is Emphatic Language: Facebook. There are several examples of Emphatic Language in this Facebook post by Hollins University. The words "provocative," "critical," "beautiful," "intimate," "grand," "fearlessly," and "passionate" all exemplify assertive language to describe the message and topic of the Facebook post. *Source*: Bennington College and Hollins University on Facebook. Screenshot captured by author.

Graphics on Facebook were used with emojis, whether it was a symbol of an arrow pointing in a particular direction, smiley face, or weather, such as a snowflake, among others. Based on the results, Graphics were only used sparingly by social media employees only if a graphic can be associated with the word or message of the post. While it is a tool available for engagement, social media employees in higher education did not use the interactive graphic frequently, instead opting to use text on Facebook. Compared to photography and text on Facebook, video was not posted much on the platform for all the 100 institutions. Colleges and universities were relying more on images as their visual content, as opposed to a video on recruitment, events, advertising campaigns, and other purposes of a message on Facebook. Thus,

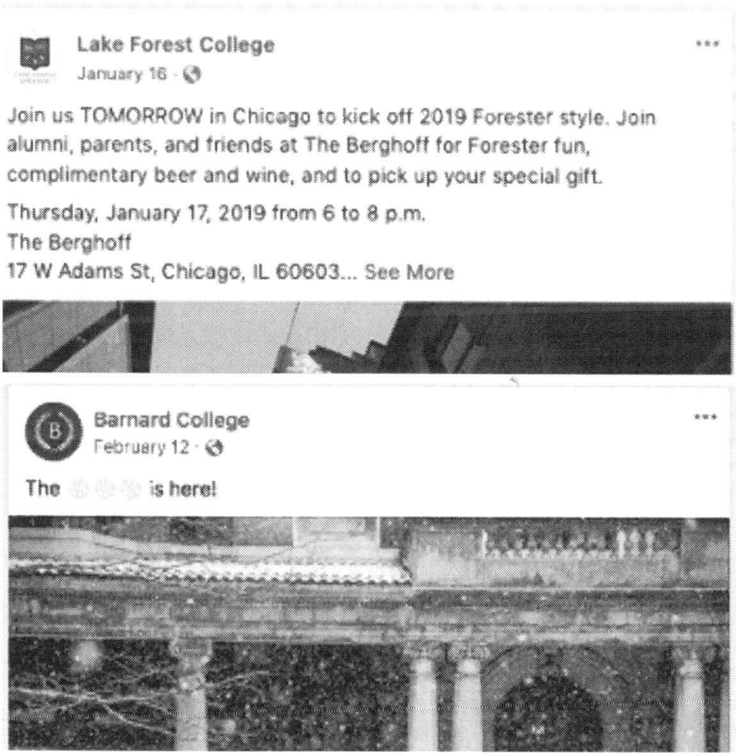

Figure 5.25 Above Is Ellipsis: Facebook. Along with all institutions using ellipsis, Lake Forest College does so at the end of their initial Facebook post. If there is more information, three periods will appear (...) and See More as a link is the very last two words. If this phrase is pressed, more information (text) will open. **Below is Graphics: Facebook.** Colleges and Universities would use graphics to replace text. In this Facebook post from Barnard College, emojis of snowflakes are used by the social media employee to replace the word "snow." *Source*: Lake Forest College and Barnard College on Facebook. Screenshot captured by author.

video is not a format regularly used on Facebook when posting a message on the social media service (figures 5.25 and 5.26).

When analyzing for genre, there are five categories of form that did not appear on Facebook. These five categories were hardly used and are not part of the genre for Facebook as each appeared fewer than one hundred times during the month of data collection. List (42) Mentions (34), Audio (11), Apologetic Message (3), and Replies (0) should not be considered a form for Facebook. Lists were posts where information appeared vertically. Social media employees for Facebook in higher education institutions preferred writing content in paragraph form. Mentions associated another business or individual by using the "@" symbol before the name or by a hyperlink. Mentions were also rarely used on Facebook by all institutions as they did not

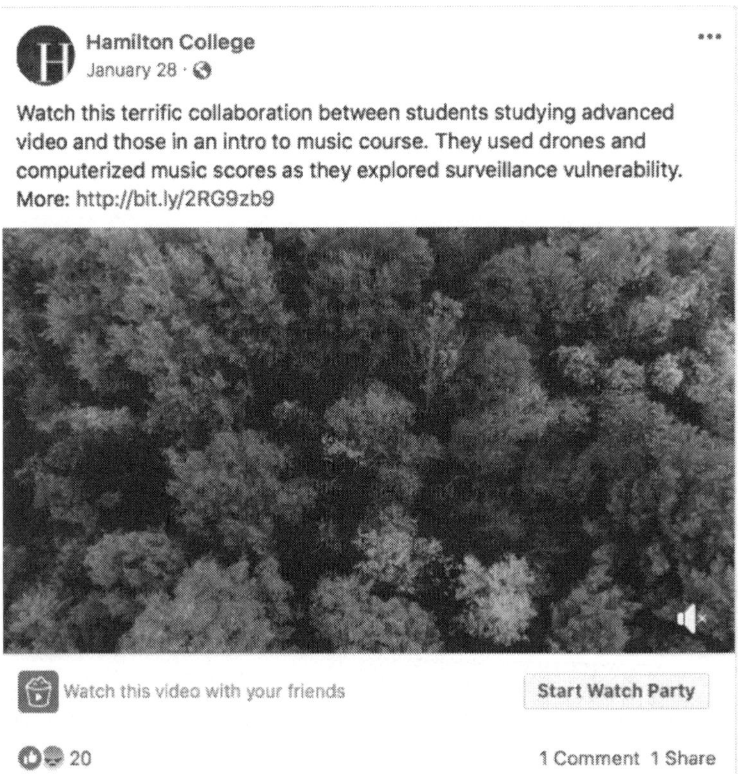

Figure 5.26 A Video Is Recognized on Facebook by Moving Images. When hovering your mouse over the image, a play button appears. Once pressing the play button, the video begins. Also, a video is also recognized on the bottom right where an audio logo appears. This allows the user to listen to the sound or turn it off. This also helps distinguish a video from a photograph, which does not have the logo. *Source*: Hamilton College on Facebook. Screenshot captured by author.

try to notify others within the message or associate a post with other social media users. Instead, many posts mentioned the college or university (figure 5.27).

Audio was not posted as a standalone type of content for Facebook in higher education institutions. Audio could be heard when video was used, but rarely was a single audio file posted. Only occasionally was a podcast promoted on Facebook. Thus, Facebook is not a platform to promote audio or post audio files for higher education institutions. Apologetic Messages were seldom used as most posts on Facebook did not show remorse or regret or retract any information. Thus, Facebook was not a platform to announce any mistakes or information needed to be discussed with the community of students, faculty, and staff. Replies were never used, but this was mostly due to the structure of Facebook. When posting on Facebook, replies work as dialogue underneath a message, as opposed to an original or shared post, which I was analyzing. This format is much more noticeable on Twitter but is not a form that can be used

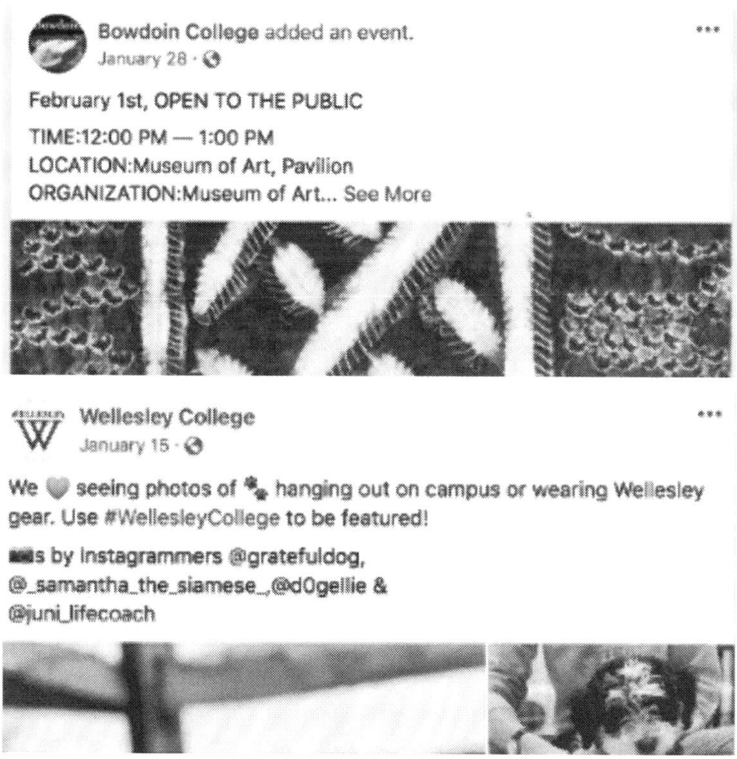

Figure 5.27 Above Is a List on Facebook and Below Is a Mention on Facebook. *Source*: Bowdoin College and Wellesley College on Facebook. Screenshot captured by author.

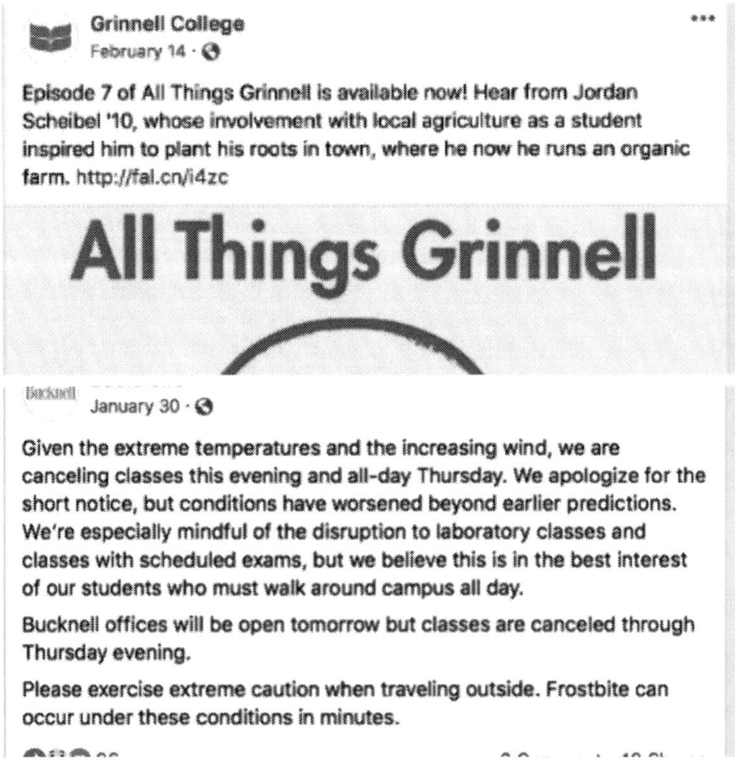

Figure 5.28 Above Is Audio on Facebook and Below Is Apologetic Language Appearing on a Facebook Post. *Source*: Grinnell College (top) and Bucknell University (bottom) on Facebook. Screenshot captured by author.

when designing a message on Facebook. All messages were original and did not state that they were replying to another user's query or statement (figure 5.28).

THEMES: SIMILARITIES AND DIFFERENCES OF FORM BETWEEN TWITTER AND FACEBOOK

Upon analysis, there were many similarities discovered between Facebook and Twitter. This is represented in table 5.2. Although in a slightly different order, the top three results for Facebook and Twitter were UCC, Pictures, and Links. To explain further the topic of visuals, both Facebook and Twitter prioritize pictures, as opposed to video. Video was rarely used for both platforms, as there were only 263 posts on Facebook and 563 tweets on Twitter using moving images. This result indicates that visuals are a format for both Facebook and Twitter, but in the form of still images.

Table 5.2 Facebook Form Results

Form Category	*Facebook Form—Total Amount of Posts*
UCC	2,909
Picture	2,552
Link	2,144
P.S.	1,666
Self-Introductory Greeting	1,360
Signature	1,129
Embedded Message	825
Greeting	771
Set Apart	713
Word/Phrase Emphasis	690
Hashtags	667
Emphatic Message	556
Ellipsis	413
Graphics	316
Video	263
UGC	84
List	42
Mentions	34
Audio	11
Apologetic Message	3
Replies	0

Source: Created by the author.

To elaborate on UCC, social media employees constructing a message preferred to post original work as opposed to sharing a message from another social media user. Original work included the message itself, along with the visual associated, such as a picture. Both Facebook and Twitter utilized hyperlinks to construct a message. The social media employees did so to share information associated with their message. On each platform, hyperlinks appeared in blue, indicating a cue to the social media user to click on the URL to read more information about the topic of the post or tweet. Therefore, based on the top three results, every Facebook post or tweet on Twitter should include a hyperlink within the message to read more information, a picture that coincides with the information, and be original work from the employee at the higher education institution.

There were two types of languages analyzed for form between Facebook and Twitter, which are Emphatic Language and Apologetic Language. On both social media platforms, Emphatic Language was used regularly in the format, but Apologetic Language was rarely, if ever, used. There were only minimal posts or tweets apologizing for something that went wrong at the institution, thus this type of language is not considered a form. However, Emphatic Language was used somewhat regularly for Facebook, and used quite often for Twitter, which means this type of language can be considered a form of constructing messages on the social media platforms. Many posts and tweets used strong, assertive words to get their point across.

Based on the results, audio is another format rarely used. Posting audio files for the online community happened only 22 times on Twitter and 11 times on Facebook. If it did occur, it was to promote a podcast. But it almost never happened within the month of analysis. Therefore, audio is a format not to include in the structure of a message. It is important to note, that out of all the ways to add media to a post or tweet, only pictures were utilized daily. Along with Apologetic Language and Audio, another format not used on both Facebook and Twitter is a List. Lists occurred 90 times on Twitter and 42 times on Facebook. This result identifies that a social media employee prefers to present information within a paragraph, as opposed to presenting text and content vertically.

Although there were several forms that can be considered as not useful for designing messages on Facebook and Twitter, the content analysis proved that several characteristics are formats for both sites. Along with Pictures, Links, and UCC, the additional formats included: Self-Introductory Greeting, Signature, Embedded Message, Greeting, and Word/Phrase Emphasis. All these formats were used by social media employees during the month analyzed. There were tweets or posts where each characteristic was omitted, but for the most part, these characteristics were used consistently. This clarifies that it is important to begin with an opening greeting such as welcome, include names of individuals the message discusses, paraphrase words when needed, embed content from a website into the original post, and end a message with a closing statement.

For the most part, Ellipsis was a format used moderately for Facebook and Twitter. However, it is important to note that Elipsis was not used to include more information about a subject or end a message. Ellipsis appeared for both social media sites within hyperlinks, meaning that there was more code to the URL that was being left out to fit the character length for Twitter and shorten on Facebook. Along with Ellipsis, I found that Graphics was used moderately on Facebook and Twitter too. It's important to note, Graphics did occur more frequently on Twitter. Therefore, the social media employee on both platforms adds emojis or animated images depending on the content of the message (table 5.3).

Upon completion of the content analysis, there are many differences between Facebook and Twitter. When reviewing the results, one can notice that Twitter has a higher number in each category than Facebook. This is because more tweets than Facebook posts were collected over the course of the one month of analysis. On Twitter, Mentions were used within a message 3,140 times, but only 34 times on Facebook for the month. This indicates

Table 5.3 Facebook and Twitter Similarities and Differences: Form

Facebook Form	*Total*	*Twitter Form*	*Total*
UCC	2,909	Picture	4,932
Picture	2,552	UCC	4,627
Link	2,144	Link	4,457
P.S.	1,666	Hashtags	3,176
Self-Introductory Greeting	1,360	Mention	3,140
Signature	1,129	UGC	2,707
Embedded Message	825	P.S.	2,642
Greeting	771	Self-Introductory Greeting	2,263
Set Apart	713	Greeting	2,242
Word/Phrase Emphasis	690	Embedded Message	1,923
Hashtags	667	Signature	1,764
Emphatic Message	556	Word/Phrase Emphasis	1,348
Ellipsis	413	Emphatic Message	1,140
Graphic	316	Graphic	1,018
Video	263	Ellipsis	946
UGC	84	Set Apart	704
List	42	Video	563
Mention	34	Reply	412
Audio	11	List	90
Apologetic Message	3	Apologetic Message	25
Reply	0	Audio	22

Source: Created by the author.

that Mentions are a form and grammar used to identify users on Twitter but not on Facebook. Facebook does have the ability to mention other users; it is simply that institutions are not using this format when constructing a message. It should be noted that although Mentions earned a substantial result, Replies were relatively low, meaning users mentioned are not responding to tweets.

Another format that was a major difference between Facebook and Twitter is Hashtags. The format of a Hashtag was counted 3,176 times on Twitter, but only 667 times on Facebook. The technique to catalog a phrase, word, or message was used within a vast number of tweets but used much less frequently on Facebook. Thus, Mentions and Hashtags were popular formats for Twitter, but for Facebook, Mentions are a format, but Hashtags were used for only some posts. For Facebook, you will find messages without a Hashtag, but for Twitter, it is very rare for a tweet not to use a Hashtag to catalog information for the social media platform.

There is also a difference between Facebook and Twitter relating to UGC. On Twitter, UGC was classified 2,707 times while on Facebook the same category only had 84 posts. This result provides clarification in that Twitter institutional web pages will share content from other users and sources (along with posting original content), while institutional Facebook pages will not post information created by users in their online community, and mostly share UCC that the institution's employees design themselves.

There were a few additional formats that provided different results between Facebook and Twitter. For Facebook, the format Set Apart was discovered in 713 posts, while on Twitter it was in 703 tweets. Although this may seem that the platforms were close in their results, this is not the case. Set Apart is a frequently used format on Facebook, as the ninth most used structure. However, on Twitter, it is the 16th most used format, and used much less frequently than many others. On Facebook, there are many posts that would separate information into two or more paragraphs, but on Twitter, information would normally stay within one paragraph, not separating topics or information. Ellipsis and Graphics are more likely to be used on Twitter than on Facebook. Lastly, the category of P.S. was identified 1,666 times on Facebook and 2,642 times on Twitter. Although Twitter had the higher number for the month, the category was used more frequently on Facebook. P.S. is ranked fourth for Facebook and seventh for Twitter. The same occurred for the format of Signature, which ranked 6th for Facebook and 11th on Twitter despite the number of tweets and posts being very similar. Used on both sites, Closing Statements and Embedded Messages are more common formats on Facebook than Twitter.

NOTE

1. Yates, Orlikowski, and Okamura, "Explicit and implicit structuring of genres in electronic communication," 87.

Chapter 6

Functionality of Facebook and Twitter

Higher Education Staff and Administration Interviews

Out of the one hundred social media employees contacted and requested participation in my study, ten individuals agreed to be interviewed. Out of the 10 participants, five were men and five were women. The interviews were conducted between February 15, 2019 and March 8, 2019, at times agreed upon with each participant. All interviews were conducted during normal business hours (9:00 a.m.–5:00 p.m.) When signing the audio and video consent forms, all participants requested audio recordings. Therefore, no interviews were recorded via video. All interviews were recorded using the voice application TapeACall Pro. The interviews ranged from approximately 10 minutes to 30 minutes. When the interviews began, I described the study again and the participant's rights.

To state an interesting finding before I introduce the results, most interviewees connected both platforms as one, not separate entities. To explain, question one asked, what is the purpose (goal, topic, and objective) for employees using Facebook in higher education? The second query followed up by asking, what is the purpose (goal, topic, and objective) for employees using Twitter in higher education? When responding, the participants answered the question by combining Facebook and Twitter together, indicating that content and information appearing on one platform appears on the other social media site as well. While some respondents answered a question describing Facebook and Twitter as separate entities, most did not.

INTERVIEW RESULTS AND DISCUSSION

After the interviews were completed, I analyzed all ten of them to look for common themes relating to the six characteristics of genre taxonomy as described by Yoshioka, Herman, Yates, and Orlikowski. In this section, the findings of each dimension in the taxonomy will be discussed through the main themes that were mentioned by the respondents relating to both platforms. I will follow up with an analysis of the themes, specifically relating to Facebook and Twitter.

Purpose (Overview of Results)

All ten social media employees were asked their purpose (goal and objective) for using Facebook and Twitter in higher education. Questions one and two of the interview asked employees the following:

1. What is the purpose (goal, topic, objective) for employees using Facebook in higher education?
2. What is the purpose (goal, topic, objective) for employees using Twitter in higher education?

Participant 1 and Participant 2 explained that the purpose for using Facebook and Twitter is to share information and news with everyone associated with the campus community including faculty, students, alumni, parents, and staff. Participant 2 said news may pertain to "college specifically or about higher education or news of interest to our audience. Specifically, not news from [redacted] but about higher education and the industry in general." Another purpose for Participant 2 is to build relationships by connecting with alumni and people already with the college. Participant 3 agreed with the previous participants by mentioning that in higher education Facebook and Twitter are used to share news about the college such as what faculty, alumni, and students are doing. Participant 3 was the first to provide a difference between Facebook and Twitter when explaining the institution's social media use: Facebook provides a glimpse of the campus with the chosen content posted, while Twitter is used to curate and provide consistent news about the institution. Participant 4 stated that the purpose for Facebook and Twitter at their institution is to recruit students to the college and connect with chosen audiences such as parents, alumni, and faculty. Participant 4 explained, "We have a variety of purposes for it but overall, our goal with anything here in our marketing and communication office would be to recruit."

Participant 5 responded for Facebook and Twitter as separate entities, as opposed to combining them as other participants had done. Participant 5 described that Facebook is best to connect with their alumni, foster a community on the social media platform, share news, and invite their audiences to interact with them on the website. For Twitter, Participant 5 uses it to connect with alumni, influencers, and organizations. Participant 5 explained, "We do tend to make connections with other influencers whether they're through alumni or organizations we work with or people who come to campus, maybe give a lecture on that kind of thing." Participant 6 posts content, specifically stories. The type of stories posted on Facebook and Twitter are sports updates, campus events, and campus news in general. While no specific Facebook goals were explained, Participant 6 said that Twitter is an excellent website for sports updates on games. Participant 7 stated that the goal for using Facebook and Twitter is to engage with their audience, which includes alumni, parents, current students, and prospective students.

Participant 8 declared that the purpose for Facebook and Twitter is to connect with their audience on both social media platforms, including alumni and students (current and prospective). Participant 8 explained a second purpose, which was using the platforms to persuade potential students to come to the college that the individual represents. Participant 9 said that the objective for using Facebook and Twitter includes engaging the community (which includes: alumni, faculty, staff, donors, and current students) and promotion. The topics that are created to promote include the institution itself, academics (majors and minors), and athletics. Closing out this section of the interview, Participant 10 revealed that the purpose for Facebook and Twitter is for engagement purposes as well. The institution hopes to engage alumni, parents, and prospective students. Participant 10 added, "I think overall we're trying to reach our multiple audiences and kind of keep them up to date on things that are happening around the campus." Although Twitter was not mentioned, Participant 10 explained that Facebook is best used for promoting stories (articles the institution has written for their website), increasing awareness of the website, increasing circulation of content that is created, and the purchase of digital advertisements on the platform.

Purpose Discussion: Emergent Themes Based on Interview Discourse

Several common themes were stated by more than half of the employees. Two themes that I continually noticed mentioned by the participants were share and engage. When sharing information on Facebook and Twitter, some of the participants stated that they were sharing news and information about audiences and constituents. When using the word "share," it is to send content (pictures, video, and articles for example), where the chosen audiences learn about a particular topic and the college itself. Cohen and Kenny defined share on social media as "a participant or creator offering content to be downloaded, viewed, and interpreted in a variety of ways through social media."[1] To explain the concept of sharing as it pertains to news, Participant 1 stated, "to use it as a vehicle to share information about the college including its faculty, students, alum, and administrators. To share that information to current students, potential students, and their parents." Another example of sharing on social media was stated by Participant 3: "Our focus on Facebook and Twitter is simply share news of the college and what our professors are doing, what our alumni are doing and what our students are doing." Both participants and social media employees highlight the type of stories written (faculty, student, and alumni based) while explaining who the intended audience is to consume such information (parents and current/potential students). Therefore, except for current students, the audience is outside sources (off campus) such as parents while the stories by higher education employees are written about faculty on campus.

The theme titled engage as it relates to the results is the way the platforms and their content interact with the chosen constituents online such as users commenting on a Facebook post or retweeting information on Twitter. Participant 7 explained engagement and whom it is with: "Our main purpose is to sort of engage the [redacted]. And I say like any community. I'm talking about a bunch of different constituencies: alumni and parents and prospective students and current students." Participant 9 mentioned that their institution engages with a wide audience: "to engage our greater community and that would be a community of current students, alumni, faculty, staff and then donors." Thus, both examples are used to indicate that specific audiences are chosen to interact and have discussions through social media platforms.

An analysis of a word frequency test of purpose revealed that the word "share" was the 14th most common word stated 43 times. The word "sharing" was the 33rd commonly used word, mentioned 24 times by the respondents. In total, the concept of share was stated 67 times during the interviews, showcasing the relevance of the theme and providing evidence as to why social media managers find the concept valuable. Earlier in the chapter, I defined the term "share" and its concept for social media as providing content to other users on platforms such as Facebook and Twitter. "Content" was stated 88 times during the interview, which not only highlights its importance in the genre taxonomy, but its connection to the social media through uploading photos, videos, documents, and other media to chosen individuals or audience with whom the institution engages. Also, "information" was the 15th most common word, appearing 41 times. Although content can relate to multimedia, information can be text-based and can relate to the institution, community, or other topics the institution wishes to share with the audience on Facebook and Twitter.

"Engagement" was the 28th most utilized word regarding purpose of Facebook and Twitter, mentioned 26 times with the query responses. As stated in the responses, engagement had to do with interacting with the institution's online audience, including students (current and prospective), faculty, staff, and administrators. In reviewing the top 25 most common words, many of the terms relate to people or a specific group with which the college wanted to engage. It is important to note that "faculty" was mentioned 20 times when participants were explaining the purpose of Facebook and Twitter. The results of this word frequency for purpose indicate that engaging with a group of online users, students, alumni, and fellow employees is a main objective for using Facebook and Twitter by the higher education institution.

While sharing and engagement were two vital goals for the higher education employees interviewed, both purposes depended on audiences: an audience to interact with and an audience to consume the content. Thus, as stated with engagement, a major purpose for employees interviewed regarding Facebook and Twitter is the audience itself (the word "audience" appeared 29 times, the 23rd most common word in the purpose node). The most discussed audience by all interviewees was alumni (by eight out of the ten participants). In the word frequency test conducted for the purpose node, "alumni" were the 9th most utilized word, stated 50 times. Although "students" were mentioned 73 times and was the 8th most mentioned word, "students" were used in a variety of ways to describe the college itself while "alumni" were an audience that institutions and social media managers were planning to reach. For example, Participant 8 stated, "I guess the biggest thing is just getting the [redacted] story out there and connecting with alumni and connecting with current students." Speaking of current students, half of the participants stated that current and prospective students were another audience with which to share and engage. One audience was not more or less important than the other. If an employee mentioned current students as a purpose, he or she followed up by including prospective students as well.

A significant purpose for higher education institutions to use social media platforms Facebook and Twitter is building relationships and connections with alumni of the college, as opposed to current and prospective students. The platforms are being used to sustain a relationship with those who have already graduated from the institution, as opposed to recruiting new students or fostering relationships with current students. In the word frequency test, although "alumni" were stated 50 times as a purpose and theme for using Facebook and Twitter, the word "prospective" was only used 12 times (82nd most mentioned word) for attracting new students. Current students are a bit harder to test as the term "current" was only revealed once on NVivo, but students (73 times) and student (23 times) came up 96 times during the interviews. However, the word "student" was used to explain a variety of topics in the higher education institution. Going back to prospective students, interview results indicated that the word "recruitment" was only mentioned twice when discussing purpose, keeping the focus on those who graduated from the institution. Participant 4 said, "We want to be able to focus on recruiting students of course although alumni are an important audience. They're very engaged on social media as well as parents and faculty and staff."

Two additional audiences for both Facebook and Twitter that four out of ten participants mentioned were faculty (20 times in word frequency) and parents (13 times in the same word frequency for purpose). Several employees mentioned sharing information regarding faculty as a major purpose of Facebook and Twitter. Four of the participants believe one of the audience members is parents because they are potentially researching higher education facilities for their own education when students are making their college decisions. Participant 10 stated, "I think overall we're trying to reach our multiple audiences and kind of keep them up to date on things that is happening around the college." So, while recruitment is not specifically mentioned as a vital characteristic of purpose, by virtue of parents being a key audience, they become part of a recruitment strategy. It is important to point out when it came to sharing and engagement, most of the employees interviewed associated the acts with specific audiences. However, three participants identified sharing news about the college as a major component of purpose. Sharing news appeared as a result because the institution hopes to keep audiences up to date on college happenings. This finding matches in the word frequency test as "news" was the tenth most stated word by the respondents, appearing 48 times.

Two participants stated that highlighting sports and athletic programs was a purpose for using Facebook and Twitter. This may indicate that the platforms are a great source for sending game updates to the masses while profiling athletes and the teams. This result matches the word frequency test for purpose as "sports" was the 111th most common word throughout the interviews only mentioned ten times while "athletes" was stated twice. One characteristic of purpose that is important to mention as a low result is academics. Although higher education institutions are associated with academic programs and departments, only one employee mentioned an academic objective. Participant 9 said: "The second goal would be to raise the stature of our institution worldwide and to promote our academic and athletic programming." In the word frequency test, "academic" appears only five times as the 214th most common used word regarding purpose. This connects to the finding that academics is not a major factor for purpose for higher education institutions utilizing Facebook or Twitter. The results indicate that sharing or providing news/information and engaging with multiple audiences through conversations over content is the purpose for Facebook and Twitter, as opposed to learning in the higher education institutions or promoting departmental major and minors.

Some of the participants reported on the specific purposes for Facebook and Twitter. The purposes for Facebook included to build community on campus, connect to alumni, share news, interact, promote the college, boost the website, increase circulation of college stories, and purchase advertisements. For example, Participant 3 stated the purpose for "Facebook is really more about connection to our alumni and students and other community members who are on that platform" while Participant 10 stated, "we mostly use Facebook to promote stories that we have written on the website to increase traffic." Based on the responses, it seems that Facebook has multiple purposes in the higher education environment.

The purpose and objectives for Twitter included sharing news (which two participants mentioned), connecting to alumni, connecting to influencers/organizations (people promoting the college or presenting at the institution), and highlighting sports. Participant 3 said, "And so we share more information on Twitter. Stories that we don't think will get much reach, we will share on Twitter and just because Twitter has a kind of limitless number of . . . there's no expectation of like, oh, you shouldn't be tweeting twice a day." Participant 5 discussed the importance of interacting by sharing news content on Twitter: "Twitter is more about sharing news in a more general way about the college. We do see slightly more interaction over the past couple of years." Therefore, the results indicate that the purpose of Twitter is to share news and information with the online community following the institution and to build connections or foster relationships with the online users interacting with the college/university through the social media platform.

Two participants agreed that connecting to alumni was a purpose for each platform. One other common purpose mentioned between Facebook and Twitter was that both were meant to share news. It is important to note that two participants stated that Twitter is meant as a news source while one interviewee stated the same regarding Facebook.

Content

Questions 3 and 4 asked participants: What type of content do employees post on college Facebook pages and what type of content do employees post on college Twitter pages? Participant 1 stated that the institution posts various kinds of content on Facebook and Twitter, such as user-generated content (UGC) (retweeting, for example) text, video, photographs, or audio created by another social media user. According to Participant 1, content shared with the online community includes news about students, the president of the college, and alumni. Regarding types of content, Participant 1 mentioned original written stories (user-created content [UCC]), media that highlights events on campus, and books that the faculty publishes. In an interesting finding, Participant 1 stated that student interns take photographs and video in the participant's office. The second participant defined content on both Facebook and Twitter as the same, which includes both UGC (photographs and video taken by others) and UCC (original stories/articles by the employee). The participant emphasized that publications must be original, but multimedia content can be borrowed from other places or users. Participant 2 described their content as, "News that pertains to what the audience might be interested in."

Participant 3 explained that accomplishments by faculty or students are the focus of the college or university's content for Facebook. Participant 3 stated, "We typically will put that on Facebook because we know that the community seems to value that information." No specific content was mentioned for Twitter, simply just that it will be different than Facebook. Participant 4 noted that Facebook and Twitter mostly contain UCC that the office/institution writes itself. Participant 4 occasionally will generate information from other sources (UGC), but the focus is on original content. This includes press and news releases, articles covering events, alumni articles, news on the local community, and things of interest such as the weather. Thus, the content is a mix of information of community interest and daily happenings on campus, while showcasing a fun atmosphere on the platforms based on various interests.

Participant 5 explained differences in content between Facebook and Twitter. The content posted frequently on Facebook includes photographs and video. Participant 5 mentioned that more photos are posted on Facebook more frequently instead of being published on Twitter. However, the primary content on Twitter is sharing news with no indication that the tweet must contain media (video or photographs). The type of content (news) that is shared on Twitter is faculty research, campus life (events and buildings), student programs (majors/minors), upcoming events, catching up with alumni post-graduation, and information created by other sources being shared on the institutional Twitter pages with their own online community. Participant 5 defined Twitter as a platform to share work from other users while Facebook is geared toward posting more original multimedia content. Participant 6 stated that the content for Facebook and Twitter is the same. The only specific type of content described for Facebook and Twitter is sharing stories (articles) with their online audience. The types of stories Participant 6 described are vague but relate to events. Participant 6 declared that the institution will only post one or two times a day on the social media networks. The reason for this according to Participant 6 is "because we really don't want to exhaust people. And thankfully we've got enough content that we can keep up with and not overload people."

Participant 7 described differences in content between Facebook and Twitter by noting how the higher education institution posts much less on Facebook than Twitter. Participant 7 explained, "We tend to post a lot of just sort of links and summaries to try to drive people to the website." Participant

7 prefers Twitter because of the creativity it offers to users. Outside of posting funny memes, Participant 7 retweets UGC from other Twitter users that are connected to the institution such as faculty, campus partners, administrators, and alumni. Participant 8 simply stated that the type of content posted on Facebook and Twitter is photographs and video. Participant 8 added, "I never send a tweet out without a photo unless it's like I'm doing like a live type of situation, event, or something like that. But we always send photos with our tweets and our Facebook posts." Participant 8 defined their social media use for higher education as requiring visual and multimedia content.

Participant 9 described the similarities in content between Facebook and Twitter. Participant 9 said, "On Facebook, it's a lot more academic focused so stories of research and scholarship; stories about our alumni successes and then select blog content as well." Twitter on the other hand was noted as having a slight difference, which is to inform and showcase campus events. Otherwise, Twitter was also used to promote research and share academic blogs written by faculty at the college. Participant 10 described the same content appearing for both Facebook and Twitter as prior interviews such as links, photographs, faculty research, and videos. However, Participant 10 identified that student interns are the ones tasked with recording video content daily. Participant 10 described student tasks as "we have 3 to 4 students that will do a video about a certain program on campus or research that a professor is doing. We have a series of like quick take interviews which is just kind of short two-minute video with a professor talking about their research, what they love about working at the college or a favorite class that they teach; things like that." Participant 10 also pointed out that the institution feels Twitter is best for promotion such as guest speakers. Twitter use is described as "promoting events that are happening on campus, lectures, speakers that are coming, and all of our student symposiums."

Content Discussion: Emergent Themes Based on Interview Discourse

Based on the ten interviews, in analyzing the differences between the two social media sites pertaining to content, Facebook is much more academic focused while Twitter is based on campus life at the college or university. Six participants explained differences between the content on Facebook and Twitter. However, four participants said the content was the same for Facebook and Twitter, which indicates that some feel what is posted on Facebook should also appear on Twitter and vice versa.

Participants who answered that the content is the same on both Facebook and Twitter stated that posting written stories is a top priority. In most cases, written stories referred to articles produced and published on the website to share on social media platforms. Participant 4 explained how written articles are developed and the type of content that is expected: "So if I write a story for the website and I've produced a news release for it, or we have an event coming up on campus or we're just talking about how nice the weather is outside. It's something that we're generating ourselves." All participants said that articles and stories published on Facebook and Twitter were created by the employees themselves; the articles were not written by other colleagues, authors, or published on websites that were not affiliated with their institutions. This finding relates back to Hinton and Hjorth (2013) who stated that social media has two forms of interaction, one of which is UCC, which is material created by the user themselves to post on social media websites.[2] Participant 4 explained that UGC is posted when the campus is quiet, possibly during semester breaks, but that they would rather focus on original content: "So during the downtimes we look externally but most of the time we want to focus on our own content."

In reviewing the results of the word frequency analysis for content, "stories" were the 17th most frequently mentioned word. The word "stories" came up in the results 38 times. The word "story" was the 29th most frequent word in the text search query and came up in the results 27 times. In total, stories were mentioned by the participants 65 times. This matches up with my analysis that stories (particularly written stories) are the most utilized content for both Facebook and Twitter. In reviewing the word frequency results further, "stories" should be ranked higher as the seventh most frequent word (content). Everything before the word has to do with people (103 times) or specific social media sites. Stories is the first specific form of content mentioned. Although the audience appears to be the main result for purpose, people continue to be a top result for content, too: participant (100) students (64), alumni (45), employees (40), audience (32), participants (30), student (24), and faculty (20). This may indicate that the written stories published on social media site pertain to these categories of individuals.

Three participants stated that photos, videos, and news were content posted on Facebook and Twitter. To explain photos and videos, Participant 8 added, "We always send photos with our tweets and our Facebook posts." This points out that social media platforms are highly visual in content. In the text search analysis, "photos" were mentioned 24 times and "photo" 18 times. In total, "photo(s)" appeared during the interviews 42 times. This matches up with my analysis of the interviews, with photography and visuals being a major form of content for both Facebook and Twitter.

In my evaluation of the interviews, "news" and "photography" were mentioned equally among the participants. However, it should be noted that in the word frequency analysis, "news" was mentioned 50 times (9th most frequent word) moving ahead of "photos," which in total was stated

42 times. Regarding news that is shared, content included students, alumni, and the community. "Community" appeared 22 times in the word frequency analysis, reinforcing my conclusion that news also was for the public wanting to be involved in campus activities, events, or community service activities. The words "student" and "students" came up in the word frequency results a total of 88 times. This is the most frequently mentioned audience in relation to content, not only highlighting that news relates to students, but that the content in general on Facebook and Twitter must be geared about or for students. According to Participant 2, information about students, alumni, and the overall community referred to "news that pertains to what the audience might be interested in." Content focused on alumni was mentioned as the type of news shared with the online community frequently (which ties in with the finding about purpose). "Alumni" was mentioned 45 times in the word frequency analysis.

At least two participants each provided content that included faculty research, events, and UGC. UGC is the second form of interaction mentioned by Hinton and Hjorth in 2013, where users share material produced by other Facebook and Twitter users. This result demonstrates that participants prefer to post original content (photos, video, and articles) instead of sharing content created by other social media users. The finding for events meant that activities on campus were a form of news to share with the online community following the institution. In the word frequency analysis, "events" were mentioned 21 times while "event" was mentioned 16 times. In total, "event/events" appeared 37 times while discussing content. This finding documents the value and importance of events for the content. Although 16 appears low in the word frequency analysis, many of the words before it, such as Instagram, Twitter, Facebook, Think, Day, and Campus, among others, do not relate to specific content. Thus, events are a major category to include. Two participants felt that it was valuable to present information about professors as a branding device, along with highlighting skills. "Faculty" was mentioned 20 times and "research" 18 times when participants were discussing content. Additional content for both platforms mentioned by at least one participant included "weather" and "hyperlinks" (stated 12 times in the word frequency analysis).

Four participants mentioned separate types of content appearing on Facebook and Twitter. For the most part, each employee mentioned something different as it relates to content. Regarding Twitter, Participant 7 stated that it was the institution's preferred platform over Facebook. Participant 7 referred to Twitter as a personal choice: "I personally prefer Twitter, so I think I kind of gravitate towards that and maybe a little bit more creative there, that's just me as a person." Two participants stated that the content appearing on Twitter was the same as Facebook. Participant 6 said, "pretty much anything that we would post on Twitter, we post on Facebook." Participant 3 agreed: "Typically if something is on Facebook, it will also be on Twitter." During the word frequency analysis, "Facebook" was the number one result relating to content receiving 222 mentions while "Twitter" was mentioned 206 times during the interviews.

One piece of content relating to Twitter that was mentioned was "news." Two participants specifically stated that news about campus life (events) was a type of content shared on Twitter. Therefore, in the word frequency results the word "campus" appeared 30 times. While I already stated that "news" appeared 50 times during the word frequency test, "share" was not far behind with 40 mentions during the interviews with employees regarding content. Additional news included faculty research, student programs, and alumni. Participant 5 responded: "So on Twitter we're sharing news. They are typically about things happening on campus or faculty research or student programs." When employees mentioned "retweets" as content shared on Twitter, it is important to note that retweeting is a characteristic of UGC since the source material is created by other Twitter users. The most common retweets included faculty, campus partners (affiliations with the college), administrators, and college alumni. Thus, these types of posts by outside sources will appear on the institutional Twitter page. Participant 5 explained their use of retweets on Twitter: "It's also a place where we share news from other sources that are about the college that we didn't write that are about us or our faculty."

A word relating to content mentioned several times was to "promote." The word was mentioned by three participants as a vehicle on Twitter to build an audience for an event or bring awareness to a subject. Three areas of promotion included faculty research, guest lectures to the college, and guest speakers at the institution. It is important to note that "promote" did not appear in the top 100 words of the content word frequency test. Participant 9 felt that promotion was important for bringing an audience to an event: "I would say our Twitter account is used for the day-to-day activities across campus so that would be promoting events." Participant 9 also mentioned additional content for Twitter including college blogs (the participant also stated this was true for Facebook). This is another example of written, original content, articles, and stories. Participant 9 explained that blogs are based on academics: "We have a blog network, so we share a lot of our academic blogs on Twitter." Although a blog seemed to be an important discussion point for a few participants, the word "blog" did not appear in the top 100 themes in the word frequency test regarding content. Evaluating Twitter based on the interviews indicates that the platform is best for sharing news and information about the institution to a mass audience, along with promoting upcoming events. Reviewing the results for Twitter, one can notice that specific content (such as photos, videos, or audio) was not mentioned. Thus, participants used Twitter as an announcement page and to "get the word out" to audiences for campus activities. Furthermore, content on Twitter uses a variety of multimedia (photos) and techniques (promoting alumni and students) to engage the audience with each tweet.

After reviewing the results for Facebook only, Participant 3 stated that the content appearing on Facebook is different than Twitter. The same participant argued that the content on Twitter will also appear on Facebook. However, Participant 6 declared that the content on Twitter is the same for Facebook. This demonstrates that content on Facebook may easily cross over to Twitter, but content on Twitter does not necessarily appeal to the Facebook audience. This may be due to the number of characters and other formats for writing a message on Twitter.

Facebook included a wide range of content. Participant 3 mentioned three types of accolades: alumni, student, and faculty. Accolades refer to accomplishments by alumni, students, and faculty. Participant 3 explained accolades as "anything that shows our students or alumni receiving accolades of any sort. We typically will put that on Facebook because we know that the community seems to value that information." Alumni once again was deemed important as Participants 2 and 9 referenced alumni content as accomplishments. Faculty accolades included any prevalent or new research conducted by the instructor. A major difference between Facebook and Twitter was the acknowledgment of specific content by participants including photographs, video, hyperlinks to other websites, and written articles/blogs. Thus, an additional finding for content is Facebook relied more on UCC—with various types of multimedia and visual content utilized—while Twitter was more likely to incorporate UGC to share news and information from the college and members of the community.

Several social media employees mentioned students as staff members in their offices who posted a variety of content. Two participants mentioned that students created and posted video to the social media sites. Participant 1 has students create video and images: "One of the things that we have been very actively pursuing is I have six students that work for me and so we use materials that they collect. Video and photo that give a snapshot of life at [redacted]." This indicated that some institutions are having students create multimedia content while the social media participants are focusing more on written work such as articles, press releases, and feature stories. Also, it illustrated that employees may not be comfortable creating certain content with little or no experience.

To summarize, participants combined Twitter and Facebook in their responses. Sharing news was important for both Facebook and Twitter, as well as multimedia content (articles, video, and photographs, among others) appeared on both platforms. To define content on Facebook and Twitter, participants and fellow employees in higher education look to educate the online community to various forms of information about the college or university. The social media pages use visual content to make the community aware of campus and academic proceedings.

Just as with the purpose of Facebook and Twitter, participants all mentioned that content related to two main audiences: alumni and faculty. Students were mentioned for those stating both platforms together and Twitter, but not Facebook. Therefore, the social media sites are used to maintain relationships with alumni through content related or interesting to them, while also featuring faculty who teach students and elevate the status of the institution through their research. The word "research" was used regularly regarding faculty and promotion when discussing Facebook, Twitter, and both institutions together. This coincides with faculty within the results while also showcasing those publications and projects are highly regarded branding opportunities to promote the college. One final theme is that the results highlight original work in written form through articles or blogs. Video and photos were mentioned by participants discussing both platforms together and Facebook, but not Twitter. Although social media uses images and video regularly (as showcased in the responses), since higher education places writing at a high standard, original works and publications are a vital piece of content among institutions posting on institutional Facebook and Twitter pages.

There are several differences when evaluating the word frequency results and the types of content that appear. However, some do coincide with one another. News and information combined were stated 89 times, becoming the highest form of content discussed during the interviews. This implies that the online community connects with institutions on Facebook and Twitter to keep up with campus happenings. Since "student" was the second highest mentioned form relating to content, one can summarize that all forms of content (written or visual) should relate to students. "Alumni" was another audience frequently mentioned, highlighting the need to relate content to those who graduated from the institution. "Photos" was mentioned 42 times while "video" was stated 23 times during the interviews. When combined, both show that online communities on Facebook and Twitter thirst for multimedia content; static visuals appear more important than moving images. "Stories"/"story" was stated 65 times during the interviews with the 10 participants. This form of content coincides with alumni, students, and other audiences as the written articles related to them. I also believe that website appearing 29 times in the word frequency results has a connection to the stories. Many of the social media participants stated that articles appear on their website first but are shared on Facebook and Twitter. Thus, while social media is important to the institution to connect to students, alumni, and community members, it is also relevant to promote and drive traffic to the website. Faculty and research are added as similarities from the word frequency test because many of the participants used the term: faculty research as a type of content for institutional Facebook and Twitter pages.

Participants

Question 5 and 6 of the interview methodology asked employees in higher education responsible with social media institutional web pages the following two questions:

5. Who are the participants posting information and content on institutional Facebook and Twitter web pages?
6. How would you describe your roles and responsibilities for posting information and content on institutional Facebook and Twitter web pages?

The first two participants stated that they were the only individuals at the college or university tasked with social media. Participant 2 is the primary person involved with posting on social media, while Participant 1 noted that posting on Facebook and Twitter depended on videographers and photographers for content and daily material. Participant 3 is the only one posting for the institution, however one colleague (the Director of Media Relations) has access to the accounts on Facebook and Twitter. Although Participant 3 takes care of posting regularly, others in the department provide story ideas for content to post on Facebook and Twitter.

Participant 4 is the primary person posting on Facebook and Twitter on behalf of the institution. Participant 5 is the primary person posting on Facebook and Twitter. While their role is to create the message to post directly on Facebook and Twitter, others help in producing content. Examples include a photographer taking campus photos and someone writing a news story for the website to share on social media. Participant 5 also added that the institution's Facebook and Twitter sites have the help of students: "I do have some interns who work for me and sometimes I'll give them assignments that often involve taking photos or video or creating posts about links that I want to share. So, it's primarily me, but others help out."

Participant 6 is the primary media person for the institution but noted that student workers help with taking photos and videos. Participant 6 made clear that all the writing on Facebook and Twitter is handled by the employee tasked with social media and not by students. Participant 6 explained, "I do all the writing. I think someone who understands the institutional voice maybe is the best to relay that information." Participant 7 is the main person posting on Facebook and Twitter for the institution, but others have access depending on the platform. For Facebook, the Director of Marketing has access to post, while for Twitter, several office members (staff and administrators) can post on the social media site including Admissions, Alumni, and Athletics.

Participant 8 is the only person posting on social media daily for the institution with no help from other departments or offices. Participant 9 is the only person posting on Facebook and Twitter but does receive help with other social media platforms from students. Participant 10 is the main person posting but does receive help from other sources, "I probably do 80 percent of actual postings, but most other people do have access." In responding to the question, Participant 10 stated that students help on Twitter by writing several tweets and scheduling tweets to be released throughout the week. On Facebook, while Participant 10 is doing most of the posting, four or five additional administrators help.

Participants Discussion: Emergent Themes Based on Interview Discourse

In reviewing and analyzing responses to the question of who posts on Facebook and Twitter, all respondents explained that they were the individual responsible for posting on the social media platforms. Half of the participants stated that they were the primary person posting for the institution. This included the two participants who stated "just me" posting on Facebook and Twitter in their response to the query. The two participants mentioned no other sources, employees, or factors. Three out of the five participants in the category for "primary person" simply stated that they were the main person tasked with the responsibility of creating the message with no other sources or colleagues mentioned. However, two social media employees stated that while they were the primary person posting on Facebook and Twitter, they received help from others at the institution. Participant 5 mentioned that help is only received when producing or creating content; all the posting on Facebook and Twitter is through the sole employee interviewed. Those offering content to Participant 5 are photographers, writers, and students who help create media (photos and video). Participant 6 responded with being the only person posting on social media, but students create photographs and video. The focus is on writing articles but depends on others to create media content. Participant 6 said, "If we had a student employee writing on Facebook or Twitter people wouldn't know that. They see that it's coming from [redacted]. So, I handle that."

Participant 3, the only one who responded, "only me," stated that the Director of Media Relations posts to both platforms while colleagues in the department develop story ideas. Coinciding with this development, Participant 7 answered with "mainly me," but also receives help in posting even though the participant is the primary person doing the task daily. Participant 7 receives help from the Director of Marketing with Facebook and employees in three offices on Twitter (Admissions, Alumni, and Athletics). Participant 7 said, "We do have people in the admissions office or the alumni office that post sports information and stuff like who are also tweeting." The final key phrase to describe participants is "mostly me" mentioned by Participant 10. The participant was tasked with social media management and strategy but received help on both Facebook and Twitter. For Twitter, Participant 10 receives help from students writing and scheduling tweets, while on Facebook other administrators in the office help with posting content and messages. Participant 10 specified, "They have access to make changes to the page, respond to comments and posts on the page as well." The participants declaring "only me," "mainly me," or "mostly me," all stated that they receive help from others at the institution with posting messages and content on Facebook and Twitter.

Based on all participants stating similar phrases, I can conclude that there is one dedicated social media employee responsible for what is posted on Facebook and Twitter. However, they have a variety of job titles. Once participants agreed to take part in the interview, I researched their job titles on public academic websites and identified the following: Social Media Strategist; Social Media Manager; Assistant Editor of Digital and Social Media; Social Media Producer; Social Media Coordinator; Assistant Director of Digital Communications; Director of Media Relations and Online Content; and Digital Content Strategist. Although there is one person associated with a social media position at an institution, there is not one clear job title.

However, 50% of participants receive help with posting and creating content to share with the online audience. Three out of the ten participants cited students as helping to create content, especially photos and video. Therefore, if any students are helping employees with social media, they are tasked with creating media content while the social media employee handles all writing materials. This was pointed out with Participant 6 mentioning the importance of one institutional voice and several employees responding with supervision over posted content. While the participants are benefiting from the help of other employees, the participants review all content that is posted by those helping, which explains why all participants answered that they were the main person posting on Facebook and Twitter.

Roles and Responsibilities

After identifying the participants in higher education who post on social media platforms Facebook and Twitter, another important aspect of the genre taxonomy is to establish what the roles and responsibilities are for posting on the sites, such as the daily tasks and requirements.

Participant 1 stated that their main role is to determine if a piece of content (visual, text) should be used and posted to represent the college or university. Also, to decide the social media platform for the post. The participant specified their role and responsibility to make social media decisions as opposed to creating content for the institutional pages. This finding coincided with Participant 2, who expressed that making decisions is a key role and responsibility when using social media within the higher education environment. Participant 2 explained: "I mean everything from strategy to tech to differentiating platforms and what content goes there." When making decisions on which content to post on social media sites, Participant 3 has a weekly calendar for tackling social media responsibilities. Participant 3 reviews all the posts for Facebook and Twitter from the prior week on Sunday night, identifying content that performed well. The results of how each Facebook or Twitter post performed are emailed to fellow employees in the department. In turn, this helps Participant 3 decide the type of stories to write and post for the upcoming week. For Facebook, Participant 3 mentioned always starting with a story related to popular culture. However, Twitter seemed to have a more precise science. Participant 3 said, "I typically start Twitter with retweeting to see what other people have shared and will repeat them and then we'll put out a link to an original story." Participant 4 agreed with the importance of planning when having to post on social media while reviewing the results and performance of a post. Participant 4 uses analytics to see how well stories are performing within their online community and the audience consuming content. Participant 4 believes their role is to make sure content is read on Facebook and Twitter, as well as consumed by a variety of audiences within their online community.

Participant 5 explained that their role is "to maintain the institutional voice for both platforms and that can mean curating the content that we are creating or sharing but also responding to other comments or content." Participant 5 did not outline specific differences in their role for Facebook and Twitter, but simply stated that Twitter can be more humorous and comedic in approach by posting emojis or GIFs. Participant 6 makes sure that content and information are up to date on both Facebook and Twitter. Also, Participant 6 creates and enforces a social media policy for employees to follow at the college/university. Participant 6 also noted that the employee discourages academic departments from creating their own social media pages, arguing that they do not fall under compliance. Participant 6 stated that there are issues with departments not following social media policies or guidelines created by the institution. Also, administrators of the social media department page may leave the college or university for other employment, therefore not providing access to their replacement. Participant 7 was the only person with different responsibilities for Facebook and Twitter. The tasks for Twitter are to find engagement opportunities (meaning to interact with their online audience) and address any concerns or complaints. As for Facebook, Participant 7 does not monitor the platform regularly since the institution uses it much less than Twitter. Participant 7 said, "We don't get a lot of messages over Facebook, but we get just random questions sometimes. I will reply to people and sort of direct them to someone who can help them out."

Participant 8 focuses on gathering stories from the college or university website, stating, "Our web team comes up with a lot of stories and stories on members of the community like faculty and staff; alumni and students, of course." Participant 8 also is tasked with creating videos, specifically ones showcasing student experiences on campus. For Participant 9, monitoring conversations is a daily task when their online community is mentioning the institution in a reply or post, as well as the conversations underneath a picture or video. Participant 9 engages their audience by joining the discussions. Participant 9 agrees with Participants 1 and 2 in creating a calendar to collect content to post for the week and into the future. Participant 10 pointed out that their main task is not social media, but to manage all web content. Social media became part of the job when other employees in the department left, and the employee was posting on social media for the institution anyway. Thus, social media is only a small part of the participant's daily tasks, which include fixing website links, managing the content management system for the website, creating, and designing YouTube pages for various academic departments, and writing feature stories for the college/university website. Participant 10 utilizes social media, but the website is the institution's priority.

Roles and Responsibilities Discussion: Emergent Themes Based on Interview Discourse

After conducting the interviews and analyzing the responses, I believe there are five employee roles and responsibilities for Facebook and Twitter. Beginning with the highest number of responses, content was noted as a vital task by five of the participants. Participant 4 manages content, Participant 5 curates content, Participant 6 assures that content is up-to-date, Participant 9 gathers content, and Participant 10 collects web content. Stories were mentioned several times by participants as a form of content that can be posted on Facebook and Twitter pages. Stories were mentioned by Participants 3, 8, and 10. Stories were shared on Facebook and Twitter to be read by their online audience. For example, Participant 10 said, "I kind of write, edit and assign the feature stories that are on the slider on the top of the website." This is an important example to point out, as many of the participants mentioned that most stories are shared from the institutional website.

The next three characteristics of the role and responsibilities for Facebook and Twitter were mentioned by at least two participants. I defined the next task as decision-making. Two of the participants interviewed stated that they make decisions on the type of content to be posted, the platforms utilized, and the definition of how each platform will be used. Participant 1 said, "I make the determination if this should be used and where it should be used." Participant 2 added a few more features to their social media decision-making: "I mean everything from strategy to tech to differentiating platforms and what content goes there." Thus, participants make decisions based on the content to be viewed by their online audience, technology that will enhance use, and how the institution should utilize free websites.

The fourth characteristic for the roles and responsibilities for Facebook and Twitter is titled analytics and was described by Participants 3 and 4 respectively. This attribute describes the performance of Facebook and Twitter posts on a weekly basis. Thus, after review, the participant may decide to make changes and additions to what they post on social media institutional pages. Participants 3 explained, "I craft an e-mail that goes out Monday morning giving everyone insight into the most popular posts from each platform for that week with a number of breakdowns." Participant 4 noted how they track analytics for both platforms, which sets the outcomes and goals that the institution expects for Facebook and Twitter. The fifth and last characteristic discussed by Participants 5 and 9 is engagement/interaction. This component describes any interaction, discussion, or conversation on Facebook and Twitter with an individual or group. Participant 5 explained interaction as, "responding to other comments or content in a way that reflects the institution as a whole." Participant 9 not only responds to the online community but monitors the conversations the audience is having with each other. Participant 9 explained, "We're engaging audiences and then responding to conversations that others are having about the institution." Thus, interaction/engagement on Facebook and Twitter tends to be a reaction based on what others are discussing about the content that the institution shares with the online audience.

Many respondents did not indicate separate assignments or tasks for Facebook and Twitter. Only Participants 5 and 7 described different responsibilities for Facebook and Twitter. Participant 5 noted that Twitter can be a bit more comedic in responding to a query or a new tweet. Participant 5 said, "Sometimes I'll respond just to an animated GIF or short comment or emoji." Participant 7 retweets (UGC) more as opposed to tweeting original content from the institutional voice. Participant 7 explained this act as, "I kind of monitor Twitter throughout the day. We'll tweet about things that we've posted on the website recently." Also, Participant 7 watches Twitter for any issue or complaint about the college or university that comes up on the site and the participant decides it needs a response. Facebook however is used to answer any questions or to direct someone looking for a specific department/office. Participant 7 explained, "We don't get a lot of messages over Facebook, but we get just random questions sometimes and I reply to people and sort of direct them to someone who can help them out." While there were a few distinctions between Facebook and Twitter, overall, participants feel that their daily duties for both social media sites were the same.

There are several key findings from the word frequency test that was conducted with the responses from the 10 participants. At least half of the respondents discussed content as a major responsibility. After running the word frequency test for roles and responsibilities, "content" ranked fifth. The word "content" was mentioned 92 times by the participants. This finding shows that content is a key responsibility for all participants. Upon further analysis of the word frequency, additional types of content can be found throughout the results: stories (62 times); news (39); information (38); photos (34); the college or university website (28); and video (20). Thus, combining content with the specific types (visual and textual), the overall number of mentions was 221. This result highlights that the participants depend on and are responsible for content on Facebook and Twitter.

I noted how participants were writing and posting stories to Facebook and Twitter as a top priority in their responsibilities. This is one way social media employees in higher education write about target audiences: students, alumni, faculty, and staff. The word "stories" were stated by participants 36 times, while the word "story" was stated 26 times. In total, the role and responsibility of writing stories resulted in 62 mentions. I also want to point out that the word "writing" was said 13 times during the interviews. Many of the employees stated that they were specifically writing stories to post on the website and social media platforms.

Most stories focused on individuals connected to the institution. In total, stories relating to a specific group or audience were mentioned 179 times by the participants. This indicates that not only are stories on Facebook and Twitter a responsibility for an individual, but the articles should be based on those who invested in the college or university. The third characteristic was making decisions on the content to post on Facebook and Twitter. The word "decisions" never came up in the results of the word frequency test. However, the words, "post," "posting," and "posts" came up many times in the conversations with the participants. In total, "post," "posting," or "posts" was discussed 143 times during the interviews relating to the role and responsibility of participants. This result strongly emphasizes that deciding what to post, what information to share, and doing the act of posting is a daily task for the participants using social media in higher education.

Analytics and review were the fourth role and responsibility stated by at least two of the participants. Although the words "analytics" and "review" were not frequent mentions by participants, two additional words can relate to the topic and task. The word "monitor" was the 78th most frequent word, appearing 12 times in the word frequency test. Another word relating to analytics and reviewing how well content does on social media platforms is "research." The word "research" was the 83rd most frequent word and was counted 12 times. In combining the results of research and monitor, the total count is 24. Since only two participants discussed monitoring how well information performs on social media, it may not be a required task for all employees, even though it is a tool possibly offered.

The last responsibility mentioned is interaction and engagement. In reviewing and analyzing the conversations, I noticed that at least two participants focused on interacting and engaging with target audiences or online communities through Facebook and Twitter. Outside of the words "interaction" and "engagement" used within many of the conversations, five additional words that are ways for participants to interact with other social media users through Facebook and Twitter include "comments," "response," "interaction," "mention," and "message."

Combining "engagement" and "interaction" results is a total of 39. Although this is may seem like a relatively low frequency, the various ways social media offers one to interact (communicate) and engage (through content) represents a much higher frequency. Forms of interaction and engagement on both platforms include sending group or private messages, commenting on another user's post, responding to a query, and sharing content from other users to the institution's social media page. Even though I discovered only two participants directly mentioning "interaction" and "engagement," other participants mentioned additional ways of communicating with an online community. This indicates that this specific task may be much more important than originally expected.

Location and Timing (Overview of Results)

The fourth characteristic in the genre taxonomy is analyzing location and timing. There were four questions from the interview that covered this section of the web genre taxonomy:

7. Where do employees/participants create, post, and consume content for Facebook?

8. Where do employees/participants create, post, and consume content for Twitter?
9. When do employees/participants expect to receive a response once a message is posted on Facebook?
10. When do employees/participants expect to receive a response once a message is tweeted on Twitter?

First, I will review results for location of participants when posting and creating content for Facebook and Twitter. Then, I will analyze the results for when participants are posting on the same two social media platforms. Since employees can access social media twenty-four hours a day, seven days week with an internet connection using chosen personal devices (mobile phones, laptops, tablets, and desktop computers), I wanted to know the location where they are posting, creating, and consuming content for Facebook and Twitter.

Participant 1 firmly declared that posts are happening all the time during the week. The only time Participant 1 posts on the weekends for social media platforms Facebook and Twitter is if an event is happening on campus. Participant 2 only posts during office hours but will use third-party software to schedule tweets to share publicly on the weekends. Participant 2 added, "But also, we have the ability to schedule in advance using different software." When participants mention "software," this means applications that allow users to schedule posts and tweets well in advance. A participant does not have to post at the exact moment that content is being created. Examples of third-party software include Hootsuite and Tweetdeck.

Participant 3 answered by saying that while social media offers 24/7 access, the employee attempts to stay within office hours, agreeing with Participant 2. Participant 3 said, "So it's a bit of a 24-hour situation seven days a week although my boss is pretty good about wanting us to make that effort to not be connected constantly." Participant 3 also brought up posting content on the weekends but stated that only comments will be reviewed; there will be no new tweets or posts. Participant 3 added, "I always try to stay on top of comments for social media platforms because you never know when someone saying something terrible." For Participant 3 it is important to reference their response again to question 1, which asked about the purpose for using Facebook and Twitter. Participant 3 asserted that while Twitter is a 24/7 platform for posting, they will limit posts to three to six posts a day. Facebook posts will be less frequent, only three to four times a week.

Participant 4 answered that the majority of posting on Facebook and Twitter was during office hours, agreeing with many of the other participants. Posting on the weekends only occurs for a major event such as homecoming. Participant 4 replied by saying, "Primarily we focus on the office hours Monday through Friday." Participant 5 also posts during office hours but will schedule posts or review comments in the evenings or on the weekends. Participant 5 explained their daily use as, "Primarily in the standard workday, although of course with a job like mine it bleeds over into other times. I try to schedule content outside those hours if I feel it's better to post something in the evening or on the weekends. I'll be posting but I do occasionally check in on posts or comments and respond more immediately if I think it's called for."

Participant 6 is the first and only participant who responded by stating that while content is created during office hours at a computer or desktop, there is no set location due to coverage of events. Participant 6 said, "I'm typically creating content on the fly in the office from my desktop. But yesterday I went to [redacted] and took photos of an event that was happening." Participant 7 is posting regularly on the weekdays between 9:00 a.m. and 5:00 p.m., which the employee described as active management. The weekends are used to schedule content for the upcoming week, while also sharing sports updates and results from athletic games. Participant 7 explained, "Obviously a lot of sports happen on the weekends, a little bit of a crutch for me. I'll just repeat the sports accounts on weekends with results." Participant 8 posts and creates content on weekends and during office hours from 8:30 a.m. to 4:30 p.m. Posting on the weekends only occurs if an important event occurs. Participant 8 pointed out, "It's rare that I'm working on the weekend unless something really important comes up and the director texts me."

Like many of the others, Participant 9 posts from the office Monday through Friday, between 8:00 a.m. and 5:00 p.m. While most of the social media posts are scheduled and created during office hours, additional work time is spent at home or on weekends because of the constant interaction. Participant 9 stated, "I would say most nights I'm working an additional hour at home on social media. Then on the weekends anywhere probably on average two to three hours a weekend." Participant 10 also posts from the office on campus between 9:00 a.m. and 5:00 p.m. Participant 10 does not post on weekends but will schedule content, agreeing with many of the other participants. Participant 10 will also review any comments on Facebook and Twitter. Participant 10 described their social media use: "As you probably know being involved with social is, could be a 24/7 thing even though I rarely post something on the weekend unless we have breaking news."

Location (Where) Discussion: Emergent Themes Based on Interview Discourse

Upon reviewing responses to the question of where participants create, post, and consume content for Facebook and Twitter, nine out of ten participants noted that they use their office for posting during the work week. An overwhelming number of participants stated that their office is their primary location, opposed to using their home or at various other locations. Although social media is a website that can be accessed from anywhere, at any time of the day, participants were not doing so. Also, personal social media accounts may be connected to work accounts, thus mixing professional and personal uses. Participant 6 mentioned that content is sometimes created during a 45-minute commute to work or while attending events. Participant 9 also noted that posting on Facebook and Twitter occurs at home (an extra hour during the week and two to three hours on the weekend). Otherwise, all participants post from their offices.

After the word search query, "office" was mentioned 20 times by the participants. "Campus" received 30 mentions from participants, highlighting the location of the office and the focus of where posting and creating content takes place. Although "campus" is the 30th most mentioned term and "office" is the 41st most frequent within the node of responses, there were a plethora of words that did not relate to a physical or digital location to use Facebook and Twitter.

As for location, I can conclude that all the participants prefer posting while on campus during regular office hours instead of at home when the employee is not "clocked in." Three out of ten participants specifically stated that posting content and information on Facebook and Twitter takes place between the hours of 8 a.m. and 5 p.m. These were participants 8, 9, and 10. Once again, this provides clarity as many participants post information during normal work hours Monday through Friday, even though the participant has access all day, no matter the location.

All the participants explained that, while the majority of posting and creating content occurs on the weekdays during their regular office hours, there are situations when they would have to work on the weekends. Four out of ten participants stated that they would use Facebook and Twitter on Saturday and Sunday for checking comments or using third-party applications to schedule messages, tweets, or posts. Comments were specifically mentioned by several participants as a way of making certain nothing negative was posted about the institution. For example, Participant 10 said, "I get notifications on my phone if there's a comment on Facebook. I receive notifications on Twitter directly to my phone, I just check it out to make sure if I need to address it." Similarly, Participant 3 stated, "I always try to stay on top of comments for social media platforms because you never know when someone saying something terrible." The term "comments" appeared 27 times in the word frequency test for the location (where) node while "comment" appeared 13 times. In total, "comments" were discussed 40 times, pushing the phrase into the top fifteen words. This matches my analysis of comments being a vital characteristic for posting on Facebook and Twitter.

When "software" was mentioned by participants, it was again in reference to scheduling tweets either for the weekend or for the upcoming week. For example, Participant 7 stated, "I try to schedule content outside those hours if I feel it's better to post something in the evening or on the weekends." Third-party software enabled participants to avoid posting or creating content on the weekends. "Software" did not come up in the word frequency results within the location (where) node because each participant mentioned different software.

Next, three out of ten participants also mentioned events as a reason for posting or creating content on the weekends. Participant 8 acknowledged events on the weekends, "It's rare that I'm working on the weekend unless something really important comes up and the director texts me." Based on the results, campus events are the only original content being created and posted on a case-by-case basis. In the word frequency test for location, "events" were mentioned 21 times by participants, while the word "event" was said 16 times during responses. In total, both words were mentioned 37 times. This word frequency analysis showcases that "events" was stated less frequently than "comments" (40 times) during participant responses.

One specific event stated in a response is "sports." Participant 7 explained how sports are covered using social media accounts on the weekend, "I'll just repeat the sports accounts on weekends with results." Thus, the participant is only retweeting or sharing scores and highlights from other affiliate social media accounts instead of producing original material. This coincides with the previous finding: If a participant is using social media sites on the weekend, it is only to post quickly as needed. As it pertains to the location (where) node in the word frequency test, sports were only discussed by 1 participant.

In conclusion, social media employees create and post content in their office on campus during the weekdays, Monday through Friday, during normal business hours (between 8:00 a.m. and 5:00 p.m.). However, weekends are utilized occasionally for important events or when a participant receives a notification that someone responded to the institution's post. Participants use Facebook and Twitter accounts on the weekend to review any content that may have a negative impact on the institution. Additionally, weekends help social media managers prepare for the upcoming work week by using third-party software to schedule a Facebook post or tweet.

Timing (Overview and Results)

Timing relates to how quickly the institution's online community (social media users on Facebook and Twitter following a college or university) respond or react to a post on the institutional page. The post is created and published by the employee tasked with social media at the college or university. Additionally, timing represents how quickly a user engages with the post or tweet and writes a message responding to the institution's post. Please note, Participants 5 and 7 provided answers specific to Facebook and Twitter. Participant 8 provided analysis for Twitter only, while Participant 10 only gave feedback for Facebook. Otherwise, all remaining participants provided answers that relate to both platforms.

The first four participants expect immediate responses to a post for the most part. Participant 1 responded emphatically that their institution expects to receive responses because it actively engages with their audience. Participant 2 simply expects to receive a response to a tweet or Facebook post instantly. Participant 3 expects an immediate response on both Facebook and Twitter; if a post or tweet is not reacted to within 30 minutes, it is viewed as a failure. Participant 4 expects a quick reaction to an important event on campus. Otherwise, most of their posts or tweets do not gain much of a reaction or comment.

For the next two results, I am going to summarize Participants 5 and 7 because both discussed similarities and differences of Facebook and Twitter pertaining to timing. When discussing Facebook, Participant 5 stated that the platform receives fewer reactions to posts than a few years ago. As Participant 5 explained, "Facebook altering its algorithm and the way the news feed is structured leads definitely to seeing a downward trend and interaction; at least organic interaction." Therefore, the institution must boost posts by purchasing advertisements on Facebook. Also, it is important to mention that Participant 5 finds that alumni are not as active on Facebook. This is interesting since most participants mentioned that a purpose of Facebook is to attract and engage alumni. Although Participant 7 stated that overall, they are proud of the engagement on Facebook, alumni content does not perform well on the platform. Participant 7 explained, "But I can kind of predict the things that are going to get like a few dozen shares and a few hundred likes." Participant 7 also mentioned that they do not really respond to a comment on Facebook unless it is a direct question.

Moving to Twitter, Participant 5 stated that there is no interaction with their online community. They receive twelve or fewer responses to a post, mostly from current students and faculty. Participant 5 explained, "Often it's the same people sharing the news. There's a handful of faculty who are active, handful of students who are active, and some alumni." Although Participant 7 is proud of the engagement through Twitter (retweeting content from their audience and receiving likes), the participant is specific about the type of content to share. Participant 7 said, "On Twitter, I tend to like most of the content we're mentioned; if it's something especially good, I might retweet it or reply to it or quote tweet it or whatever."

Participant 6 expects most of their posts and tweets to have a specific time span, which is three days. After that, their audience on Facebook and Twitter will not interact with their content. Participant 8 expects an immediate response from their online community, as other participants stated. Participant 8 provided details about audience feedback and responses to tweets. According to Participant 8, their audience is always engaged on Twitter; followers regularly interact with their institutional Twitter account by re-tweeting or "liking" their content. Participant 8 did state that they expect engagement within the first hour. The participant added, "The folks following us on Twitter, they're just really interested, and they love us." Participant 10 expects to receive positive comments to their posts and tweets on Facebook and Twitter. The participant did mention the need to buy ads on Facebook for their content to be seen or receive any sort of interaction. Participant 10 clarified: "Depending on what the particular audience is, we have to promote or boost a lot of our posts either to people already following our page or kind of you know, using keyword targeting."

Timing (When) Discussing: Emergent Themes Based on Interview Discourse

Several themes emerged from analyzing the interview responses. First, four out of ten participants stated that they expect an instantaneous reaction from their online community after posting on Twitter and Facebook. Participant 2 said, "instantly." Participant 3 concurred, "So I think I lean on the immediacy of a response." Participants 8 and 9 expected instantaneous feedback. It should be noted while more of the participants expected immediate response to their content, two participants felt that they got no response from their online community and audience. This included Participants 4 and 5. Participant 4 said, "Yes, we'd like your comment every once in a while; we'll have a question or a comment come in. In which case I'm here to respond and I do it fairly quickly."

Based on the results of my interviews, participants expect to receive an immediate response from their online communities and audiences. But two of the participants stated that they do not expect any responses; there may be institutions who post content that rarely interact with their community on social media platforms. Thus, using Facebook and Twitter as an extension of their websites.

There are three additional themes related to timing that came up several times during the interviews. The first theme is that participants expect a response from their online communities and audiences because of their high level of engagement. Participant 1 stated, "I actively engage my audience," while Participant 7 said, "I think we've got pretty good engagement.

I'm usually pretty proud of how much engagement we're getting." While Participant 8 was confident in their engagement, it depends on a specific time frame (time of day, for example) when material is posted.

Specific time of interaction is the second theme that developed in the interviews. Four participants discussed time periods when interaction is successful. As mentioned with Participant 8, interaction occurs for the most part in the very first hour of publication. Participant 8 said, "They usually retweet or sometimes may reply to a tweet or something within the first hour or so." Participant 9 agreed and stated that a response will occur within the first hour, but it depends on the type of content posted. Participant 9 clarified, "It really depends on the topic. I would say almost instantaneous. I would expect it at least within an hour." Participant 3 thought that Facebook and Twitter should have a quick response when content is shared. Regarding Facebook, Participant 3 mentioned, "Typically if I haven't received any comments within a half an hour on Facebook, I view that as this is not going well." When evaluating Twitter, Participant 3 also expects a 30-minute time window. Participant 3 pointed out, "Usually within half an hour if I don't have a few either likes or reactions or a heart on Twitter or retweet on Twitter, then I feel like, OK, this is likely not going to go much further." Participant 6 felt much differently and believed that content can last longer than one hour, perhaps a couple of days, when the online community is engaging with the institution and responding to posts. Participant 6 said, "I think our stuff kind of has a three-day lifespan. I say typically after three days people aren't really continuing to engage with it."

The last theme was that two participants (4 and 10) stated that the only way to receive a response from the online community and audience was to boost posts. This response was only pertaining to Facebook, not Twitter. The respondents felt that a boosted post is the only way for information to be seen by the largest number of people on Facebook. A boosted post is a way to buy an advertisement that will appear on a set number of Facebook users' newsfeed. The type of ad depends on how much an institution is willing to spend. For example, Participant 10 stated, "So most stories that we want to get out, we do put a little bit of money behind." Based on the results for timing, interaction is expected to occur quickly and instantaneously. Specifically, regarding Facebook, instant reaction from the online audience requires help from a boosted post, such as a paid advertisement.

Functionality

The main goal for conducting the one-on-one interviews with participants working on social media was to discover the functionality of Facebook and Twitter in the higher education environment. Several questions covered two areas of functionality: expectations of use and efficiency. Employees were asked the following questions pertaining to functionality:

11. What are your overall expectations of using Facebook?
12. What are your overall expectations of using Twitter?

After responding to the two queries based on expectations for using the two social media sites, participants answered two additional questions based on functionality:

16. Is Facebook an efficient web page to use for higher education? Why?
17. Is Twitter an efficient web page to use for higher education? Why?

Expectations of Use—Facebook and Twitter

In asking the 10 participants their overall expectations for using Facebook and Twitter, only two participants gave separate answers for each social media platform. The remainder of the participants answered this query by having the same expectations for Facebook and Twitter, as opposed to having different expectations for them. First, I will begin analyzing the different expectations for Twitter and Facebook. For definitive expectations for using Twitter (in no particular order), Participant 8 stated that the social media website has a specific audience. Participant 8 explained the audience as: "a mix of students and alumni, friends and people who are just interested in what [redacted] is doing." A second expectation for using Twitter specific to Participant 8 is that the social media platform is best for posting and sharing information regarding campus events. Campus events include anything from workshops, social outings, and student activities that occur on campus. Participant 8 stated, "If there is an event going on, I'll be more likely to post it on Twitter because it just moves. It's just the nature of Twitter." Stating that a post "moves" better on Twitter indicates that information is easily shared among the online community faster than it may on Facebook. Thus, the information reaches the audience wanting to find out about a specific event.

Participant 3 expected to use the platform to tell the college story using multiple voices. This means that there is not one person posting, but the online community (audience) sees, hears, and listens to multiple points of view by the way messages are designed. There were two reasons Participant 3 provided that response. First, the participant stated that multiple voices do not work as well on Facebook: "We don't really re-post a great deal on Facebook simply because we've seen that the numbers don't bear out in terms of engagement." Secondly, Participant 3 re-tweets and shares opinions, thoughts, and perspectives on Twitter from other users by the practice of a re-tweet. Student, faculty, or community member tweets are placed on the institutional Twitter page on a regular basis. Participant 3 clarified further: "We try to make original posts on Facebook and retweet a lot on Twitter." Having re-tweets on the institutional Twitter page is an example of an online community reading messages and telling the story of the college from multiple voices.

The same two participants who provided precise expectations for Twitter, did the same for Facebook. There were three statements that were specific to Facebook. Participant 3 felt that it is expected that each post is an original message written by an employee of the institution. This indicates that it is important for this specific institution (and potentially others) that one voice represents the thoughts and perspectives of the institution on Facebook. This differs from the multiple voices common on Twitter.

Participant 8 also added specific expectations for using Facebook. Although Twitter was mentioned by Participant 8 as being best for current students and alumni, the same participant believed that Facebook is best for alumni, not current students. This is connected to another expectation the same participant has when using Facebook: most messages focus on alumni stories. This is because the online community on Facebook is made up of more alumni than current students. Participant 8 explained, "If I post about an alum who's doing something great, I know it's going to get probably a lot of engagement as opposed to like an event. We don't post mini flyers on Facebook because it can get oversaturated and then people just really aren't interested in events." Therefore, Participant 8 does not post campus events on Facebook, but rather what their alumni are doing for the community and in their careers since graduating from the institution. This is a contrasting outcome for Twitter, as the participants are expected to post about events on Twitter.

Expectations of Use—Themes for Both Social Media Platforms

Aside from Participants 3 and 8, the remainder of the participants described the same expectations for Facebook and Twitter, as opposed to having varied expectations for them. Although the participants appeared to have different expectations for using Facebook and Twitter, similar themes emerged through the combined discussion of both.

I discovered four main themes from the combined discussion of both platforms. The themes for expectations of use with Facebook and Twitter in higher education are share, interaction/engagement/communicate, telling the college story, and promotion.

Out of the 10 participants, 6 discussed the importance of interacting, communicating, and engaging their online community, which consists of students (current and prospective), alumni, faculty, staff, and the local community.

Participant 2 described this as building a relationship with people through the platforms. Participant 2 responded, "to provide information to people and to deepen relationships and connect with people who are seeking information." The participants believed that connecting with people by using the social media platforms is building community around the institution. This will not only help current students, but prospective students as well. Participant 5 followed up by stating, "I know a lot of high school students may not have heard of [redacted] although we obviously feel we have a lot to offer, so we try to broadly give a sense of what we are like as an institution and who the people are that make up our faculty, student body, and alumni so they can feel they can make some kind of connection." Facebook and Twitter build community through daily interactions with current and prospective students.

Participants 7 and 9 stated that communicating and interacting with the online community keeps those individuals engaged on the social media sites. Participant 7 stated that every year a goal for the institution is to keep engagement up with their community who is following them. Participant 9 agreed, stating, "My overall expectations would be again to build engagement with our constituents and our community." Participant 9 provided the amount of engagement the institution expects to receive stating, "I like to see about 20 percent of our audience receiving the story and then about another 10 percent actually engaging with it." Not only does Participant 7 want to increase engagement every year but also to increase the number of followers on the platform and to help with recruitment. Participant 7 said, "Get maybe some prospective students to go over the hump and actually click submit with their applications" is a major expectation for using Facebook and Twitter. Participant 10 agreed with recruitment: "Kind of, you know, get the word out to prospective students in terms of student recruitment and kind of actively courting them and their families and keeping them updated on the college." By continually keeping the community engaged and conversing with them, Participant 10 believes that it will keep their recruitment numbers higher.

In conducting the text search analysis for expectations, two words stood out within the results. The 21st most frequent word mentioned in the test was "engagement," receiving 31 statements. However, much lower on the word frequency was "interaction, " which was the 73rd most frequent word, receiving 12 mentions. "Communicate" was not on the word frequency results. In total, the theme received 43 mentions during the interview. This will put the words "engagement" and "interaction" among the top 15 frequent words. However, based on the word frequency results, "engagement" seems to be an expected use of Facebook and Twitter opposed to interacting with the online community.

I mentioned in the theme that interaction, engagement, and communication occur with the online community consisting of students and employees (faculty and staff). As with prior queries, specific people always appeared in the top fifteen results of a word frequency test. Student and students combined received 89 mentions during the interview, alumni 42, and employees were mentioned 40 times. Faculty was mentioned 16 times during the interview, thus giving a total of 187 mentions. This showcases that engaging with the target audience (students, faculty, staff) is an expectation of using Facebook and Twitter within higher education.

The concept of sharing information, news, and content was another theme discussed by three of the participants. Participant 1 described six ways and types of content that the individual expects to share with their online community: news, events, campus life, and faculty, students, and staff. Participant 1 explained, "I guess my goal is to share the wide variety of events and news and various associations of the college with as many people as I can." Participant 6 agreed that it was their responsibility to share news with the online audience and community they have on Facebook and Twitter. Participant 6 added, "Expectations are that we are reporting on and sharing stories that show people that we continue to be good stewards of the resources that we have." Although sharing news seems to be a major expectation for most employees tasked with social media, Participant 7 said that it is vital for alumni, more specifically. Participant 7 wants alumni always to be thinking about their institution with the news posted.

In reviewing the word frequency test pertaining to expectations, the word "share" was mentioned 35 times while "sharing" received 20 mentions. In total, 55 mentions relating to share match my analysis that this concept is a major expectation for using Facebook and Twitter in higher education. Most of the participants stated that news, information, and content were among the items shared with the online community on institutional Facebook and Twitter pages. Based on the literature review, an employee requires content to share on social media platforms. "Content" was mentioned 84 times by participants, while "news" and "information" each received 40 mentions. Therefore, news and information totaled 80 mentions regarding expectations based on the text search analysis.

The third theme I established from the results was telling the college story or as Participants 3 and 6 described, a comprehensive view of the college. Participant 3 stated, "The goal is always to give a comprehensive view of the college." Two important areas of telling a story that Participant 6 described are being a good resource and fulfilling its mission as a liberal arts college. Participant 6 discussed being a good resource: "There's always more than one story to a story. So, my goal is to kind of balance all of that and just have enough key words or like triggers for our audience that they see that story from their own experience or what they expect to see I guess, not neglecting any important aspects of the story." Outside of being a good resource for information and continually telling a story, Participant 10 thinks you must keep the audience informed and update prospective students on campus happenings. Telling the story, according to Participant 10, is actively getting the word out to prospective students about what the institution offers and what is happening on campus.

Although only three participant responses related to telling stories, the word frequency test indicates that stories were discussed much more consistently between participants in the node for expectations. The word "stories" were mentioned 30 times, while "story" was discussed 30 times. In total, "stories" were mentioned 63 times during the discussion of this specific question. Because of the number of times that stories were discussed during the node, this result matches the researcher's analysis and establishes this concept as an expectation for using Facebook and Twitter in higher education.

The final theme established from the interviews when participants were discussing their expectations for using Facebook and Twitter is to promote. Participants 3, 5, and 10 said that their expectation was to promote using Facebook and Twitter. An area to promote on Facebook and Twitter is the college itself. Participant 10 stated that their expectation was to "increase awareness about the college" using Facebook and Twitter, while Participant 5 is using both sites to "get the name of the institution" out to the public, thus raising awareness. Participant 2 mentioned that they are "providing information to people," which promotes what the college is doing and what they offer to current and prospective students, as well as the community. Though promoting the college or university was described by three participants, the word "promote" did not present itself during the text search query. I should point out that the word "college" was mentioned 44 times in the expectation node. The word "university" was not within the first 100 frequently used words in the expectation node when running the text search query.

Efficiency—Facebook and Twitter

Questions 16 and 17 asked participants if Facebook and Twitter are efficient web pages for higher education. The goal for this question was to determine whether Facebook and Twitter facilitate completing any tasks. Five out of 10 the participants provided separate results for Facebook and Twitter. First, I will discuss the efficiencies for Twitter, followed by the results for Facebook. Before comparing the two social media sites, Participant 6 definitively stated that both social media sites are efficient overall.

Three participants gave specific reasons why Twitter is a functional website for the social media employees in higher education. The efficiencies described did not match the specific expectations for Twitter such as telling the college story in multiple voices, keep current students and alumni engaged, and posting tweets about events. Participant 2 stated that both Facebook and Twitter are efficient websites, but for different reasons. I will discuss Facebook in the next section, but this participant believes that Twitter is efficient for sharing news and information with an online community and social media users who follow the institution. Participant 3 was unsure if Twitter is efficient for the higher education institution, but it is good for having an ongoing conversation with an online community and followers on the platform. The interactivity and communication with students, community members, alumni, and others are continuous. Participant 5 mentioned that Twitter is effective for brand awareness among different audiences and cultures. Participant 5 stated, "I think Twitter is useful for getting brand awareness for different segments of the population than we might typically see." Participant 10 was undecided whether Twitter is an efficient website for higher education. The participant explained how Facebook can be efficient but did not discuss Twitter in their answer to the query.

Only one expectation matched an efficiency for Facebook, but from different participants. Participant 8 stated that alumni engagement was an expectation for Facebook, but Participant 2 said that it is a characteristic for the platform to be efficient. When discussing efficiency for Facebook, more than one participant said that interaction and communication with their online community is the best use for the social media site. Participant 3 explained that Facebook is efficient because it is a fast way to communicate with their online community adding, "I do think that certain segment of the public view the Facebook page generally as a way to connect to someone more quickly than an institutional website. I will go to see if they have a Facebook page first because so often, they are monitoring it much more closely than maybe a messaging platform they have built into their website." Participant 3 felt that social media employees may respond to their online audience quicker on Facebook as opposed to the college or university website. Participant 4 stated that their interactivity is best for Facebook because the online audience participates with the content the institution posts and they get the best responses for action items. Participant 4 explained the practice: "Our purpose for sharing a post is getting people into a website where they can discover more about our programs and apply. Facebook is generally the best vehicle for doing so." One difference between the participants is that Participant 3 believes Facebook has become the main online presence for the institution while Participant 4 wants to use Facebook to drive people to the college or university website.

As stated, when analyzing Twitter, Participant 2 concluded that Facebook and Twitter are both efficient websites for higher education, but for different reasons. Participant 2 stated that Facebook is best for engaging or interacting with alumni. The same participant did not feel this was the case for Twitter.

Another area where Participant 3 felt that Facebook is an efficient social media site for higher education is for receiving messages from the public and those interested in attending the college or university. Participant 3 was also surprised by how some of the messages received on Facebook pertain to older posted material and not recent campus happenings. Participant 3 explained the abundance of messages received daily on Facebook: "I'm actually really amazed at the number of questions that come through the Facebook page of people wanting to know just basic information about admissions or scholarships."

Participant 10 discussed how Facebook is an effective tool in communicating with current and prospective students. This is because the institution created specific "class pages" for every incoming academic year. Participant 10 said, "I think particularly the Facebook pages that are class pages has been a really effective way for us to communicate with our student body and particularly communicate with our potential students too." To engage with students who are deciding to go to the higher education institution and convince them to apply and accept, the institution created a closed Facebook group that is not open for everyone to join. Students introduce themselves in the Facebook group and plan social events with one another. Engagement continues after acceptance, as it becomes a "Class Facebook Group" for the students' four years at the college or university. Although this is a relevant response to mention, it is important to state that the Facebook groups do not appear on the institution's main Facebook channel. This is a separate tool that Facebook offers and is outside of the scope of my research. However, it does point out that Facebook offers colleges and universities additional tools that may be efficient for the institution to use to complete tasks.

Efficiency—Themes for Both Social Media Platforms

Overall, most of the participants felt that Facebook and Twitter are both functional platforms for higher education. Although one participant stated that they were unsure about Twitter, the remaining nine participants overwhelmingly felt that Facebook and Twitter are efficient to complete tasks for many reasons. As Participant 8 said during the interview, "Social media is definitely necessary for higher education institutions." In this section, I will discuss the overall themes for how Facebook and Twitter are efficient platforms for the completion of specific tasks. When participants discussed how Facebook and Twitter were efficient in getting tasks done, six themes emerged: promotion, building an audience, interaction and engagement, free website, student applications, and authenticity.

Out of four expectations described for both platforms, two were also revealed to be a theme for efficiency. Promotion and interaction/engagement were expectations revealed to be functionalities for both Facebook and Twitter. Several of the participants discussed how Facebook and Twitter were efficient for promoting the college or university. The main concept mentioned for promotional purposes is that both social media platforms offer boosted or sponsored advertisements. Facebook and Twitter enable an institution to purchase digital ads on the sites to reach specific audiences on the platform. The online ad can be seen by selected locations, communities, demographics, and ages. Participant 5 stated that it is important to purchase ads through Facebook or Twitter or else no one would ever see their content. Participant 5 said, "Unless we put money into promoting it or using it in a different way, we understand that whatever we share here is not necessarily going to be seen by the people we want to see it."

Participant 7 agreed that boosted posts are important to grow an online audience that would not be discovered otherwise. However, the same participant felt that Facebook is better than Twitter for boosted posts when they want their posts to be more organic. Participant 7 stated, "We occasionally buy boosted posts on Facebook, not too often, only for specific purposes but not in every post. And I think that's worth it because we don't spend that much, and we do see it get boosted to a bigger audience."

Because Twitter was mentioned as organic information, I added authenticity as a theme. Participant 6 discussed that it is important for all their social media posts to be original, because they want the audience to feel as though the posts are coming straight from the source or institutional voice. Participant 6 explained, "We would like to do more paid content. I just worry a little bit about that authenticity. I think if you continue to see the sponsored under that post, I just think that that's something that might not say something that inspires trust." Outside of boosted or promoted posts/tweets, another participant stated that digital tools are vital for Facebook and Twitter to be efficient. Participant 9 responded that Facebook and Twitter are not efficient "without a third-party tool." Participant 9 said, "I utilize Hootsuite for scheduling content and tagging content. Tagging content helps me keep track of different metrics." Hootsuite is third-party software that allows a college or university to schedule tweets or posts. It creates a schedule for posts for several days, weeks, or months. Also, it provides free analytics on how well the posts and tweets are performing. Thus, the scheduling software provides ways to make the daily tasks easier for the participant.

Another theme that emerged from the participants was to build and grow an audience online who follow the higher education institution on Facebook and Twitter. As Participant 1 explained, "It is a valuable tool to reach a wide audience." The goal for Participant 5 is to use Facebook and Twitter for more than simply keeping in touch with alumni, but to connect with prospective students looking to apply to the institution. Participant 8 explained, "I think it's just a very high visibility opportunity because people are there." If people are consistently using social media for all aspects of interaction and communication, colleges and universities can use the sites for building their audiences for recruitment purposes.

"Interaction" and "engagement" were mentioned quite frequently when participants explained their expectations for using social media. According to several participants, it is successfully executed on Facebook and Twitter. Participant 1 thinks that there is so much value in Facebook and Twitter as successful social media sites for interaction and engagement. Participant 1 said: "You can have a great news story in say the *New York Times* or on a morning news show. And that's extremely valuable. But I think that there is a lot of value in engaging with your constituents. Whether it be, you know, alums or potential students or current students or parents, I think having that interaction means something to your audience." Participant 8 agreed, stating that an institution cannot reach a high level of engagement simply by using its website.

Two participants explained that part of the reason why Facebook and Twitter are efficient and functional for their institution is that they are free websites for the college or university. Participant 1 quickly responded by saying the two websites are free. Participant 7 added, "I think they're efficient in that they don't really cost us anything." This result indicates that the participants might consider not using Facebook and Twitter if they had to pay a fee to use the websites.

As with the prior queries, the top two words in the results of the text search query were "Facebook" and "Twitter." In the efficiency node, "Facebook" received 219 mentions, while "Twitter" earned 193 mentions from the participants. Although this may not mean that Facebook is more important, the fact that the participants discussed Facebook more frequently may indicate that the employees utilize and prefer the service more than Twitter. Of the five themes explaining why both Facebook and Twitter are functional platforms for higher education, two words (promotion and authenticity) did not come up in the text search results. This does not indicate that the themes are not relevant as they were discussed many times by the respondents. I believe the reason for this result is because of the many different terms the audience associated with promotion and authenticity. For instance, promotion was used to describe digital advertisements, sponsored ads, and boosted posts, among other ways to purchase ads on Facebook and Twitter. All the phrases describe the same topic. The issue came up with authenticity as participants described original posts, as well as not re-tweeting and sharing from other users. Thus, the themes remain vital to the functionality of Facebook and Twitter in that promotion and authenticity are two of the main characteristics.

The second theme for both Facebook and Twitter as efficient platforms for higher education is building an audience. As discussed in prior nodes, participants and the audience within the college or university online community are always among the most frequent terms. In total, the term "audience" was mentioned 32 times. However, the specific audiences were discussed much more frequently. Students (50), alumni (40), employees (40), student (23), community (20), and faculty (15) were all target audiences described by participants. In total, audience, combined with all target audiences, were discussed 220 times. This would make this theme the second most discussed, right above Facebook and Twitter. Also, this result illustrates that building the online audience is one of the most important ways Facebook and Twitter are efficient in higher education.

The third theme, interaction and engagement, is becoming a top priority for functionality in using Facebook and Twitter in higher education. "Engagement" was discussed 27 times while "interaction" received 14 mentions. However, additional interaction and ways to communicate came up with the results of the text search query. Post (88), posting (30), posts (23) share (35), comments (24), and sharing (20) are all ways to interact and engage with an online community using Facebook and Twitter. With all the ways to communicate with an online audience using Facebook and Twitter, "engagement" and "interaction" emerged with 261 declarations among participants discussing functionality of Facebook and Twitter. This result reveals engagement and interaction as the main reason why Facebook and Twitter are functional and efficient for the participants using the sites within higher education.

The last characteristic of functionality analyzed was that Facebook and Twitter are free websites. Although the term "free" did not come up within the top 100 most frequent words among the participants, "website" was mentioned 27 times and discussed quite often during the responses. This result matches my analysis that using Facebook and Twitter as free platforms is another characteristic of the efficiency.

Structure (Form)

All participants were asked how Facebook posts or tweets on Twitter are formatted. Questions 13, 14, and 15 asked participants the following:

13. What is your format when constructing a post on Facebook? What are the textual and visual requirements?
14. What is your format when constructing a tweet on Twitter? What are the textual and visual requirements?
15. Do you have any formatting or linguistic requirements in your post or tweet?

Facebook and Twitter Form—Characteristics of Each Platform from Interview Results

For previous interview questions, most participants combined Facebook and Twitter. The same continued for questions 13, 14, and 15. However, four out of ten participants explained differences constructing and formatting messages between Facebook and Twitter. Three of the participants responded only by giving specific characteristics for Twitter. For the analysis, I will explain how each participant answered the questions regarding structure, followed by formatting features and themes that stood out from the discussions. Additionally, I will compare the structure of a Facebook and Twitter post.

Participants overwhelmingly stated that both Facebook and Twitter should include pictures in every post. Five participants stated that Twitter should utilize pictures, while four interviewees mentioned that Facebook posts should add a picture as part of the message. Participant 3 explained, "We rarely share anything on Facebook without a photo of some sorts." Participant 4 highlighted the importance of a photo for Twitter: "We do like to have pictures with whatever we post especially on Twitter." Another similar characteristic for both Facebook and Twitter are the addition of a link. Link is short for hyperlink, which is text usually highlighted in blue, that re-directs the social media user to another source, usually a corresponding website related to the topic in the post or tweet. Participant 5 described the use of links on Facebook as: "We're making sure that our news links show up with an appropriate photo or video." Although links are used as well on Twitter, Participant 5 explained that the institution tries to use links a bit less because of the never-ending feed that Twitter provides its users. Participant 5 said, "I also recognize that a lot of people are scrolling through tweets and not necessarily clicking on the links. Also, I try to frame it in a way that gives some nugget of information, in case, if they just read the tweet." This quote by Participant 5 indicates that users do not want to leave the social media website to read more on another web page.

Hashtags were mentioned for both Facebook and Twitter, but for completely different reasons. Half of the participants mentioned hashtags as an important characteristic of Twitter. Most participants felt that hashtags provide a search feature for the users to locate information on a topic. Participant 1 explained that the use of hashtags is to categorize their institution's programs: "And we do have initiatives or campaigns I guess you could call them, that require hashtags." Participant 3 agreed that hashtags can be valuable for initiatives, stating: "We use hashtags when we are clear on how the hashtag ties into the tweet. For example, we have certain campaigns that we know, oh this post ties in perfectly with our four campaigns. so, we're going to hashtag it, but we don't use hashtags with every post." Participant 3 discussed that while hashtags are used on Twitter, the institution is careful in adding them to a message, making sure that the text and information within the post are cataloged.

Hashtags were a bit different in responses for Facebook. Two of the participants stated that hashtags do not work on Facebook and should not be used. Participant 6 explained that the audience does not respond to hashtags: "Hashtags on Facebook just kind of isn't like that successful. I do include them sometimes just because I want to kind of clue people who are reading it. But we will see more people kind of participating in those hashtags on Instagram and Twitter."

Although most of the participants find success using hashtags on Twitter but not on Facebook, Participant 6 mentioned that the structure of a hashtag should include capitalizing the first letter of the word. For instance, "If I was to like hashtag climate change or something or research matters it would be capital Research, capital Matters or Climate Change or whatever." Participant 6 explained that when the initial first letter of each word is not capitalized, it can be misread by the social media user, thus causing a misunderstanding of a public post by the college or university.

After the top three characteristics (pictures, links, and hashtags) participants discussed additional features regarding Facebook and Twitter. Participant 5 stated that Facebook should include some sort of visual element: "So for Facebook I would say that I always have some visual element whether that's just sharing a straight up photo or a video." Although Participant 5 specifically mentioned photos and videos, visual elements can include memes, GIFs, graphics, or animations. Thus, the phrase includes all types of still and moving images. Even though one participant highlighted visual elements along with the four participants who described pictures as being important on Facebook, two participants stated that there are times when a post can be text only. Participant 2 identified this as: "There are exceptions of course when they would be just a text, but I would probably just do that on Twitter as infrequent circumstances." Participant 2 further explained that it is important to add an image to a message for the most part; there must be a reason behind why text only is used.

There were two ways other visuals were mentioned with Facebook and Twitter. Participant 5 uses videos for Facebook and emojis (graphics) for Twitter. Emojis include graphical elements of facial expressions and objects to convey a message or express a feeling to the online audience. Regarding emojis on Twitter, Participant 5 explained, "I found that in some cases those posts have another visual element in the text that's a little bit more interactive."

Two additional features that were mentioned for Facebook and Twitter separately are call to action and condensing stories. Participant 4 described a call to action as, "Read more at our website. Discover more about this program: here." Participant 4 said a call to action creates interactivity because it encourages the social media user to do something. Therefore, I added interactivity as a characteristic because participants mentioned it several times for Facebook; audience participation has an impact in formatting a post on social media. The reason for condensing stories on Twitter is the limit of 280 characters per tweet set by the platform. Participant 5 added, "On Twitter, given the constraints of a tweet, in terms of size, I try to condense down whatever it is I'm sharing to as short a caption as possible." This connects to the previous characteristic for Twitter, where an emoji or other graphic can shorten the text of a message.

The final characteristic for Twitter is writing standards. Participant 7 strongly believes that the writing standards of the college needs to be upheld because of the public nature of tweets. To explain, Participant 7 stated, "[redacted] is a place that prides itself on having a long literary tradition and reading and writing. I think it's OK if our tweets fit with that. If our tweet is a little bit more complex and obviously like we have high standards for grammar and punctuation and everything because of that." Participant 7 stated that the institution will not re-tweet anything from a social media user that mentions the college or university if there is a spelling or grammatical error in the tweet.

Facebook and Twitter Form—Overall Characteristics of Form (Combined)

This section highlights the top characteristics of form when participants were discussing Facebook and Twitter combined. Several participants viewed the form of Facebook and Twitter to be the same, as opposed to separate literacies. All ten participants stated that photographs were an essential aspect for designing a message on Facebook and Twitter. Participant 10 explained this simply by stating, "We always try to post something that has an image with it to increase engagement. For the most part, we do try to get an image to help bring people to the story." Many of the participants felt that a picture is just as important to the message as the text. Only two participants stated that text alone is an important trait. This was only mentioned for the social media site Twitter. Therefore, based on the ten participant interviews, visual images are an important part of constructing a post on Facebook and Twitter. A second most mentioned feature for Facebook and Twitter combined is the use of hashtags. Six participants mentioned hashtags when describing the structure of a tweet or Facebook post. Hashtags had much more of an impact on Twitter than Facebook, as discussed in the previous section. Participants 3 and 6 stated that hashtags do not work on Facebook and that they should not be used. However, five participants stated that hashtags are an important format for composing a tweet on Twitter.

Links, also known as hyperlinks, are a third form for Facebook and Twitter combined. Two participants each for Facebook and Twitter stated that hyperlinks leading to another website are important to the structure of a message on both social media platforms. Participant 4 described the overall format using Twitter as an example: "Twitter I would say pictures, links to a website and some sort of hashtag." The use of links on Facebook is described as giving a user something to do, which connects to the theory of a call to action for the social media site. Participant 5 said, "I'll also include a link so that they can go off to do something whether that's sign up for an event or go read this article about us." The difference seems to be that links on Facebook are to encourage an action, while links on Twitter provide further details to the story.

The last common characteristic for Facebook and Twitter is the importance of good spelling and grammar, use of a style guide, and keeping with writing standards of the institution. Many of the participants stated that it's extremely important to have a consistent writing style when constructing a message on Facebook and Twitter. Because of the nature of higher education and the expectation of quality writing, grammar is reviewed regularly. Participant 8 described the use of a writing style for Facebook and Twitter as, "We use AP style in general and then we have a [redacted] style. We always capitalize the B in black and we just like to do things that nobody else does." Participant 7 added, "We just want our brand to be very prestigious when it comes to writing." This also connects to Participant 6's statement that social media employees should be posting on Facebook and Twitter to represent the academic or institutional voice on the platforms. Students are best utilized to post for authenticity purposes when the time is right or for particular social media sites for younger audiences, such as Instagram. Additionally, many participants felt that they wanted to continue to oversee text, as students can be best utilized and trusted more frequently with the visuals. Participant 6 explained this notion: "Students kind of respond well to that authentic voice. And when you see a student speaking directly to you, you really get that. But if we had a student employee writing on Facebook or Twitter people wouldn't know that." Since the social media sites represent the institution as opposed to the student, the participant wants to make sure that the message on the sites is clear and understood by all audiences.

I ran the word search query to see if the results matched the analysis. The top 100 words were analyzed. Upon reviewing the results, many words associated with people came up, such as alumni, employees, and participants. However, I only reviewed the words associated with my analysis of the interviews and text that relate to the structure or functionality of a message.

Within the combined results for Facebook and Twitter, I did not find interaction to be a frequent topic or theme of discussion. Interaction was found to be valuable for those participants discussing the format for Facebook. When the text search analysis was conducted, "interaction" resulted in 14 mentions. However, other ways of interacting came up in the results. Post (91), share (35), posting (30), engagement (30), posts (35), and comments (24) are all actions to communicate with an audience or online community through social media. Therefore, "interaction" was discussed 226 times regarding formatting messages for Facebook and Twitter. Although this is not a specific technique or tool to construct a message, it is important and relevant to state since the messages are created to engage and interact with a chosen audience.

In total, "content" received 86 mentions throughout the interviews relating to format. This indicates that creating and using content is the most important characteristic of formatting a message on Facebook and Twitter. The forms of content that received the most frequent mentions were news (40) and information (40) with a total of 80 statements. This is intriguing, as news for both platforms combined was not an important form of content within the initial analysis. However, news was discussed frequently as shown in the text search analysis.

This may relate to the next characteristic within the results as stories (59) and story (28) were stated 59 times among participants. Condensing stories was noted as a characteristic for Twitter, as opposed to Facebook. This result shows that when constructing a message on Facebook and Twitter, news or stories are a valuable link or form of content to be inserted within the message.

The words photos (26), photo (18), and image (12) were mentioned 56 times during the interviews. This matches the analysis in which all participants discussed the importance of still photography for both social media platforms and the expectation that there should be an image with every post or tweet. Hashtags (17) and hashtag (14) were mentioned 31 times. This matches the analysis that hashtags are used for both Facebook and Twitter, even though participants stated that the practice works better for Twitter than Facebook. The word "video" received 21 mentions during the text search query. This is an intriguing result, as Facebook was the only platform where video was a valuable digital tool. This indicates that video is potentially used much less than photography but is an important form of content that participants may use when creating a Facebook post.

The word "visuals" were mentioned 18 times by respondents. This word is difficult to categorize, since it can relate to several items such as: photos, video, memes, GIFs, or animations. Thus, individuals may be stating one or both (photography and video), as well as additional types of visuals when using this word. This establishes that along with the frequent mentions of photos and videos, participants will use both text and imagery in their messages on Facebook and Twitter.

"Links" was frequently mentioned as a format for both Facebook and Twitter. However, it was stated much less than visual content. "Links" was mentioned 13 times during the interviews regarding functionality. Although it may be less mentioned as a format than photos or videos, it is still frequently utilized among participants and matches the results of my analysis, as most participants mentioned the use of links.

"Writing" is the last word to highlight in the text search analysis. The word "writing" was used to discuss a style guide or format for constructing messages. "Writing" was mentioned 13 times during the participant interviews regarding format, thus showing that while some participants have a rulebook at their institutions, it may not be a tool that all colleges or universities utilize regularly.

Additional Results from Responses

During interviews with the 10 participants, additional themes and topics emerged outside of the genre taxonomy. The following section highlights the relevant topics that may potentially impact or correlate to the findings. The additional topics (participant responses) also may be useful for future research about genre studies and social media in higher education.

Before analyzing the direct question asking respondents to provide additional information on the topic, there was one important point consistently made by participants: Instagram was their preferred social media channel over Facebook and Twitter. Participant 7 stated, "We emphasize Instagram a lot more even though that's not your focus. It feeds into the content of the other platforms more because whenever we post there, we usually also pull that post over to Twitter." The same participant admitted to focusing on Facebook less because of using Instagram on a more regular basis. Participant 7 also mentioned that while Twitter does not seem to have a large audience compared to their other platforms, the participant preferred to use Twitter. The findings highlight employees may select social media platforms based on their personal preference and interest, as opposed to what may be best for the institution.

Participant 8 explained that the audience on Instagram is mostly students rather than faculty. The online community typically consists of current and prospective students, along with "young alumni," meaning graduates who have received their degrees recently. Participant 7 also stated that engagement is much better on Instagram than on Facebook and Twitter stating: "We get our best engagement on Instagram. We are getting like over a thousand likes on a photo and we never really get that on the other platforms." This statement highlights the fact that Instagram may be getting more audience interaction on a post (picture, video, text) than the other social media platforms. This finding was reinforced by Participant 6: "We do give students the ability to take over on our Instagram stories and I think that plays into that audience, too, where students kind of respond well to that authentic voice." Many of the other participants agreed with Participant 6 about the realism or authenticity that images and video offer to students.

After analyzing the comments that interview participants made about Instagram, the question is: Should Instagram be analyzed as a genre? Based on my research of genre studies, I believe that it is too early to analyze Instagram as a genre for several reasons. According to prior research, Barnes and Lescault concluded in 2011 that Facebook and Twitter are the best platforms for sharing information with current and potential students. While this justifies the study focusing on Facebook and Twitter, Instagram has yet to be examined as a recruitment and informative website.[3]

Secondly and more importantly, as Participant 6 pointed out, most employees at higher education institutions are not using Instagram on a regular basis. Instead, students were hired as interns to post on Instagram. For example, Participant 9 said, "We also utilize an Instagram account in which I actually empower students to help with." This statement relates to Participant 6 who stated that students are hired to create visual content on Instagram, while Facebook and Twitter are used by social media employees who make sure the online writing is grammatically correct. Furthermore, Instagram is not a genre because the participants do not utilize the site on a regular basis to complete tasks, instead having others, in this case students, post the information for them. As discussed in the literature review, while Instagram is being used in an academic setting, which agrees with Bhatia, it goes against the definition I developed for genre from many scholars including Lehtinen and Palli.[4] The authors defined genres as a way for employees to get things done and accomplish tasks personally, as opposed to others doing the work for the employee. Since students post content on Instagram—not the employees with the social media titles—Instagram is not yet ready to be considered a genre in higher education.

The last question I asked all participants was: Do you have any closing comments you wish to mention before the interview concludes? This offered participants an opportunity to add additional feedback pertaining to Facebook and Twitter in relation to genre studies. Outside of the theme of Instagram evaluated above, all other responses were individual topics discussed by each participant. Therefore, I will interpret and examine each response in order of interview. While no other major theme developed, it is important to mention the topic because of its potential future impact on social media, higher education, and genre studies.

Participants 2 and 8 did not have additional comments to add to the discussion. Participant 1 felt it was important to mention that while Facebook and Twitter are excellent tools for sending positive information out to the masses, it is equally vital to utilize when a crisis comes up and the information is not positive. Participant 1 explained, "I think that rather than seeming like we're staying silent on an issue, it allows us to share it more widely as opposed to just having it on our website." Thus, Facebook and Twitter allow the participant to send messages quickly and respond to their audience, who may have direct questions or concerns. Participant 3 felt that social media is still evolving and is still a work in progress: "I feel like there are some institutions that respond very quickly to breaking news because it ties into their like whatever it is they sell and of course in higher education you have to kind of walk a fine line about pop culture things you want to jump on." Participant 3 said that institutions should be very careful when posting about controversial topics such as politics or entertainment because stories continually develop. Also, with the different cultures and backgrounds of students, there are many political and religious affiliations on campus. Institutions must be aware that there are multiple audiences with different backgrounds and cultures. While one audience may understand or find a pop culture reference funny, another audience could be offended. Thus, Participant 3 is providing a warning about pop culture references and news stories.

Participant 4 was also cautious about privacy, specifically mentioning Cambridge Analytica's theft of data for 50 million Facebook users. Users downloaded what they believed was a psychology application. Instead, the application sent data to Cambridge Analytica, which then created political profiles on all users based on how they were likely to vote in upcoming elections. Thus, Participant 4 argued that with the continual privacy issues Facebook is having, institutions may become afraid to use the platform or social media in general. To combat privacy, Participant 4 proposed being more personable with their audiences on both Facebook and Twitter: "We do have to have conversational posts. We do want to get people excited about (the college) and we want to be proactive about listening as well." Participant 4 suggested that personal communication will be a valuable trait and function for the future of both Facebook and Twitter for higher education use. It provides an authentic voice.

Participant 5 responded that social media platforms are still evolving, meaning that they are still in their infancy and beginning stages; their true definition of use is still developing. Participant 5 said, "It's important to stay on top of them and pay attention to what we're doing there." Based on the response by Participant 5, Facebook and Twitter are still new entities. Their uses are still shaping and the impact of the massive amount of data on the systems is yet to be realized. Although social media may be evolving, Participant 6 responded to the last question by explaining the importance of reviewing competitors and other colleges or universities that use social media. The review will help an institution understand the type of conversations an online community is having relating to content on the platform. It may help inspire or give ideas about how best to utilize social media in a higher education environment.

Participant 9 advocated that social media sites should make it easier to delete offensive comments attached to a post. Participant 9 explained that on Twitter, there are many instances when a tweet is published, and an audience member responds with an offensive tweet. There is nothing that the institution can do to delete it. Participant 9 added: "Of course we're trying to protect students and promote free thinking. For example, I tweeted about something this week and somebody commented with a racist statement. And there's nothing that I can do, and they tagged a handful of students in it. I wish that there was some way to remedy that but there's not." Lastly, Participant 10 noted that social media is still a new development, agreeing with Participant 5; it can be hard to explain the importance of its use to the administration of a college or university. Participant 10 stated, "Overall social media at the college is a new thing, kind of a hard sell to explain, at least explaining the importance of it to some of our higher administration." Although social media is regularly utilized for personal use, there are still employees who do not see sufficient value in its use to warrant such attention and daily responsibilities.

When discussing the employee role for using Facebook and Twitter at the institution, Participant 10 described how social media is part of the individual's website position. The participant initially was hired to create content for the website to update the homepage, web pages, and write feature stories. Social media became integrated into the position when the Director of Public Relations (who previously worked on social media) left the institution. Participant 10 proclaimed, "Social media is kind of just like technically a third of my job responsibilities." This may indicate that the participants have other titles, tasks, and responsibilities at the institution outside of only social media. Future research will have to evaluate whether social media should be its own position at higher education institutions as a sole responsibility, instead of being combined with other digital platforms.

Participant 3 detailed how the sites work differently when posting content: "If something is on Facebook, it will also be on Twitter. And if something is on Twitter, it won't necessarily be on Facebook." In reviewing the results from Participant 3 in more detail, Facebook is defined as an extension of the university website, whereas Twitter offers a more creative environment for posts. Also, this response highlights how the platforms work differently, which could affect the structure of a message. Twitter only offers a message up to 280 characters, whereas Facebook offers no limit. The difference in structure may point out how Twitter posts may not work the same in the Facebook environment. Participant 6 desires to keep the number of daily posts low: "I try to keep the number of posts on any platform to 1 or 2 per day because we really don't want to exhaust people. And thankfully we've got enough content that we can keep up with and not overload people." However, Participant 7 posts less on Facebook, but much more frequently on Twitter. According to Participant 7, the goal for Facebook is to bring the audience to the institution website, whereas on Twitter, posts increase because of the creativity offered on the website. The data collection in the content analysis agrees with this statement as daily postings on Twitter far exceeded the number of posts on Facebook for all institutions. It also is pertinent to mention that when conducting word search queries for all of web genre from the participant interviews, Facebook was stated more than Twitter with every theme or topic.

Compare and Contrast Purpose Interview and Content Analysis Results

The genre characteristic of purpose was analyzed twice in the study. Participants in the interview were asked their purpose for using Facebook and Twitter, then I analyzed the purpose of each post and tweet based on the seven functions of higher education. Several similarities and differences appeared when comparing the interview with the content analysis results. First, it was clear that all institutions are sharing information on Facebook and Twitter. In the interview, all participants stated that their goal is to share information with their audiences on Facebook and Twitter. Whether it was highlighting faculty research, promoting an upcoming event, showcasing an art gallery, or posting a lecture, information was shared daily on Facebook and Twitter.

A major difference between the interview and content analysis of purpose pertains to communication and collaboration. All participants in the interview responded that engagement and interaction with their online audience are major purposes for using Facebook and Twitter in higher education. However, the content analysis for both platforms did not agree with the statements made by the participants. On Facebook, "collaborate" had 24 posts for the month and "communicate" had 12 posts for the month. On Twitter, "communicate" had 361 tweets and "collaborate" had 76 tweets. Although on

Twitter there was more dialogue and discussion between the institution and its followers, for the most part, colleges and universities were barely engaging their constituents on both social media sites. Thus, the participants interviewed felt engagement was a priority, but it did occur in the content analysis.

A third stated goal for both Facebook and Twitter were connecting with their audience, which includes alumni, students, faculty, and staff. Throughout the month of analyzing tweets and posts, this theory proved to be true as at various points, the messages were directed to all those constituents. The least likely posts or tweets were about staff, but there were messages directed toward students (event announcements), faculty (research), alumni (recent job announcements), and staff (starting new positions at the institution). The institution did focus on all audiences when creating messages for Facebook and Twitter.

It is important to note that the interviews made no mention of any of the seven functions of higher education. No participant mentioned fostering socialization, promoting culture, conveying knowledge, conducting research, conferring credentials, sustaining the institution, or providing public service as a purpose for using Facebook and Twitter. However, the content analysis describes how each function plays a pivotal role in messages posted on institutional Facebook and Twitter pages. In one response, a participant identified a purpose for Twitter as providing sports updates. This statement was proven to be true as fostering socialization was a priority for Twitter, but also received a fair number of posts for Facebook. Both sites promoted games for the audience to attend as well as giving the final scores. A purpose specific to Facebook that participants mentioned during interviews was to share written articles. The content analysis highlighted that this is true for both Facebook and Twitter, as articles written by campus employees that were posted and featured on the website also were shared on the social media sites. Additionally, faculty journal articles and student blogs were shared on Facebook and Twitter. Regarding Facebook, participants also stated that promotion was a purpose for using the site. This was proven true for both Facebook and Twitter in the content analysis as the social media sites were regularly used to promote such things as events, academic departments, concerts, exhibitions, lectures, and sports.

Compare and Contrast Form Interview and Content Analysis Results

While form was specifically analyzed with a content analysis of posts and tweets for Facebook and Twitter, it also was discussed during the interviews. Participants were asked if there was a form or structure to writing a message on each social media site, as well as specific grammar or writing styles utilized when communicating information to the masses. Upon review, there are similarities between the two methods but disparities as well.

There are two important distinctions between the interview and content analysis results. After I analyzed the types of form used to create a message on Facebook and Twitter, the two most important characteristics are pictures and hyperlinks. This connected to the responses in the interview as participants stated that pictures and links are important to include in a Facebook post or tweet. One participant even stated that they will rarely post anything on Facebook without a picture of some sort. This result indicates that both pictures and hyperlinks should be included in creating a message on Facebook and Twitter.

In the prior section, the researcher explained how video was not a format frequently used on Facebook and Twitter. This was a bit of a discrepancy with the interviews, as one of the results noted how Facebook uses video frequently within a post. Although "video" was used in 263 posts during the month, it was one of the lowest structures used. The same discrepancy in media occurred with graphics, specifically emojis. An interview participant mentioned that emojis are used frequently within tweets. This was proven to be true somewhat as graphics were identified 1,018 times. It should be noted, though, that graphics were used less frequently than other formats. Therefore, video on Facebook and emojis on Twitter were used as forms based on the interviews, but not utilized enough or on a consistent-enough basis in the content analysis.

During the interview, most of the participants stated that hashtags do not work on Facebook but are important to incorporate on Twitter. After the content analysis, this response was proven to be true as a plethora of hashtags were discovered within the tweets for the month and used less frequently on Facebook. It is significant to point out that although participants stated that hashtags should not be used on Facebook, it was identified 667 times in the month and was a form somewhat used, just much less when compared to Twitter. Regarding Twitter, the interviews noted that tweets can be text-only, but Facebook posts should always include multimedia. The research noted that this ended up being accurate for Twitter as there were tweets using text without an image (for instance, simply responding to someone in the online community or a direct statement), whereas Facebook posts always included an image or video. Also, it should be clarified that more tweets had images than text-only posts.

Another result from the interviews pertaining to the format of a Facebook post is the inclusion of a call-to-action, giving the audience something to do. An example is asking the audience to "click here" for more information at the end of a Facebook post. After the content analysis, this approach is used for both Facebook and Twitter. Messages on both platforms regularly requested the audience to watch something or read more about a particular subject. Instead of labeling this theme as a call-to-action, the term "signature" was used instead. "Signature" was identified 1,764 times on Twitter and 1,129 times on Facebook as a frequently used format during the month. Another way to structure a message based on the responses of the participants was to add captions to photos. This structure was not necessarily discovered on Facebook or Twitter, as every tweet or post had some text above the image. Images did not have any text on them or underneath as a caption.

Another goal for participants in the interviews was to condense stories. While this is difficult to decipher based on the content analysis, the only difference between platforms was that messages on Twitter had to remain in 280 characters, while on Facebook there is no limit to how long a story could be. Thus, condensed stories were a statement made by participants regarding Facebook; it is more of a requirement for Twitter. Another form frequently discussed in the interviews was video. The word frequency places an importance on visuals as well, which ties into pictures. Pertaining to links, the words "stories," "writing," and "news" were frequently mentioned based on the text search analysis. This ties into the content analysis, since links was a priority of form and all links related to articles on the institutional website or elsewhere. However, this does not match up with the content analysis as video was not utilized continually on either platform.

NOTES

1. Cohen and Kenny, *Producing New and Digital Media*, 254.
2. Sam Hinton and Larissa Hjorth, *Understanding Social Media* (Sage, 2013).
3. Barnes and Lescault, "Social media adoption soars as higher-ed experiments and reevaluates its use of new communications tools," 2.
4. Lehtinen and Palli, "Conversational use of genres in managerial meetings," 287.

Chapter 7

Conclusion

Facebook and Twitter as Genres

The study had four research questions that can now be answered after completing the interviews and content analysis. The first research question asked: Based on the seven functions of higher education, what appears to be the purpose of Facebook and Twitter institutional social media web pages? After completing the study, I can declare that there are clear purposes for Facebook and Twitter, but for different reasons. The purposes of each social media platform are not the same; each has distinct goals and objectives for using the sites within the higher education environment. Before highlighting the distinctions, each characteristic in the seven functions of higher education was a goal for using Facebook and Twitter at some point, as discussed in interviews, or discovered during the content analysis. Nonetheless, some functions are more relevant than others. This connects to Bhatia (1993) who stated that genres can have more than one purpose.[1]

For Twitter, the most relevant function is to foster socialization. In order of relevance, the remaining top purposes for Twitter are other, promote culture, convey knowledge, and conduct research. I label these five categories as the primary goals and objectives for using Twitter in higher education. These five functions should be used by all colleges and universities using institutional Twitter web pages. The remaining five include the last three categories of the seven functions of higher education and added traits based on the findings. These last five traits are alternative goals and objectives for using Twitter in higher education and are utilized less frequently. In order of relevance, the functions are confer credentials, communicate, sustain the institution, provide public service, and collaborate.

Regarding Facebook, the most relevant function is to promote culture. The following four purposes for Facebook are the primary goals and objectives presented in order from highest to lowest: other, convey knowledge, foster socialization, and conduct research. Although promoting culture is the primary goal, the other four functions were all used regularly within the month of analysis and should be considered when colleges and universities are utilizing Facebook institutional web pages. The remaining five purposes are defined as alternative uses for the goal of a post or tweet on the respective social media platforms. Three functions remain as the secondary options, along with the two additional options based on the literature review. In order of most used to the least used, the alternatives are confer credentials, sustain the institution, provide public service, collaborate, and communicate.

To conclude, the primary purposes for using Facebook and Twitter are the same: foster socialization, other, convey knowledge, promote culture, and conduct research. These five should be included for both. However, the difference is the priority of the function. For example, on Facebook the first focus is to promote culture, while on Twitter it is to foster socialization. Additionally, the secondary and alternative purposes are the same for Facebook and Twitter: confer credentials, provide public service, sustain the institution, collaborate, and communicate. The difference is that for Facebook collaborate and communicate received so few responses that they are not needed for the genre of Facebook, while for Twitter collaborate was the only function that was rarely a priority.

I added communicate and collaborate as characteristics to analyze purpose based on Russo, Watkins, Kelly and Chan's (2008) study revealing that both are functions of social media sites.[2] However, both were rarely discovered within the content analysis of purpose and are not part of the genre of Facebook and Twitter.

The second research question asked: Using the linguistic and formatting features of social media as assessment instruments, what can be said about the form of Facebook and Twitter institutional social media web pages? This question was answered by using a content analysis of the 21 categories of form to identify the structure of a message. All 21 categories were a form of a message at some point within the one-month analysis of each tweet and post. However, coinciding with purpose, some traits were more relevant than others when designing a message to inform an audience. Although there are similarities, Facebook and Twitter have separate forms to construct a message on the platforms. The results do not coincide with Cohen and Kenny (2015) in that social media should feature text, pictures, sound, and video.[3] The findings of this study explain that social media uses text and pictures as a format, but rarely uses video and almost never uses sound.

Beginning with Twitter, first I wanted to explore whether content on institutional Twitter pages is user created by the social media employee or is shared content created by others. For Twitter, both types of posting information are used very regularly, but more preference is given to user-created content. Based on the results of the content analysis, there are four levels to the relevance of form on Twitter. The two primary formats include pictures and links, as both appeared in a significant number of tweets. Additional primary formats include hashtags and mentions. As a result, a tweet should include a picture, link, hashtag, and mention for all posts.

The second level of relevance or secondary purposes of form using Twitter in the higher education environment are P.S., self-introductory greeting, and greeting. The secondary formats are presented in order of relevance in the content analysis. These are all frequently used formats on Twitter, just used less than the primary traits. They can, however, be used when needed for a tweet.

The third level of alternative options of formats when structuring a message or tweet include an embedded message, signature, word/phrase emphasis, emphatic message, and a graphic. All options were used semi-regularly, but not as consistently as the prior two levels.

The fourth and final level includes possible format options that were sometimes used, but not on a regular basis, by social media employees. In order of results, this includes ellipsis, set apart, video, and reply. All were used at various points within the month as a form on Twitter, but only when needed. Three formats were rarely used in the construction of a tweet: list, apologetic messages, and audio.

Following up with Facebook, preference is given to creating original posts as user-created content was the most relevant category. It was discovered that user-generated content is rarely used and should not even be considered a format for sharing information on Facebook. The two primary formats used on Facebook in order of relevance are pictures and links. Thus, every post should include a picture and link within the message. Secondary formats on Facebook in order of relevance include P.S., self-introductory greeting, and signature. All formats are used frequently within a post on Facebook by social media employees designing the message. The third level of Facebook posts includes (in order of relevance): embedded message, greeting, set apart, word/phrase emphasis, hashtags, emphatic message, ellipsis, graphic, and video. All are formats somewhat used on Facebook when needed by social media managers. The remaining formats are ones that are not needed when designing a Facebook post. The formats include list, mentions, audio, apologetic messages, and replies. All formats were rarely used or sporadically appeared in a post during the month of analysis.

In conclusion, the top two formats for Facebook and Twitter were the same, pictures and links, along with information being original content (UCC) designed by social media employees of the higher education institution. The statement regarding links connects with the research of Crowston and Williams (2000) when they discovered that over 80% of web pages contain hyperlinks.[4] Thus, this finding is also proven true on social media platforms, which are also web pages. However, on Twitter, it is also a priority to share content from outside sources (UGC), while on Facebook this is not a format. It was stated by Lüders, Prøitz, and Rasmussen (2010) that web genres should have participation from the online community to create content.[5] This is only proven for social media web pages on Twitter, but not Facebook due to the practice of the institutions re-tweeting and sharing content created by their online audience. In Kwasnik and Crowston's (2000) research, the authors believed it was difficult to define a genre by interacting with the online audience.[6] This study was able to prove that Twitter is not only a genre, but has a characteristic of form, in which information is shared from other online users outside of the institution (user-generated content or UGC). Twitter also connects with Hinton and Hjorth's (2013) research in that social media should encompass both user-generated, and user-created content.[7] Facebook mainly utilized user-created content only. However, a big difference between the two are that hashtags and mentions are primary formats on Twitter, with both used much less frequently on Facebook. Facebook and Twitter both share similar formats that are rarely used, such as a reply, list, apologetic message, and audio.

A similarity is that many of the same formats are used on both platforms, but the preference in format changes whether using Facebook and Twitter. Although media content (pictures and links) were the top two formats, it was also proven that Facebook and Twitter are a combination of text and media content. This finding agrees with Lüders, Prøitz, and Rasmussen (2010) as their study revealed that online genres are a combination of media and text.[8] This is established on Facebook and Twitter as both were a combination of text, such as greeting, self-introductory greeting, signature, and media including pictures, hyperlinks, and graphics throughout the entire month of analysis. However, it should be noted that media is preferred on Facebook and Twitter, even though text is intertwined.

The third research question asked: Using the genre taxonomy as an assessment instrument, what is the functionality of Facebook and Twitter institutional social media web pages? The genre taxonomy was utilized during the interview with participants, regarding specific questions relating to functionality. As discussed in chapter 6, a question specifically asked participants about the functionality of Facebook and Twitter. It was discovered that Facebook and Twitter have similar functions for participants, but also that there are separate efficiencies for each social media site.

For Facebook, the functionality is for interactivity and engagement with alumni, answering questions from those within the online community about the institution, and to communicate with students. The functionality for Twitter is to share news, have an ongoing conversation with the online community, and raise brand awareness toward an institution. The similarities for both institutions regarding functionality when participants discussed both together include interaction and engagement, building an audience to follow what the college or university is doing, the fact that both Facebook and Twitter are free websites to utilize, both platforms offer authenticity, and they promote an institution. In conclusion of functionality when compared with the results of the content analysis, Facebook and Twitter is most efficient to share news, as the platforms were used to spread daily information to their online community consisting of students, faculty, and others associated with the institution.

The fourth and final research question is: Based on the similarities of purpose, form and functionality, are higher education Facebook and Twitter institutional social media websites a genre? Through the results of the interview questions and content analysis, I can state that both Facebook and Twitter are a genre but are for different reasons. As previous scholars defined, a genre is established thorough similar purpose, form, and functionality. For example, Dillon and Gushrowski (2000) declared that purpose and form must be similar.[9] Beginning with colleges and universities, it was discovered that each institution uses Facebook and Twitter differently. For example, one institution would primarily use Twitter to foster socialization, but another college or university would focus on conducting research. All institutions have a different purpose, form, and functionality for using the sites. However, the interviews and content analysis describe each site as a distinct genre. This is because Facebook and Twitter have similar primary purposes for using the platforms, as well as having related formats and functionalities described in the prior research questions. But even though there are similarities in the results, the platforms have differences in how they are used, based on the priorities of each institution's goals and objectives for using the platform (similar results of purpose, but different hierarchy), as well as having differences in how to format a message on Twitter. Thus, a genre is established for a specific social media site by itself. For example, Twitter is a distinct genre because the format needs to have a hashtag and mention to go along with pictures and links. This is different than the format of Facebook, which only should include a picture and link to go along with the information being sent to the online community. This also coincides with functionality, as the participants had similar ways the platforms are efficient, but also described separate reasons why they are valuable for higher education institutions.

After presenting the research questions, I believe that Facebook and Twitter are separate, distinct genres. This turned out to be the result that both are genres for similar characteristics of purpose, form, and functionality, but also for separate individual reasons. Hence, the social media platforms work differently from one another having their own goals and objectives, individual ways to arrange the format of a post or tweet and have independent efficiencies on how to use the sites successfully for the college or university. The conclusion for genre in social media higher education institutional web pages also agrees with Santini (2007), who stated that web pages do not fall under one genre.[10] Thus, Facebook and Twitter fall under the definition of social media but were proven to be separate genres on characteristics of purpose, form, and functionality.

SOCIAL MEDIA AND GENRE

The findings of this study present both institutional Facebook and Twitter web pages as separate genres. Thus, the phrase social media cannot be considered its own genre. Instead, each platform is its own genre due to having its own purpose, form, and functionality. After completing the study, the research discovered that social media sites do not have a common format, objective, or efficiency for a higher education institution. Instead, the platforms all work differently from one another, even if there are similarities between them.

A question to follow up: Is social media a genre in higher education? According to genre studies, a genre should have the same purpose, form, and functionality. The answer is yes, but Facebook and Twitter are identified as separate genres. There are a vast number of similarities, but also a fair number of differences, too, in each of the three characteristics. Thus, the platforms themselves are genres, as opposed to the universal term of social media.

Another substantial social media finding in the higher education environment is that Twitter was used much more frequently than Facebook. Based on the data collection and content analysis of purpose, Twitter had a total of 7,607 tweets, while Facebook had 2,961 posts. This is a massive difference and indicates that social media employees are posting much more frequently on Twitter than on Facebook. What is even more significant about this result is that most Facebook pages analyzed from the 100 colleges and universities have more followers than the institutions Twitter accounts. It was very rare to discover that a Twitter account had more followers than Facebook. Thus, even though Facebook has a larger online community, Twitter is used more frequently by social media employees. Nonetheless, Facebook is still used daily, but there are not as many posts during the day. I noticed that Twitter could have multiple tweets throughout one day, while Facebook would have maybe one or two for the same institution.

One last revelation in the results is that social media employees have varied preferences relating to platforms and reasons for using them. Social media could not be identified as one genre because every institution uses the platform differently, each having different purposes and formats in designing a message. In addition, the interviews disclosed that participants, as well as social media employees, may post more on social media sites based on personal preferences and platforms the individual favors, as opposed to an institution telling them to use one more than the other.

HIGHER EDUCATION AND GENRE

The focus of this study was to investigate whether Facebook and Twitter are a genre within the higher education environment. This is defined as colleges and universities creating a profile to post information on Facebook and Twitter, respectively. Then, to define their purpose, form, and functionality as described in the beginning of this chapter. It is important to state in conclusion that this is separate from in-class use and how potentially an instructor would use the services for pedagogy, class lessons, or assignments. When conducting this study purpose, form, and functionality did not pertain to any approach an instructor would use for the services. Hence, a separate study should be conducted on whether social media web pages for higher education courses have become a genre.

The results of this study can be a model for colleges and universities currently using Facebook and Twitter institutional web pages, or that wishes to create channels in the future. I hope that the results of the three phases of genre (purpose, form, and functionality) can be applied to strengthen information sharing with an online community by having a clear goal for the platform (purpose) and improved structure of the message (form). This is also valuable for anyone reading information and consuming content on Facebook and Twitter. The results of functionality can help social media employees understand how Facebook and Twitter can be effective in the higher education setting.

RELEVANCE FOR INFORMATION STUDIES

The completed research on genres and social media (Facebook and Twitter) is of importance to the field and discipline of information studies. As more online users continue to use platforms such as Facebook and Twitter as their main source of knowledge, it is imperative for scholars and researchers to examine them for their impacts on society. Social media sites contain a vast amount of information posted daily by users, brands, and organizations. This study has relevance for information studies by establishing new platforms as genres to process, search, and retrieve information. Additionally, organizations, such as higher education, can use this study as a model when deciding what to post on social media sites and how to design the message as well. Both the purpose (goal) and the format of a message impacts information in the system.

This study is linked to several concepts within information studies, such as information retrieval, information services, and organizational information management. Information services is connected to this study as the organizations sharing information with others are higher education institutions providing knowledge publicly online for others to consume. This study is also linked to information retrieval as the information being shared is collected by the researcher in the content analysis, as well as the online audience viewing the messages or acquiring information the institutions provide. Furthermore, this study is also intertwined with organizational information management as the results can be a guide for higher education institutions and other industries wishing to post information in the social media landscape. I have identified that the platforms were also being used as a form of archives, because of the use of hashtags for students, faculty and other members of the community to search, retrieve, and locate information, when needed.

LIMITATIONS OF THE RESEARCH

After completing the study, I recognize that there a few limitations to the research. First, I am aware that the content analysis only contained a month of tweets from Twitter and posts collected from Facebook. Although this is a valid sample to study, it is acknowledged that the results of each platform could alter month by month. For example, if in the month of February an institution offers many events, fostering socialization may be the highest category of purpose. But if a new art exhibit opens on campus, it may change to promoting culture. Thus, future studies should focus on whether purpose alters throughout a semester and if the format of a message on Facebook and Twitter institutional web pages modifies in any way.

Another area of the data collection I recognize as a limitation is when the content analysis began. The goal with start date of January 15 was to begin when colleges and universities started for the spring semester. However, there were still some institutions on winter break until the end of January. Also, there was a holiday during the data collection as well, Martin Luther King Jr. Day. The holiday may have affected events and programs on campus, besides closing institutions for the day. Thus, future research should make sure that all colleges and institutions are back in session when analyzing Facebook and Twitter institutional social media web pages, as well as avoiding holidays that can potentially affect results of any category in purpose and form.

One last limitation of the research pertains to the participant interviews. The researcher is aware and understands that this is only the perspective of ten social media employees in higher education and may not represent how all social media employees or institutions feel about the efficiency of Facebook and Twitter. Also, this study also represents only 100 colleges and universities nationwide. I understand that there are many other viewpoints and potential uses from colleges and universities not represented in the study, as well as social media employees not interviewed.

RECOMMENDATIONS AND TOPICS FOR FUTURE STUDY

There are many directions to still evaluate for future research. First, many of the participants stated in the interviews that they use Instagram as an institutional channel for posting information. When beginning this study, Facebook and Twitter was chosen based on the research of Barnes and Lescault (2011), who discovered that Facebook and Twitter were the most used among students and employees.[11] However, the findings showcase that social media is evolving and with new platforms, employees may prefer to use different sites to communicate with an online audience when there are advancements in technologies. At some point in the future, it will be important to investigate whether Instagram is a genre or not. A second area to focus on is whether classroom uses of Facebook and Twitter are a genre. For instance, a college course (such as Business 101) creating a Twitter profile to post course updates and have discussions with students is an area to evaluate for genre studies. As with Facebook, many instructors create groups as a digital classroom to share and discuss course content, as well as being a setting to answer any queries pertaining to assignments. Facebook groups as digital classrooms are another direction for future research. This study focused on institutional social media web pages that represent the entire college or university, but future studies can also investigate not only in-class Facebook and Twitter accounts, but also departmental or office channels, such as Athletics, Library, Psychology or Communications Departments.

Pertaining to the structure of the study, I recommend creating categories in addition to the seven functions of higher education. This recommendation is because the other category received one of the highest numbers of purpose in the content analysis. Thus, categories to include can be weather, campus updates, sports, inspirational quotes, and other topics that were discovered within the findings. Another recommendation is to evaluate the genre for a longer period, as it would be interesting to see if results from each category stayed the same or changed over the course of a semester or academic year.

NOTES

1. Bhatia, *Analysing Genre*, 3.
2. Angelina Russo, Jerry Watkins, Lynda Kelly, and Sebastian Chan, "Participatory communication with social media," *Curator: The Museum Journal* 51, no. 1 (2008): 21–31.
3. Cohen and Kenny, *Producing New and Digital Media*, 253.
4. Crowston and Williams, "Reproduced and emergent genres of communication on the World Wide Web," 208.
5. Lüders, Prøitz, and Rasmussen, "Emerging personal media genres," 953.
6. Barbara H. Kwasnik and Kevin Crowston, "Introduction to the special issue: Genres of digital documents," *Information Technology & People* 18, no. 2 (2005): 79.
7. Hinton and Hjorth, *Understanding Social Media*, 55.
8. Lüders, Prøitz, and Rasmussen, "Emerging personal media genres," 953.
9. Andrew Dillon and Barbara Gushrowski, "Genres and the web: Is the personal homepage the first uniquely digital genre?" *Journal of the American Society for Information Science* 51, no. 2 (2000): 202.
10. Santini, "Characterizing genres of web pages," 7.
11. Barnes and Lescault, "Social media adoption soars as higher-ed experiments and reevaluates its use of new communications tools," 2.

Appendix

Interview Questions (Script)

GENRE TAXONOMY QUESTIONS

1. What is the purpose (goal, topic, objective) for employees using Facebook in higher education?
2. What is the purpose (goal, topic, objective) for employees using Twitter in higher education?
3. What type of content do employees post on Facebook institutional pages?
4. What type of content do employees post on Twitter institutional pages?
5. Who are the participants posting information and content on Facebook and Twitter institutional web pages?
6. What are the roles and responsibilities of the participants posting information and content on Facebook and Twitter institutional web pages?
7. Where do employees/participants create, post, and consume content for Facebook?
8. Where do employees/participants create, post, and consume content for Twitter?
9. When do employees/participants expect to receive a response once a message is posted on Facebook?
10. When do employees/participants expect to receive a response once a message is tweeted on Twitter?
11. What are your overall expectations of using Facebook?
12. What are your overall expectations of using Twitter?
13. What is your format when constructing a post on Facebook? What are the textual and visual requirements?
14. What is your format when constructing a tweet on Twitter? What are the textual and visual requirements?
15. Do you have any formatting or linguistic requirements in your post or tweet?

FUNCTIONALITY QUESTIONS

16. Is Facebook an efficient web page to use for higher education? Why?
17. Is Twitter an efficient web page to use for higher education? Why?

CONCLUSION

18. Do you have any closing comments you wish to mention before the interview ends?

Interview Transcript—Participant 1

Question 1 & 2: What is your purpose (goal and objectives) for employees using Facebook and Twitter in higher education?

Participant 1: There are several goals. One is to use it as a vehicle to share information about the college including its faculty, its students, its alum, its administrators, to share that information to current students, potential students, and their parents, and alum, and just I guess the public in general.

Question 3 & 4: What type of content do employees post on Facebook and Twitter institutional pages?

Participant 1: Different kinds of content. Some of it is comes from outside sources; say an alum or the president or the college or a student was mentioned in a news story. Or something they did was the subject of a news story. I'll give an example. Say a professor was interviewed because they have a new book out. So, I would use that on social media. Some of the stories are generated by us and so I would share those sometimes. There are events that are happening on campus. I would also share that on social media. One of the things that we have been very actively pursuing is I have six students that work for me and so we use materials that they collect. Video and photo that give a snapshot of life at [redacted]. So, we'll put that stuff mostly on Twitter and Instagram. But since we're just talking Twitter and Facebook, I don't use a lot of that material on Facebook.

Question 5: Who are the participants posting information and content on Facebook and Twitter institutional web pages?

Participant 1: I mean when we have bigger events, we'll have photographers there and we'll use the materials that they take. I shoot video and edit videos. Those will be on there. But we have also had videographers. We had a videographer in our department and we're going to be having another one soon. And the materials that person develops, we'll also share those on social media.

Question 6: How would you describe your roles and responsibilities for posting information and content on Facebook and Twitter institutional web pages?

Participant 1: OK, I make the determination if this should be used and where it should be used. And when.

Question 7 & 8: Where do employees/participants create, post, and consume content for Facebook and Twitter?

Participant 1: All time. Because we'll have some night events last night. There was a video that I shot that started at six o'clock at night because there are events scheduled all morning, afternoon, and evening. And so those materials will be shared.

Question 9 & 10: When do employees/participants expect to receive a response once a message is posted on Facebook and Twitter?

Participant 1: I expect to receive responses and I actively engage my audience.

Question 11 & 12: What are your overall expectations for using Facebook and Twitter?

Participant 1: My expectation. I guess my goal is to share the wide variety of events and news and various associations of the college with as many people as I can. It's to show a slice of [redacted] life both for people currently on campus and what's happening with our alums as well.

Question 13, 14, & 15: What is your format for constructing a post on Facebook and Twitter? What are the textual and visual requirements? Any formatting or linguistic requirements?

Participant 1: They have to be some sort of visual or has to be some sort of art. I won't post otherwise because no one would pay attention to it. And we do have initiatives or campaigns I guess you could call them that require hashtags. So, one of our hashtags is #[redacted]. And so, we will use that especially on Twitter. And that's a lot of the student content. For instance, when we had a big snowstorm and one of my students took a quick video of another student sledding down this big hill. And so that would be #[redacted]. So, I guess that's one way that I know use specific language. I would say definitely the hashtag. Other than that, it's important that in most instances it's grammatically correct because we will get called out on it. You know sometimes that I might use like a colloquialism or something like that. But on occasion, depends on the conversation, I will use emojis or GIFs. I use them sparingly.

Question 16 & 17: Do you think Facebook and Twitter are efficient web pages for higher education?

Participant 1: Yes. So, one thing it's free and we obviously do have others such as Instagram and YouTube, but it is a valuable tool to reach a wide audience. And to have them interact with the college you can have a great news story in say the *New York Times* or on a morning news show. And that's extremely valuable. But I think that there is a lot of value in engaging with your constituents. Whether it be you know alums or potential students or current students or parents, I think having that interaction means something to your audience.

Question 18: Do you have any closing comments you wish to mention before the interview ends?

Participant 1: One value in it (Facebook and Twitter) is you know certainly when great things are happening. It's great to have that interaction but sometimes you have crises come up and I think that social media allows you to engage with people even when it's not good news. You can share maybe what the college is doing to combat a specific crisis. Maybe a letter that the president wrote, and we will get "well, what are you doing about this [redacted]?" And then I will share that letter from the president, with each individual who will ask that question. So, I think that rather than seeming like we're staying silent on an issue, it allows us to share it more widely as opposed to just having it on our website. It allows us to push out those messages. And respond to people who have concerns.

Interview Transcript—Participant 2

Question 1 & 2: What is your purpose (goal and objectives) for employees using Facebook and Twitter in higher education?

Participant 2: Primarily we had to boil it down to two or three purposes. I would say sharing news about the college specifically or about higher education or news of interest to our audience. Specifically, not news from [redacted] but about higher education and the industry in general. I would also say sharing relevant photos and images from the college that connects alumni with the college. Also connecting people with the college as well and making them feel connected and making them feel like they could be here. Relationship building with the college.

Question 3 & 4: What type of content do employees post on Facebook and Twitter institutional pages?

Participant 2: News and photos that we specifically wrote. News that pertains to what the audience might be interested in. Photos and videos that either come from the college or that were made from our audience that we shared.

Question 5: Who are the participants posting information and content on Facebook and Twitter institutional web pages?

Participant 2: Primarily me.

Question 6: How would you describe your roles and responsibilities for posting information and content on Facebook and Twitter institutional web pages?

Participant 2: I mean everything from strategy to tech to differentiating platforms and what content goes there.

Question 7 & 8: Where do employees/participants create, post, and consume content for Facebook and Twitter?

Participant 2: So, about three thousand of our members of our Facebook audience are consuming it from [redacted]. But those are certainly the largest two geographic areas. So that would be the same across platforms. And then typically scheduling from when I'm in the office. But also, we have the ability to schedule and advance using different software.

Question 9 & 10: When do employees/participants expect to receive a response once a message is posted on Facebook and Twitter?

Participant 2: Instantly.

Question 11 & 12: What are your overall expectations for using Facebook and Twitter?

Participant 2: To provide information to people and to deepen relationships and connect with people who are seeking information.

Question 13, 14, & 15: What is your format for constructing a post on Facebook and Twitter? What are the textual and visual requirements? Any formatting or linguistic requirements?

Participant 2: I mean we definitely have a style guide the college follows. So, we would follow that. And also, it would be a rare circumstance where I wouldn't have either a photo or image card with a post. There are exceptions of course when they would be just a text, but I would probably just do that on Twitter as infrequent circumstances.

Question 16 & 17: Do you think Facebook and Twitter are efficient web pages for higher education?

Participant 2: Certainly, but for different purposes. Facebook for alumni and Twitter for news.

Question 18: Do you have any closing comments you wish to mention before the interview ends?

Participant 2: No.

Interview Transcript—Participant 3

Question 1 & 2: What is your purpose (goal and objectives) for employees using Facebook and Twitter in higher education?

Participant 3: Sure. So, with Facebook we're actually in kind of an interesting situation here because the school where I worked before coming here was in [redacted] a branch of the [redacted] and the focus of the social media there specifically Facebook and Twitter and other platforms, Instagram, Snapchat, was to increase enrollment size. It was to spread the name of this particular satellite of the larger campus and to let prospective students know what the college offers. And here at [redacted] it's a little different because when at least specifically in certain circles, people and students are already familiar with [redacted] and there isn't ....

Participant 3: I don't know that admissions will say this, but I get the impression that they aren't struggling to get applicants. Now it may be they have other concerns in terms of diversity and economic diversity. That is a different kind of topic but in terms of numbers in the way that the other place I worked for was concerned, it's not quite the same. So, our focus on Facebook and Twitter is simply sharing the news of the college and what our professors are doing.

Participant 3: What our alumni are doing, what our students are doing. The Facebook audience in particular we have seen (because I've been here for two and a half years) with the changes in the algorithm our reach has dwindled quite a bit and engagement is OK, we don't do any advertising. We don't do any boosted posts or anything. And so, we're just relying on organic reach. We've noticed our numbers dropping. But we also are trying to curate our Facebook in a way that when someone visits our Facebook page they can get a sense of the campus community, what our professors are researching and students who have received fellowships and scholarships. Those are high impact stories for us, we get a lot of responses to those. We also get a lot of response to photos. We don't do a lot of photos on Facebook that are just campus beauty shots. We do those on Instagram constantly. On Facebook, we don't share photos by themselves although I have started doing that more frequently simply because the audience seems to enjoy them so much. So, for Facebook the audience is a much broader audience. We have a lot of community members from [redacted] town, prospective students, we have parents, we have people who follow our sports teams, and it can be tricky trying to find a message that resonates with all of them. So, we just do the best we can with our story choosing from week to week. We post three times a week on Facebook at this stage and sometimes a little bit more but typically not more than four times a week. We try to alternate days Monday, Wednesday, and Friday. Then on Twitter, we're viewing more as almost like a new service for [redacted]. We have faculty on Twitter and a lot of alumni who are in media. And so, we share more information on Twitter. Stories that we don't think will get much reach, we will share on Twitter and just because Twitter has a kind of limitless number of . . . there's no expectation of like, oh, you shouldn't be tweeting twice a day.

Participant 3: And Twitter, it's just, it seems the more prolific you are the better. And so, we keep that in mind, we're still not as prolific as some of our counterparts. We tweet maybe three to six times a day if we're lucky. And we view it as kind of a news source, as a place to share stories news stories about faculty, alumni, students, and we re-share a lot of content from there as well from the local newspaper, from other departments, the sports department, the arts museum, and others.

Question 3 & 4: What type of content do employees post on Facebook and Twitter institutional pages?

Participant 3: Typically, if something is on Facebook, it will also be on Twitter. And if something is on Twitter, it won't necessarily be on Facebook. For example (Facebook) we just put out a story earlier this week of a student who received a fellowship to study at [redacted] for her law degree and any sort of information like that is on our Facebook page and on Twitter. Especially Facebook where the engagement is kind of inconsistent, gets incredible engagement, so anything that shows our students or alumni receiving accolades of any sort. We typically will put that on Facebook because we know that the community seems to value that information. The same goes with faculty research and faculty accolades, community response to that. Recently we just published our spring magazine, and we will publish stories from our magazine and those will kind of hit and miss. Some of them will have a lot of resonance with our audience. Others will be like crickets chirping. But anything that goes on Facebook is automatically going to be on Twitter. Facebook is more of our curated location.

Question 5: Who are the participants posting information and content on Facebook and Twitter institutional web pages?

Participant 3: Sure. So, it's me and my counterpart [redacted]. He is the director of media relations. It used to be four of us that did it. Me, my boss who is the editorial director and then our communications officer. Then a new chief communications officer came in, we decided to change it up a bit. Now it just alternates between me and the director of media relations which worked out well because he has his ear out for stories all the time or he is aware of press releases that are coming up. So, it just seemed to make the most sense to just have it go back and forth between the two of us.

Participant 3: Yeah, it's basically he and I for the most part. And then others in the department will share information or share stories that might be of interest for social and they'll just email them to me. But in terms of posting, it's just me and him.

Question 6: How would you describe your roles and responsibilities for posting information and content on Facebook and Twitter institutional web pages?

Participant 3: Sure. So, every Sunday night I go through all our posts from the previous week and our insights for Facebook, Twitter, and Instagram. I craft an email that goes out Monday morning giving everyone insight into the most popular posts from each platform for that week with a number of breakdowns. And then if I'm on social, I typically come in, we have a free Trello account, we have it scheduled by week, and we pop in just any kind of stories that we've seen come through our new searches that might be interesting. I'd rather err on having too much than too little. So, everyone kind of just throws everything in there and I will come in on Monday morning and look at what has been posted the previous week. On Facebook it's an imprecise science in terms of we typically try to put the first thing in the morning on Monday at nine o'clock or so because there is the thought that people are arriving to work and checking Facebook. So, I try to think about those timeframes. I've never really seen a huge difference when I try to put in different times or in the evening. And so, we just kind of stick to nine o'clock in the morning Mondays and Wednesdays, especially Friday, it's always a slow day for us on Facebook. So, we may try to do something on Thursday instead. I look at what's been scheduled. Look at what we have available and try to judge whether or not it would be something useful for Facebook which again I typically tend to think of something in pop culture or praising a student or something unusual. Then, we'll just post accordingly. I don't schedule a lot; I typically post things at the time. I know a lot of people use the scheduling platforms. I don't regularly use Hootsuite. I use it mostly for social listening and then I do the same thing for Twitter. I typically start Twitter with retweeting to see what other people have shared and will repeat them and then we'll put out an original link to a story.

Question 7 & 8: Where do employees/participants create, post, and consume content for Facebook and Twitter?

Participant 3: So that's a great question. Twitter that can be a bit of a 24-hour kind of thing because it feels so easy. So, when I'm at home I will get alerts about Twitter. Someone mentioned us or shared information and tagged us and depending on what it is, I may just log in and tweet immediately. There's a lot of sporting events that my colleagues cover, and I should say the athletics department are Twitter masters. They tweet constantly though they will be working at a game or something and they'll be tweeting stuff and tag us, and I will usually go in and try to find the tweet pretty quickly just because it's so timely. Facebook, I don't engage with as often unless we get a comment. I always try to stay on top of comments for social media platforms because you never know when someone saying something terrible. I will get a ping through the Facebook pages saying you've got a comment and I will typically check it very quickly. It's something that needs to be dealt with immediately and so it's a bit of a 24-hour situation seven days a week although my boss is pretty good about wanting us to make that effort to not be connected constantly. So that's why I have limited Facebook to say I will only look at Facebook if I've noticed that someone is commenting on something we posted.

Question 9 & 10: When do employees/participants expect to receive a response once a message is posted on Facebook and Twitter?

Participant 3: Typically, if I haven't received any comments within a half an hour on Facebook, I view that as this is not going well. I think that I tend to view it as pretty immediate and of course some of them cumulate throughout the day and then I see how people are responding. But usually within half an hour if I don't have a few either likes or reactions or a heart on Twitter or retweet on Twitter then I feel like, OK, this is likely not going to go much further. So, I think I lean on the immediacy of a response.

Question 11 & 12: What are your overall expectations for using Facebook and Twitter?

Participant 3: So, I think the expectation is both and it's to tell the story of [redacted], cohesively, and using multiple voices. And that is specific to Twitter because we don't really repost a great deal on Facebook simply because we've seen that the numbers don't bear out in terms of engagement. We try to make original posts on Facebook and retweet a lot on Twitter. But the goal is always to give a comprehensive view of the college. I would say telling a comprehensive story of the college as much as we can.

Question 13, 14, & 15: What is your format for constructing a post on Facebook and Twitter? What are the textual and visual requirements? Any formatting or linguistic requirements?

Participant 3: We use hashtags when we are clear on how the hashtag ties into the tweet. For example, so we have certain campaigns that we know oh this post ties in perfectly with our four campaigns so we're going to hashtag it, but we don't use hashtags with every post, and we don't use imagery in every Twitter post. I know that photo tweets on Twitter get a lot of engagement and we probably would do good by trying to make that effort. So, a lot of times we don't have it and we need to share the story. On Facebook, rarely share anything on Facebook without a photo of some sorts. We never use hashtags on Facebook.

Question 16 & 17: Do you think Facebook and Twitter are efficient web pages for higher education?

Participant 3: I do think that, especially Facebook. Twitter, a lot of people just kind of have an ongoing conversation but I get a lot of messages to the Facebook page of people asking questions that are typically in the past. If I had been in their shoes, I would have gone to the website to ask or to look for the answer. And so, I'm actually really amazed at the number of questions that come through the Facebook page of people wanting to know just basic information about admissions or scholarships. And so, I do think that certain segment of the public view the Facebook page generally as a way to connect to someone more quickly than an institutional website. Speaking for myself, I know that like restaurants that I want to reach out to, I will go to see if they have a Facebook page first because so often, they are monitoring it much more closely than maybe a messaging platform they have built into their website.

Question 18: Do you have any comments that you want to add that you wish to mention regarding Facebook or Twitter that we haven't discussed?

Participant 3: I feel like it's a work in progress. I know that I see a lot of opportunities. Social media is one role I have here. The other is an editor. I helped put together the magazines which I'm in the midst of doing now. I feel like there are sometimes some missed opportunities in terms of responding to breaking news or a pop culture reference that's going out just because I've missed it or its the next day and its old news. But I don't want to just jump on the bandwagon because I can and because I feel like there are some institutions and a lot of them are all like businesses that respond very quickly to breaking news because it ties into their, like, whatever it is they sell, and of course in higher education you have to kind of walk a fine line about pop culture things you want to jump on. But no, I think you covered a lot of great stuff and it's just kind of a constant work in progress for us.

Interview Transcript—Participant 4

Question 1 & 2: What is your purpose (goal and objectives) for employees using Facebook and Twitter in higher education?

Participant 4: Well, we have a lot of audiences that we want to be able to reach. We want to be able to focus on recruiting students of course, although alumni are an important audience. They're very engaged on social media as well as parents and faculty and staff. So, we have a variety of purposes for it but overall, our goal with anything here in our marketing and communication office would be to recruit.

Question 3 & 4: What type of content do employees post on Facebook and Twitter institutional pages?

Participant 4: Mostly stuff that we write ourselves. So, if I write a story for the website and I've produced a news release for it, or we have an event coming up on campus or we're just talking about how nice the weather is outside. It's something that we're generating ourselves. Although during our down times of the year we also might be sharing news articles about alumni or something that's happening in the city that we can relate to the college. So, we want to be able to post on a daily basis during the week. So, during the downtimes we look externally but most of the time we want to focus on our own content.

Question 5: Who are the participants posting information and content on Facebook and Twitter institutional web pages?

Participant 4: We have a very decentralized communications structure as many colleges and universities do. That being said I'm the primary person who posts on behalf of marketing communication and then we have different departments and units on campus who manage their own social media accounts. So, I manage a social media users' group that has a total of about 60 people who participate in some way shape or form on social media, primarily Facebook and Twitter. Although Instagram is growing very quickly, and I believe there are still a couple that are using Snapchat as well.

Question 6: How would you describe your roles and responsibilities for posting information and content on Facebook and Twitter institutional web pages?

Participant 4: I would say it's an intense daily responsibility. It's not something that we would assign an intern to and expect them to be able to track all the analytics and the outcomes that we want to focus on. We want to be able to show a return on investment. We want to be able to have editorial calendars that manage how our content is handled and we want to be able to speak with a variety of audiences and that's something that we want somebody who's experienced in communications to be able to do.

Question 7 & 8: Where do employees/participants create, post, and consume content for Facebook and Twitter?

Participant 4: Well, that depends. Most of the time I'm posting during the week during office hours. Every once in a while, we'll have an event like a career summit that draws folks from all across the country to campus to talk to our students in which case they're staying here late on Friday and then participating again on Saturday, or we have a homecoming week for example where we're working late at night during the week and then all-day Saturday. So, the short answer is it varies but primarily we focus on the office hours Monday through Friday.

Question 9 & 10: When do employees/participants expect to receive a response once a message is posted on Facebook and Twitter?

Participant 4: Usually it's an exclamatory reaction to something that we've posted that is very exciting for our community. So, for instance if we just posted a story on our volleyball coach retiring, we expect to hear congratulations [redacted] on your retirement well-deserved. Something like that. So, it's not something that we necessarily need to be responding to other than affirming. Yes, we'd like your comment every once in a while; we'll have a question, or a comment come in. In which case I'm here to respond and I do it fairly quickly.

Question 11 & 12: What are your overall expectations for using Facebook and Twitter?

Participant 4: Overall expectations. Every time I post I expect to be reaching about 20 percent of my audience with any given post. Obviously, there are some exceptions based on things like timeliness, based on things like community interest, based on things such as current events. So, we'll see some spikes and fluctuations, but I like to see about 20 percent of our audience receiving the story and then about another 10 percent actually engaging with it.

Question 13, 14, & 15: What is your format for constructing a post on Facebook and Twitter? What are the textual and visual requirements? Any formatting or linguistic requirements?

Participant 4: Well, we do like to have pictures with whatever we post especially on Twitter. With something like Facebook, we generally include a call to action. Read more at our website. Discover more about this program here. I guess it depends on what type of story we're talking about. And then on Twitter we'll include a link or where people can go for more information or maybe a hashtag. Again, it depends on the post but going back to your original question; Facebook, I look for pictures and I look for calls to action. Twitter, I would say pictures, links to a website and some sort of hashtag.

Question 16 & 17: Do you think Facebook and Twitter are efficient web pages for higher education?

Participant 4: Yes, especially Facebook. We generally get the best responses in terms of what we want them to do with Facebook. I'll give you an example. If we want people to learn more. Our purpose for sharing a post is getting people into a website where they can discover more about our programs and apply. Facebook is generally the best vehicle for doing so. Facebook produces the best result for us in that fashion and we do a little bit of advertising as well that helps us capture prospects.

Question 18: Do you have any closing comments you wish to mention before the interview ends?

Participant 4: I think there is some skepticism when it comes to dealing with a brand especially in the wake of what's happening with things like Cambridge Analytica and even digital concerns that are related to the collection of data. So, I think we do have to have personable responses. We do have to have conversational posts. We do want to get people excited about [the college] and we want to be proactive about listening as well. So that when somebody sent a response, we pay attention to what they're saying and if they're posting about us without necessarily tagging us or with the intention of reaching us specifically. We still know what they're saying, how to reach them, and how to respond.

Interview Transcript—Participant 5

Question 1 & 2: What is your purpose (goal and objectives) for employees using Facebook and Twitter in higher education?

Participant 5: So, what is our goal for each platform. They're slightly different, we have different audiences on each. Facebook it's really more about connection to our alumni and students and other community members who are on that platform. And again, that audience has changed over the past 10 years. It's giving opportunities for those people to feel like they're part of the community especially if they're alumni who moved on. You know, we want to make sure that they still feel connected. So, fostering community I think is a primary goal there. And we do a lot of things that invite interaction and share news with them. But in a way that is a little bit more insider information. On Twitter it's really more about brand awareness. We don't get a ton of interaction, certainly not as much as Instagram or Facebook. Twitter is more about sharing news in a more general way about the college. We do see slightly more interaction over the past couple of years. I would say among a younger audience. But again, it's minimal. We don't invest a ton of time on the platform, it's just kind of necessity, I think, to share news there. We do tend to make connections with other influencers whether they're through alumni or organizations we work with or people who come to campus, maybe give a lecture on that kind of thing. So, we kind of try to do cross promotion there too. Again, it's more about brand awareness in general.

Question 3 & 4: What type of content do employees post on Facebook and Twitter institutional pages?

Participant 5: There is some similarity in what we're doing. So let me start with Twitter just because that's the most straightforward, I think. So, on Twitter we're sharing news. Again, part of our communications operation is creating news stories for our website. They are typically about things happening on campus or faculty research or student programs. They serve a variety of functions. We try to share those. We share those on Twitter with an eye towards a general audience. And again, making connections wherever we can to broader news trends in particular and then I guess secondary, we are also again sharing things about the college that relate to things happening in the news cycle in general or responding to news events or sharing things that our alumni are doing as well. It's also a place where we share news from other sources that are about the college that we didn't write that are about us or our faculty. We do some of the same things on Facebook again with an eye toward an inside audience alumni, students, parents, who know a little bit about us, and we might frame the story differently. Invite them to comment or reminisce about how things were when they were here. And then we share a lot more photos I would say on Facebook. A little bit of context as well. So just because there's more opportunities for visual, we also do more video content on Facebook than we do Twitter.

Question 5: Who are the participants posting information and content on Facebook and Twitter institutional web pages?

Participant 5: Concerning the main institutional channels [redacted], those are primarily me. Some of the content being shared is not produced by me but by others in my office whether it's a photographer taking photos or our news person writing stories for the website. I do have some interns who work for me and sometimes I'll give them assignments that often involve taking photos or video or creating posts about links that I want to share. So, it's primarily me, but others help out. I'm the one mostly creating the post directly.

Question 6: How would you describe your roles and responsibilities for posting information and content on Facebook and Twitter institutional web pages?

Participant 5: My role would be to maintain the institutional voice for both platforms and that can mean curating the content that we are creating or sharing but also responding to other comments or content in a way that reflects the institution as a whole, and that's another aspect that I think I do on Twitter more often than Facebook particularly, kind of try to inject a sense of humor, particularly if I know the counter person sharing something about the college. Sometimes I'll respond just to an animated GIF or short comment or emoji.

Question 7 & 8: Where do employees/participants create, post, and consume content for Facebook and Twitter?

Participant 5: Primarily in the standard workday, although of course with a job like mine it bleeds over into other times. I try to schedule content outside those hours if I feel it's better to post something in the evening or on the weekends. I'll be posting but I do occasionally check in on posts or comments and respond more immediately if I think it's called for.

Question 9 & 10: When do employees/participants expect to receive a response once a message is posted on Facebook and Twitter?

Participant 5: It's changed a lot over the past few years with Facebook altering its algorithm and the way the news feed is structured leads definitely to seeing a downward trend and interaction at least organic interaction. We do occasionally boost posts that we definitely want people to see or interact with. If we're doing as much or promoting an event or we have some really cool video content, we want to make sure people see it. My gut tells me that our population in particular alumni are not as interactive as some other institutions. You know, we've had a lot of discussions here about why that is but it's a little bit to other areas of interaction like giving or event attendance and varies a lot with an institution that is as old as we are. We have older alumni from the 50s and 60s who are here when it was an all-male institution; they have a very different feeling about the college. And when it became coed in the 70s. And there's other things that play into that, I think.

Interviewer: Same for Twitter?

Participant 5: We've never gotten a lot of interaction on Twitter, so I don't I don't tend to tweet with the expectation that I'll have more than a dozen likes or retweets. I'm always pleasantly surprised when it's more than that. Often, it's the same people sharing the news. There's a handful of faculty who are active, handful of students who are active and some alumni in particular. A couple of people I know to be trustees or other stakeholders in the college who are happy to share our news and excited about it.

Question 11 & 12: What are your overall expectations for using Facebook and Twitter?

Participant 5: I think overall it's again about building community and getting our name out there. That's one of our primary goals in driving communications to prospective students. I know a lot of high school students may not have heard of [redacted] although we obviously feel we have a lot to offer so we try to broadly give a sense of what we are like as an institution and who the people are that make up our faculty, student body, and alumni so they can feel they can make some kind of connection.

Question 13, 14, & 15: What is your format for constructing a post on Facebook and Twitter? What are the textual and visual requirements? Any formatting or linguistic requirements?

Participant 5: So, for Facebook I would say that I always have some visual element whether that's just sharing a straight up photo or a video. We're making sure that our news links show up with an appropriate photo or video. With text, I try to invite some kind of interaction. It's not always straightforward but it's worth sharing a story about a new program or new building on campus. So, invite alumni in particular to respond and comment on what it was like when they were here. Sometimes there are posts on Facebook I started doing a few photo posts. We have a large archive of photos that we pull from and some of them are quite interesting, so I'll just throw the photo up and invite them to caption it. That's all I say. So, it gives them something to play with, I guess. And if it's not asking a question, I'll also include a link so that they can go off to do something whether that's sign up for an event or go read this article about us or things like that.

Participant 5: On Twitter, given the constraints of a tweet, in terms of size, I try to condense down whatever it is I'm sharing to as short a caption as possible. And often if it's a news story about the college I'll try to make the tweet interesting enough that they might want to click through. But I also recognize that a lot of people are scrolling through tweets and not necessarily clicking on the links. Also try to frame it in a way that gives some nugget of information, in case, if they just read the tweet. I started more and more over the past year or two in particular just inserting emojis because the platform has made it easier to do that. And I found that in some cases those posts have another visual element in the text that's a little bit more interaction.

Question 16 & 17: Do you think Facebook and Twitter are efficient web pages for higher education?

Participant 5: I think it depends on the audience. I think, and again, this has changed over the last 10 years. I think we've moved from any sort of reliance on either platform for doing anything in particular. It's the reliability of someone seeing posts that we've put up has dwindled a bit. So, unless we put money into promoting it or using it in a different way, we understand that whatever we share here is not necessarily going to be seen by the people we want to see it. At the same time, the tools in terms of promoting things to a particular audience I think have also allowed us to expand our reach a little bit at least in reaching people outside our traditional base of alumni emails or with prospective students that we purchase to communicate via email. So, it's a slightly different audience that's a slightly different way of communicating. I think the fact that there is the ability to interact and have some understanding of who is doing the interaction is useful. And again, I think Twitter is useful for getting brand awareness for different segments of the population than we might typically see.

Question 18: Do you have any closing comments you wish to mention before the interview ends?

Participant 5: Yes. They're both evolving platforms in a lot of ways. So, it's important to stay on top of them and pay attention to what we're doing there.

Interview Transcript—Participant 6

Question 1 & 2: What is your purpose (goal and objectives) for employees using Facebook and Twitter in higher education?

Participant 6: So, I'll limit this to Facebook and Twitter, but we're also on LinkedIn, Instagram, and we do a little bit of Buzzfeed too. We tailor each of those platforms really to the demographics of the people who are on them. So, as we develop content for Twitter. We take a look at those. Analytics of how people are participating with the content. And also, we look at the data that is provided to us about those followers from Twitter. And from Facebook which are very different in the way that those are reported back to us as institutions. So, we look at our followers on Twitter. We know that the majority of those people fall into older age groups. They tend to be pretty much split 50/50 men or women. And those people tend to have higher incomes. So, we take that to mean that they are more established in their careers like that. And they also kind of share their general interest with us so we know people on that platform are interested in sports and dogs and coffee. My people. So, as we look at content that succeeds on that platform that really is like stories about some of our student athletes who are driven to do big things in their career or things like that.

Participant 6: We talk about campus events and we're sharing news.

Participant 6: So, I tend with that platform, I use language that is that is a bit more direct. I guess I kind of take that to mean that when people are on Twitter especially the people who are following us, they're really looking for sports updates. They're looking for funny content, not necessarily looking to hear from their alma mater, but when we have stories like we just did, we're, we are one of the top bright producers among four-year baccalaureate colleges or whatever. Those are influencers and alumni. That's kind of how we categorize that group and so that informs all the decisions we make there and then when we look at Facebook, we know that we've got a lot of our followers in the [redacted] metro area. A lot of them list us as an institution that they went to or whatever. So, we think that we take that to mean that a lot of parents of current students and alumni and also recent alumni and alumni in general are following up on Twitter. There are also a lot of current students that follow us. We know that parents are kind of a primary influencer with their students. College decisions, and so we also kind of use like a more informative, like, we try to, of build community there. We'll share more fun photos or use more like insider type content and language like we say [redacted], which is part of our school song. I think it's the only school song out there that has a waltz. And the reason they say [redacted] is like the students singing it forgot the words and so they just say that. Like that and kind of assume people know what it means. Also call ourselves [redacted] which is our mascot. And that's kind of a derivative of [redacted]. So, like we feel comfortable using that kind of language on Facebook because we believe that a lot of the people who follow us there are on the inside then and if they're not, like we want to pique your curiosity. So, we kind of dabble in all kinds of stuff on Facebook but the place where we are the most playful is Instagram because we know from those demographics that it is more like about 30 percent of the people who follow us on Instagram are young and live in [redacted].

Participant 6: So, we take that to mean that they probably live on campus geographically.

Question 3 & 4: What type of content do employees post on Facebook and Twitter institutional pages?

Participant 6: We have a pretty active news page on our website. And so, we're always sharing those stories as they come out. I also do like monthly reports that kind of cover our four main social channels Facebook, LinkedIn, Instagram, and Twitter.

Participant 6: I'll take a look at our engagement, which is always pretty standard. One month to the next Twitter and Facebook we get a lot more engagement. We get a lot of engagement on Instagram, but we get about 40 percent of engagement from our users on Facebook and about 10 percent on average on Twitter and about a third of our content when we post it on Facebook reaches its intended audience and about 20 to 30 percent, I guess. Let me say that about 20 percent on average I guess for Twitter. So that has an impact to what we share.

Participant 6: And pretty much anything that we would post on Twitter, we post on Facebook. Sometimes we do live tweeting. But it's not like if people can't attend the event, they're tuning in we don't necessarily think that happens.

Participant 6: We live tweet convocation, sometimes that resonates with the influencers and alumni on Twitter. And then we also if we have a fundraising event, like, we'll pretty, we'll do something. I try to keep the number of posts on any platform to 1 or 2 per day because we really don't want to exhaust people. And thankfully we've got enough content that we can keep up with and not overload people.

Question 5: Who are the participants posting information and content on Facebook and Twitter institutional web pages?

Participant 6: I have a dedicated social media position. I do have some student workers that work in our office. And so, we've got kind of a variety of people who are taking photographs that I might use for social. But I do all the writing. And my predecessor did have students writing more on those platforms. In my opinion, I think someone who understands the institutional voice maybe is the best to relay that information. I just think that when people are attending a school, we tend to attract people who are driven to graduate school who has an interest in global issues. They're really smart. They're kind of at top of their game.

Participant 6: We employ a number of them to write content that isn't edited by some of our staff in marketing communications before it goes online. But like a raw, direct to the people kind of writing like I just would prefer to do that when it's kind of a lasting statement of our college. So, because there's all this nuance and history that you have to be mindful of. We do give students the ability to take over on our Instagram stories and I think that plays into that audience too where students kind of respond well to that authentic voice. And when you see a student speaking directly to you, you really get that. But if we had a student employee writing on Facebook or Twitter people wouldn't know that. They see that it's coming from [redacted]. So, I handle that.

Participant 6: And then previous to this I used to work as a communications manager for [redacted] and I kind of had an all-purpose role there. I was looking at their social and writing stories. I was kind of writing on behalf of the Dean. But being at this school is very unique. I get to do more deep diving into the kinds of data that helped drive the way that we continue to do things.

Question 6: How would you describe your roles and responsibilities for posting information and content on Facebook and Twitter institutional web pages?

Participant 6: I would say that I'm kind of trusted to make sure that that everything stays up to date. I also maintain a list of writing and enforcing a social media policy for the school kind of falls under me. And then right now, I'm kind of in the process of bringing people into compliance. I have a list of people throughout the Internet who have created social profiles on YouTube, Twitter, Facebook, whatever.

Participant 6: That includes the words [redacted] that people just landed on it like why would they be thinking about us or whatever. And I've got kind of like subcategories for those up like, is this student [word] or is that where it's kind of governed by student government association where I have to participate with them to get people under compliance. Intercollegiate Athletics Conference something for the Midwest where athletics teams meet people to get under compliance. I am kind of drafting recommendations for people.

Participant 6: Right now, when it comes to Facebook, we're really discouraging people from creating independent pages because those do not fall under governance and for those tend to not bridge generations, like student quits college or graduates. I guess nobody has access to the page. That's what I see, scattered information all around the Internet. It might surprise you. Let's say we've got about 3000 students at a time. We've got 400 social media accounts roughly tied to this. Yeah. And some of them are accounts that people have created twice because they didn't know that they had one.

Participant 6: Yeah, I mean there's only so much you can do, and I know that when I was working at [redacted] and the type of deep diving I'm doing. I'm sure their social media person wouldn't have the appetite to take on what I do because it's a million people or whatever. I feel like I can do that. I should do that.

Question 7 & 8: Where do employees/participants create, post, and consume content for Facebook and Twitter?

Participant 6: I've got a 45-minute commute to campus. I live in [redacted] and a bunch of my colleagues actually live in the [redacted] and commute down to about an hour commute. I'm typically creating content on the fly in the office from my desktop. But yesterday I went to [redacted] and took photos of an event that was happening. It was like a job or internship fair where people were doing back-to-back interviewing. It was adorable, like all these teenagers in briefcases waiting to talk to Target!

Participant 6: I was there and took photos and then I used my Canon camera and that kind of creates like a wireless network unto itself that I can then transfer photos wirelessly to my phone and then I use Instagram to share those. Sometimes I am doing kind of on the fly stuff like that but typically I'm sitting drafting things like in the moment at my desk.

Question 9 & 10: When do employees/participants expect to receive a response once a message is posted on Facebook and Twitter?

Participant 6: Yeah, I think our stuff kind of has a three-day life span. I say typically after three days people aren't really continuing to engage with it. When I am doing my monthly reports, I like to wait two weeks until after the post is done before like collecting data on it because it's pretty much done or won't change after that. A lot of stuff doesn't come back to life after that unless we have received some funds from a donor who earmarked it to go to sports facilities. And so, any time I would post about that this year like there would invariably be somebody who would say well that's fine and dandy, but this school is well known for performing arts. [Redacted] is known for choir and Christmas Festivals. It's kind of like this lingering issue sometimes people come back to old posts and comments or whatever but that's very rare. I typically post something at night. I check for comments before I go to bed and then I check the next morning.

Participant 6: Typically, they just kind of trickle in. In that time span that sometimes over a weekend it might take them a couple more days.

Question 11 & 12: What are your overall expectations for using Facebook and Twitter?

Participant 6: Expectations are that we are reporting on and sharing stories that show people that we continue to be good stewards of the resources that we have; that we're fulfilling our mission to make college and liberal arts education affordable for the students; to show and demonstrate financial need including stories. It all ties together really closely at this school. A donor will fund a student who goes on to do some really interesting research or whatever. There's always more than one story to a story. So, my goal is to kind of balance all of that and just have enough key words or like triggers for our audience that they see that story from their own experience or what they expect to see I guess, not neglecting any important aspects of the story. And I guess just showing people that we are alive and kicking! That's really easy to do in school like this. Everybody's happy to participate. Students are really excited to be showcased. So, professors are really responsive.

Question 13, 14, & 15: What is your format for constructing a post on Facebook and Twitter? What are the textual and visual requirements? Any formatting or linguistic requirements?

Participant 6: That's actually interesting because when I started out, I was at a different school and then I took about a year or two between positions and in that time, I wasn't tweeting every four and a half minutes or whatever, but I used to have more verbal cues, but Twitter changed a little bit and Facebook too. So now you can put a URL into a Facebook post and it will generate the image.

Participant 6: Some sample text or whatever from the post and then you can just delete that URL and it doesn't need to be part of the post. So that's been a really cool development. Hashtags on Facebook just kind of aren't like that successful. I do include them sometimes just because I want to kind of clue people who are reading it. If they discuss these on their own channels, like this is what you would use or whatever. But we will see more people kind of participating in those hashtags on Instagram and Twitter.

Participant 6: So, I like to use hashtags on Twitter. I will try to use them in place of standalone words. So, if I was to use the word like research, potentially, I would do #research and then it's my personal preference that when I'm doing a hashtag, I like to make the initial letter capitalized. If I was to like hashtag climate change or something or research matters it would be capital Research, capital Matters or Climate Change or whatever. We just have this hashtag campaign called [redacted] where we wanted people to share their stories of how they met their best friends or significant other or whatever on campus. If you just look at all in lower case, it reads like delicious meat.

Participant 6: So, it was something like that it became somewhat essential to capitalize. I like to include them in a tweet throughout the text but most our platforms we generally have enough characters like at the tailwind.

Participant 6: And I tend to think especially on Instagram, and I guess I know this because I've seen a lot of people comment on it but if you post a really funny string of hashtags, people are delighted by that. It's kind of like poetry or something.

Question 16 & 17: Do you think Facebook and Twitter are efficient web pages for higher education?

Participant 6: Facebook yes and Twitter yes. I think they all participate.

Participant 6: You can't just do a billboard. You should also be doing social, or you should do print. You have to go online. That's part of the holistic approach to higher education where we understand that students are being inundated with information at all aspects of their lives. So, they're all kind of a necessary contributor for us getting in front of them and showcasing like why this is a great place to further their education. And we don't do a lot of boosted content. We mostly do organic content. We would like to do more paid content. I just worry a little bit about that authenticity. I think if you continue to see the sponsored under that post where, I just think that that's something that might not say something that inspires trust.

Question 18: Do you have any closing comments you wish to mention before the interview ends?

Participant 6: So, one of the institutions I would like to look at is [redacted], like what are they up to?

Participant 6: I like ran the same kind of formula that I do to figure out our user engagement and stuff for them on Twitter and on Facebook something that I think is really interesting with them is that they generate a lot of conversation especially on Facebook or whatever. But it's not always positive. I think they have a placed themselves to such a high position and people feel like they could stand to be taken down a peg. People on our social channels are generally sweet, especially within the past couple months, I started to receive our YouTube comments direct to my inbox. That's not a channel that I manage because we have a digital guy who does videos and stuff. I asked to be on this list. YouTube especially is like a hotbed for rude and mean people.

Participant 6: And we get the sweetest comments, we get people saying like especially because we're like we're known for music, people comment on our music pieces and say I listened to this song every morning, it gets me started. I wish I had a beautiful male voice. I would love to join the choir or just people like taking time out of their day to be genuine and kind. I just don't think you see that in a lot of other places online and I feel very happy at least that this institution inspires some people.

Interview Transcript—Participant 7

Question 1 & 2: What is your purpose (goal and objectives) for employees using Facebook and Twitter in higher education?

Participant 7: Our main purpose is to just sort of engage the [redacted] community. And I say like any community. I'm talking about a bunch of different constituencies alumni and parents and prospective students and current students.

Question 3 & 4: What type of content do employees post on Facebook and Twitter institutional pages?

Participant 7: On Facebook we post less often. I think compared to our peer institutions we post on this less frequently because we don't like overwhelming people, but we tend to post a lot of just sort of links and summaries to try to drive people to the website. On Twitter, we post much more frequently and it's kind of a bigger mix. And part that's honestly just because like I personally prefer Twitter, so I think I kind of gravitate towards that and maybe a little bit more creative there, that's just me as a person. But we also post links to the website that we want to drive people to, but we'll post kind of more fun things; we don't do a lot of, like, memes. We will occasionally engage with stuff like that retweeting some of our campus partners, retweeting faculty and administrators who are active on Twitter, and things like alumni birthdays and stuff that's maybe less of a clear driver to the website or less a clear purpose. That is sort of fun and goes with our brand.

Question 5: Who are the participants posting information and content on Facebook and Twitter institutional web pages?

Participant 7: Mainly me. I report to our director of marketing. She will also sometimes post things and obviously if I'm on vacation or something, she'll sort of take over. On Facebook we really only maintain the one sort of flagship [redacted] page. On Twitter, we've got multiple official accounts. We've got the [redacted] account which is verified and that's the main one that I run. We do have people in the admissions office or the alumni office that posts sports information and stuff like who are also tweeting, and I talk to them, kind of advise them. Mainly me, but not entirely.

Question 6: How would you describe your roles and responsibilities for posting information and content on Facebook and Twitter institutional web pages?

Participant 7: I mean Twitter I monitor pretty closely. I mean I'm staring at TweetDeck like on my screen right now. And I used to have a rule where like I tweeted at least three times a day on weekdays, like that was when I was at the start of a job, and now that I've been doing it for a while, I sort of relaxed and I just kind of tweet what needs to be tweeted and less tweet for the sake of having a tweet. And I also kind of rely more on retweeting others and doing less like actual tweets. So, I kind of monitor Twitter throughout the day. We'll tweet about things that we've posted on the website recently. Kind of look for engagement opportunities; obviously monitor Twitter if there's any sort of crisis that pops up or someone with a complaint or concern. Facebook, I spend less time looking at Facebook. We post less on Facebook. We really try to maintain a schedule of it. We usually post on a weekday afternoon, and I don't monitor that as much. We obviously monitor the comments but that's about it. I monitor any messages that come in, we don't get a lot of messages over Facebook, but we get just random questions sometimes and I reply to people and sort of direct them to someone who can help them out.

Question 7 & 8: Where do employees/participants create, post, and consume content for Facebook and Twitter?

Participant 7: Well, I definitely do most of the active management sort of 9–5 on the weekdays. I'm more likely to schedule things in advance or I might just check in a couple of times during the day on Saturday and Sunday and catch up and maybe see if any tweet has occurred. Obviously, a lot of sports happen on the weekends, a little bit of a crutch for me. I'll just repeat the sports accounts on weekends with results.

Question 9 & 10: When do employees/participants expect to receive a response once a message is posted on Facebook and Twitter?

Participant 7: I think we've a pretty good engagement. I'm usually pretty proud of how much engagement we're getting. Let's see, on Facebook. Some content obviously doesn't perform as well. But I can kind of predict the things that are going to get like a few dozen shares and a few hundred likes and other comments, and we don't respond to most comments. If people are directly asking the question or if they say something like really nice but we just don't respond to everything. On Twitter, I tend to like most of the content we're mentioned; if it's something especially good, I might retweet it or reply to it or quote tweet it or whatever. But yeah, I mean again we actually get our best engagement on Instagram. I think we do OK but Instagram we are getting like over a thousand likes on a photo and we never really get that on the other platforms.

Question 11 & 12: What are your overall expectations for using Facebook and Twitter?

Participant 7: Well, we set goals every year to increase our followers and try to keep engagement up. Like I said it's already pretty good, but we would notice if it started going down. So, I actually probably have a bit different perspective from most managers because I actually try not to get obsessed with numbers and analytics and growth because I think that if you focus too much on that it starts to seem less authentic, like the content. We don't worry too much about growth, but we do want to see our numbers keep going up on both of those platforms and we're doing pretty well. We do really well on our account compared to peer institutions on Twitter even adjusting for like size of the execution. On Facebook, we sort of lag behind a little bit. I found that it seems like everyone with a page grows at the same rate, so I don't really know if there is a way to leapfrog that. I think it's just it's like how many constituents you have on Facebook, and you can't really change that. Every year we set these goals for growth monthly, ideal reports and just sort of look at what performed well during the previous month and share that with some of the people in my office. We just, we just like a good way to show off. What makes [redacted] special and try to keep alumni thinking about the college in the back of their minds and get maybe some prospective students to go over the hump and actually click submit with their applications

Question 13, 14, & 15: What is your format for constructing a post on Facebook and Twitter? What are the textual and visual requirements? Any formatting or linguistic requirements?

Participant 7: Yeah, I definitely don't have requirements because again I try to keep it fairly authentic and kind of loose and less like an institution and more like a person, I guess we do use hashtag [redacted] in our own tweets just because it's kind of a subtle signal that other people should use that, and we will see their content. That's really not a hashtag that gets a lot of use. I don't know how useful it is for us to keep using it. We usually tweet with a photo because that tends to get better engagement. If you look at our feed, I think most things have a photo unless there just wasn't one available. I mean we always use links and Bitly to track them. In terms of formatting or textual stuff. Our tweets probably are longer than maybe they ideally should be if you are really trying to optimize. But [redacted] is a place that prides itself on having a long literary tradition and reading and writing. I think it's OK if our tweets fits with that. If our tweet is a little bit more complex and obviously like we have high standards for grammar and punctuation and everything because of that. I mean, there are other colleges I see, I don't want to name names, but less strict about that. But if someone tweets at us even if it's a really nice tweet about how much they love candy and if there's even a small error in it, I probably won't retweet it because we just want our brand to be very prestigious when it comes to writing.

Question 16 & 17: Do you think Facebook and Twitter are efficient web pages for higher education?

Participant 7: I think they're efficient in that they don't really cost us anything. And it's also hard to measure exactly how much benefit you are getting from them, but I definitely don't think it hurts. I mean I guess it hurts if you tweet something really bad and then delete your account. But we try not to do that. We occasionally buy boosted posts on Facebook not too often, only for specific purposes but not in every post. And I think that's worth it because we don't spend that much, and we do see it get boosted to a bigger audience. We haven't done any promoted tweets or anything on Twitter, that's all organic. And again, as a sort of skeptic when it comes to numbers, I'm not quite sure how much I trust Facebook's analytics in terms of how these people are really watching your videos. So, it's a little bit hard for me to know how it's really getting out beyond those boosted posts. At the end the fiscal year, we tend to maybe boost the post for the alumni annual fund gift or if we sort of have a flagship video that comes out that we really want people to see, we might boost that post.

Question 18: Do you have any closing comments you wish to mention before the interview ends?

Participant 7: I definitely think we deemphasized Facebook a little bit just because the past few years, you've seen Facebook's reputation change. And I guess it just seems a little bit less relevant. I guess you can argue that Twitter is also not that relevant because it doesn't have as big of a user base as far as Facebook does but it seems like a better fit for us. And I just think it's kind of a better platform for what we do in terms of engagement and how we use it and it's easier for me to use. And again, we emphasize Instagram a lot more even though that's not your focus. It actually feeds into the content of the other platforms more because whenever we post there, we usually also pull that post over to Twitter to try to benefit from both audiences if they're not following us. Also, we have a very beautiful campus, sort of one of our main selling points. And so, for us like I already said that we focus a lot on our writing, but I would also say that for social media the visual is very important to us because just the physical location of [redacted] and our campuses is a selling point. So, photo-based platforms are something we focus on too.

Interview Transcript—Participant 8

Question 1 & 2: What is your purpose (goal and objectives) for employees using Facebook and Twitter in higher education?

Participant 8: I guess the biggest thing is just getting the [redacted] story out there and connecting with alumni and connecting with current students. And then of course connect with prospective students who might be interested in [redacted] and using our social media as a tool to I guess subtly or not so subtly persuade them to want to attend [redacted].

Question 3 & 4: What type of content do employees post on Facebook and Twitter institutional pages?

Participant 8: So, we use video across all of our social platforms so that of course includes Twitter and Facebook. We use photos. I never send a tweet out without a photo unless it's like I'm doing like a live type of situation, event, or something like that. But we always send photos with our tweets and our Facebook posts.

Question 5: Who are the participants posting information and content on Facebook and Twitter institutional web pages?

Participant 8: Yeah, it's just me.

Question 6: How would you describe your roles and responsibilities for posting information and content on Facebook and Twitter institutional web pages?

Participant 8: So, I guess the way I get my information is through a few different channels. Our web team comes up with a lot of stories on members of the community like faculty and staff, mostly faculty, alumni, and students of course. There is an area on our website called "our stories" where they upload those stories and so sometimes, I'll pull content from there. We also have a [redacted] connection which is a weekly e-newsletter that goes out to 30,000 people or something like that. And like there is five stories in there that revolve around people in our community and so forth.

Participant 8: My job also now, which it didn't initially set out that way but the way that social media just kind of evolved, is creating video a lot more. So, I'll go out and kind of create random videos and sometimes I'll kind of create more things. We had a video series called My [redacted] experience. So, I shot a lot of those videos, it involved students. It's just showcasing the different types of[redacted] experiences that students have here.

Question 7 & 8: Where do employees/participants create, post, and consume content for Facebook and Twitter?

Participant 8: I work 8:30–4:30 and I try and keep it within those hours. So yeah, it's rare that I'm working on the weekend unless something really important comes up and the director texts me. Yes, primarily like 9–5 when I'm creating content unless there is an event.

Question 9 & 10: When do employees/participants expect to receive a response once a message is posted on Facebook and Twitter?

Participant 8: It's usually depending on what it is. We usually get a pretty immediate response. The folks following us on Twitter, they're just really interested, and they love us. Yes. They usually retweet or sometimes may reply to a tweet or something within the first hour or so. I would say probably that time frame is most of our engagement.

Question 11 & 12: What are your overall expectations for using Facebook and Twitter?

Participant 8: Well, maybe the expectations with our social media channels and I don't know if this is the case for the other institutions you may come across in your research. But for our different social channels there are very specific audiences, concentrated audiences. For Facebook, it's mostly alumni. For Twitter, it's a mix of students and alumni, friends and people who are just interested in what [redacted] is doing. Then Instagram, which isn't part [of your] research is primarily students and prospective students and young alumni. Which kind of speaks to the folks who are on those channels, in general, I guess. So as far as expectations go, I mean engagement. I know what I like to post on Facebook and Twitter. For example, if I post about an alum who's doing something great, I know it's going to get probably a lot of engagement as opposed to like an event. We don't post mini fliers on Facebook because it can get oversaturated and then people just really aren't interested in events. Then on Twitter, it just kind of like, not a free for all but it's just you know, I can post more things. If there is an event going on, I'll be more likely to post it on Twitter because it just moves. It's just the nature of Twitter.

Question 13, 14, & 15: What is your format for constructing a post on Facebook and Twitter? What are the textual and visual requirements? Any formatting or linguistic requirements?

Participant 8: So, we use AP style in general and then we have a [redacted] style. [Redacted] style guide thing that I never utilized. We always capitalize the B in black and we just like to do things that nobody else does. And like I mentioned, a photo in every post.

Question 16 & 17: Do you think Facebook and Twitter are efficient web pages for higher education?

Participant 8: Absolutely they are. I mean social media is where it's at obviously. And I think it's just a very high visibility opportunity because people are there and I just, like for instance, I've created a short little 45 second video at the beginning of the semester in January and like no one talking. I just asked students to write down on a white board some goals that they had for 2019. And I mean the video reached one hundred ninety-six thousand people and it just got crazy engagement. I mean there's would have been no other way to get that type of engagement like through the website or you know, any other medium that we have control over. Absolutely yes. Social media is definitely necessary for higher education institutions.

Question 18: Do you have any closing comments you wish to mention before the interview ends?

Participant 8: No.

Interview Transcript—Participant 9

Question 1 & 2: What is your purpose (goal and objectives) for employees using Facebook and Twitter in higher education?

Participant 9: We have a small team, but we have multiple goals. So, one would be to engage our greater community and that would be a community of current students, alumni, faculty, staff, and then donors. And of course, the community that surrounds our campus. The second goal would be to raise the stature of our institution worldwide and to promote our academic and athletic programming.

Question 3 & 4: What type of content do employees post on Facebook and Twitter institutional pages?

Participant 9: We actually tend to post similar content to both. I would say our Twitter account is used for the day-to-day activities across campus so that would be promoting events and sharing academic research. We have a blog network, so we share a lot of our academic blogs on Twitter. And then of course athletic programming. On Facebook, it's a lot more academic focused so stories of research and scholarship; stories about our alumni successes and then select blog content as well.

Question 5: Who are the participants posting information and content on Facebook and Twitter institutional web pages?

Participant 9: Sure. On Facebook and Twitter, it is me and I work for the Office of Public Affairs and Marketing. We also utilize an Instagram account in which I actually empower students to help with.

Question 6: How would you describe your roles and responsibilities for posting information and content on Facebook and Twitter institutional web pages?

Participant 9: My daily tasks are monitoring conversations and mentions and those sorts of things. Looking at our calendar, and we do use some sort of an editorial calendar, and so looking at any content that's coming up for the following couple weeks that we need to be starting to talk about that we're engaging audiences on and then responding to conversations that others are having about the institution.

Question 7 & 8: Where do employees/participants create, post, and consume content for Facebook and Twitter?

Participant 9: I have a regular eight to five working hours. I would say most nights I'm working an additional hour at home on social media. Then on the weekends anywhere probably on average two to three hours a weekend.

Question 9 & 10: When do employees/participants expect to receive a response once a message is posted on Facebook and Twitter?

Participant 9: It really depends on the topic. I would say almost instantaneous. I would expect it at least within an hour.

Question 11 & 12: What are your overall expectations for using Facebook and Twitter?

Participant 9: So, my overall expectations would be again to build engagement with our constituents and our community. And then of course we measure conversions for different events that we have by attendance or the number of forms submissions somebody returns or that an event returns rather or even the number of applicants that we might receive for admission.

Question 13, 14, & 15: What is your format for constructing a post on Facebook and Twitter? What are the textual and visual requirements? Any formatting or linguistic requirements?

Participant 9: I do not use any linguistic format for that actually. We know that we have standard hashtags that we try to incorporate, and they mean different things. I do try to mention when we have faculty who are active Twitter users or Facebook users or there are departmental pages [Facebook or Twitter accounts], we will try to incorporate their handles and mention them as well. But those are probably the only standards for composing content that I would use, other than making sure we include a link or a photograph when we have one or a video.

Question 16 & 17: Do you think Facebook and Twitter are efficient web pages for higher education?

Participant 9: Not without a third-party tool. I utilize Hootsuite for scheduling content and also tagging content. Tagging content helps me keep track of different metrics.

Question 18: Do you have any closing comments you wish to mention before the interview ends?

Participant 9: I don't think so. The one frustration I think I have that other folks working in Higher Ed may also have is when conversations turn offensive or borderline or cross the line. Like on Twitter, there is really nothing that you can do to make that go away and I don't mean like saying something that you disagree with but borderline racist and hate speech. Twitter does an OK job as a community. Of course, we're trying to protect students and also promote free thinking. For example, I tweeted about something this week and somebody commented with a racist statement. And there's nothing that I can do, and they tagged a handful of students in it. I wish that there was some way to remedy that but there's not.

Interview Transcript—Participant 10

Question 1 & 2: What is your purpose (goal and objectives) for employees using Facebook and Twitter in higher education?

Participant 10: I think overall we're trying to reach our multiple audiences and kind of keep them up to date on things that is happening around the college. And I think it's a good way to engage alums, parents, perspective students and all of our core audiences. So, we mostly use Facebook to promote stories that we have written on the website to increase traffic. We'll pay for a boosted post [ad] to increase that circulation.

Question 3 & 4: What type of content do employees post on Facebook and Twitter institutional pages?

Participant 10: We are posting links to stories on the website, multimedia content so photos taken and videos that are created by our team. Here we work with a lot of student workers that help with social media stuff. We have 3–4 students that will do a video about a certain program on campus or research that a professor is doing. We have a series of like quick take interviews which is just kind of short two-minute video with a professor talking about their research, what they love about working at the college or favorite class that they teach; things like that. We also use Twitter especially for promoting events that are happening on campus, lectures, speakers that are coming, all of our students symposiums which are pretty frequent especially during this spring semester.

Question 5: Who are the participants posting information and content on Facebook and Twitter institutional web pages?

Participant 10: I mean my role is Web Content and Social Media Manager. I'm kind of in charge of our overall social strategy. On Twitter it's mostly me posting.

I do have a student worker that does help write tweet and schedule things within TweetDeck. I usually work with him once or twice a week for a couple of assignments and go over everything before they actually post. From when they're scheduled, making some slight adjustments, to the style and stuff like that. On Facebook, we do have I think four or five different people within my office that are administrators. I'm doing most of the posting, but a few other people help out posting stuff. My boss who's the Director of New Media, our overall boss who's kind of VP of Marketing Communications. So, they have access to make changes to the page, respond to comments and posts on the page as well. I probably do 80 percent of actual postings, but most other people do have access.

Question 6: How would you describe your roles and responsibilities for posting information and content on Facebook and Twitter institutional web pages?

Participant 10: My role is pretty interesting. I did not start off doing the social media when I was hired here at the college and then just my role overall involving social media has changed a lot in the three years I've been doing it. I was brought on to basically manage web content. So, the home page of [redacted] website is kind of my main domain. I kind of write, edit, and assign the feature stories that are on the slider on the top of the website. Just kind of give a big picture overview of things that students are doing. Highlights of the school stories from our alumni magazine audiences. The home page really focuses on perspective students, that's we're trying to reach. The social media was originally done by the Director of PR, and it was mostly just taking things from the website and posting them directly to Twitter and Facebook. She left that position a little over three years ago. So, the social kind of got integrated into my role when it kind of made sense as I was kind of being the curator of web content. I was kind of engaging with social stuff anyway and doing a lot of our prospective student-centered stories and so we kind of shifted our social strategy particularly to a perspective student outreach with a lot of Instagram and Snapchat which I know isn't part of your dissertation but I kind of have folded that into my work as well. So, I do that and then the other part of my day is I also manage the content management system that we use to run the website. So, I do trainings and you know fix broken links, help departments, Biology Department, English Department; update, redesign their pages, add YouTube videos we created and embed them in their home pages. So that's basically most of my day. But social media is kind of just like technically a third of my job responsibilities. It ends up taking up a lot of time, a lot more time but I do kind of enjoy doing that. So that's why we do have some help even though I am in charge, I'm not the only person that is responding to everything.

Question 7 & 8: Where do employees/participants create, post, and consume content for Facebook and Twitter?

Participant 10: Good question. I mean most of my actual posting is done 9–5 when I'm on campus. Most days I work around a 40-hour work week actually in the office. As you probably know being involved with social is, could be a 24/7 thing even though I rarely post something on the weekend unless we have breaking news. We have tweets and Facebook posts that are scheduled earlier during the week, they come up on the weekend and there's obviously comments and things that come up. Things that students might post on Twitter and then we see it. Take a screenshot and delete it later and we have to deal with that. So, when I'm not in the office; kind of at home, at night on the weekends. You know, checking in on our pages making sure everything is OK. I get notifications on my phone if there's a comment on Facebook. I receive notifications on Twitter directly to my phone, I just check it out to make sure if I need to address it.

Question 9 & 10: When do employees/participants expect to receive a response once a message is posted on Facebook and Twitter?

Participant 10: That's a good question. I mean with Facebook it changed so much in just five years. Unfortunately, we have to buy in, if that's a story we really want to get maximum reach, we have to put money behind it. So, kind of depending on what the particular audience is, we have to promote or boost a lot of our posts either to people already following our page or kind of you know, using keyword targeting. If it's a story about an English professor, you know trying to target to people interested in literature and writing and stuff within [redacted]. So, most stories that we want to get out, we do put a little bit of money behind and that's definitely different than when I started three years ago. I was kind of rarely doing that but we kind of needed to get eyeballs on our content. Put a little bit of money behind it with Facebook advertising stuff. So, we don't get a ton of comments on a lot of our stuff. Unless it's mostly positive. Occasionally there'll be something relatively controversial which will bring out trolls. Usually, it's just a cool story. Thanks for letting us know or something along those lines.

Question 11 & 12: What are your overall expectations for using Facebook and Twitter?

Participant 10: I think the expectation is just to increase awareness about the college, keep all of our audiences informed on what's going on and then kind of you know get the word out to prospective students in terms of student recruitment and kind of actively courting them and their families and keeping them updated on the college.

Question 13, 14, & 15: What is your format for constructing a post on Facebook and Twitter? What are the textual and visual requirements? Any formatting or linguistic requirements?

Participant 10: Yeah, I mean we always want to have a photo to increase engagement. So, I mean that's something that I often come across particularly with Twitter, if I have someone who wants to help me or reach out to me to help promote an event on campus. There always has to be an image to go with that because I work in Public Affairs and Communications office, we have a database of photos or photo shoots that goes back years and years that I can bring up if we don't have a poster/image of the speaker. I usually will crop an image in Photoshop to get it to the dimensions, you know 10 x 24 range. That's the preferred form on Twitter. Yeah, we always try to post something that has an image with it to increase engagement. Every once in a while, there's a piece of news or something that doesn't have that. For the most part, we do try to get an image to help bring people to the story.

Question 16 & 17: Do you think Facebook and Twitter are efficient web pages for higher education?

Participant 10: That's a good question. I think particularly the Facebook pages that are class pages has been a really effective way for us to communicate with our student body and particularly communicate with our potential students too. One cool thing about these closed Facebook groups is we see a ton of engagement during the field season. So, from the end of March when decisions go out to that May when all of our regular applicants have to make that decision. We see this really fun couple of weeks when we send out invitations every day, there's 20 new people or more joining the group and kind of introducing themselves. And it's funny to see over the years how it kind of evolved almost like this standard post where they're saying their name, what they're interested in, bands that they like, including three or four pictures of themselves, always linking to their Instagram or Snapchat. Like almost 100 percent of the time. And then we see these students kind of organizing and talking about reasons why they're interested in [redacted] even if it's not their top choice or they don't end up going there. Then, what they liked when they visited a certain class that they sat in on and even arranging meet ups in other cities. Last year a group of 10 or 12 college students that were from the [redacted] all got together and met even though they had never met on campus. They all met up in the [redacted] and hung out on the weekend meeting through the Facebook group. So, I think it's been a really effective way for us to work with those incoming students to kind of help our numbers on Facebook.

Question 18: Do you have any closing comments you wish to mention before the interview ends?

Participant 10: It's kind of just always adapting. One thing I struggle with is to kind of stay up on trends and stay ahead of the curve, a little bit in terms of Facebook advertising stuff. We have kind of worked a lot in the past year for our giving campaigns using Facebook and using Facebook ads and actually uploading a list of young alumni or something that we're trying to reach out to. So that has been relatively successful but also a little bit of kind of reaching new territory. Overall social media at the college is a new thing, kind of a hard sell to explain, at least explaining the importance of it to some of our higher administration. Something that I am constantly working on and evolving.

Bibliography

Afros, Elena and Catherine F. Schryer. "The genre of syllabus in higher education." *Journal of English for Academic Purposes* 8, no. 3 (2009): 224–233.

Andersen, Jack. *Genre Theory in Information Studies*. Bingley: Emerald Group Publishing Limited, 2015. *eBook Collection (EBSCOhost), EBSCOhost.* Accessed February 3, 2018.

Anderson, Monica and Jingjing Jiang. "Teens, social media & technology." Last modified May 31, 2018. https://www.pewresearch.org/internet/2018/05/31/teens-social-media-technology-2018/.

Askehave, Inger and Anne Ellerup Nielsen. "Digital genres: A challenge to traditional genre theory." *Information Technology & People* 18, no. 2 (2005): 120–141.

Bakhtin, M. "The problem of speech genres." In V. W. McGee (Trans.), C. Emerson and M. Holquist (Eds.), *Speech Genres and Other Late Essays*, 60–102. Austin, TX: University of Texas Press, 1986.

Bal, Anjali S., Dhruv Grewal, Adam Mills, and Gary Ottley. "Engaging students with social media." *Journal of Marketing Education* 37, no. 3 (2015): 190–203.

Barnes, Nora Ganim and Ava M. Lescault. "Social media adoption soars as highered experiments and reevaluates its use of new communications tools." *Center for Marketing Research*. University of Massachusetts Dartmouth, North Dartmouth, MA, 2011.

Bauman, M. L. "The evolution of Internet genres." *Computers and Composition* 16, no. 2 (1999): 269–282.

Bazerman, C. *Shaping Written Knowledge. The Genre and Activity of the Experimental Article in Science*. Madison, WI: The University of Wisconsin Press, 1988.

Bazerman, C. "Systems of genres and the enactment of social intentions." In A. Freedman and P. Medway (Eds.), *Genre and the New Rhetoric,* 79–101. London: Taylor & Francis, 1994.

Bazerman, C. "Discursively structured activities." *Mind, Culture, and Activity* 4, no. 4 (1997): 296–308.

Bazerman, C. "Speech acts, genres and activity systems: How texts organize activity and people." In C. Bazerman and P. Prior (Eds.), *What Writing Does and How it Does It: An Introduction to Analyzing Texts and Textual Practices,* 309–339. Mahwah, NJ: Lawrence Erlbaum Associates, 2003.

Beghtol, Clare. "Classification theory." In *Encyclopedia of Library and Information Sciences Third Edition*, 958–973, CRC Press, 2009.

Berger, Arthur Asa. *Media and Communication Research Methods: An Introduction to Qualitative and Quantitative Approaches.* Sage Publications, 2015.

Berkenkotter, Carol and Thomas N. Huckin. *Genre Knowledge in Disciplinary Communication: Cognition/Culture/Power.* Routledge, 2016.

Bhatia, Vijay Kumar. *Analysing Genre: Use in Professional Settings.* Longman: Harlow, 1993.

Bicen, Huseyin and Nadire Cavus. "Social network sites usage habits of undergraduate students: Case study of Facebook." *Procedia-Social and Behavioral Sciences* 28 (2011): 943–947.

Boese, Elizabeth Sugar and Adele E. Howe. "Effects of web document evolution on genre classification." In *Proceedings of the 14th ACM International Conference on Information and Knowledge Management*, 632–639. ACM, 2005.

Bradley, Anthony. "Re: A new definition of social media [Web log message]." Last modified January 7, 2010. Accessed October 7, 2018. Retrieved from http://blogs.gartner.com/anthony_bradley/2010/01/07/a-new-definition-of-social-media/.

Bretan, Ivan, Johan Dewe, Anders Hallberg, Niklas Wolkert, and Jussi Karlgren. "Web-specific genre visualization." *World Conference on the WWW and Internet*, 1998.

Bucher, Elaine, Christian Fieseler, and Anne Suphan. "The stress potential of social media in the workplace." *Information, Communication & Society* 16, no. 10 (2013): 1639–1667.

Busch, Ryan. "Unlocking the voice of the university: The convergence of course, content, delivery, and marketing through social media." In *Teaching Arts and Science with the New Social Media*, 141–166. Emerald Group Publishing Limited, 2011.

Carr, Caleb T. and Rebecca A. Hayes. "Social media: Defining, developing, and divining." *Atlantic Journal of Communication* 23, no. 1 (2015): 46–65.

Cohen, James and Thomas Kenny. *Producing New and Digital Media: Your Guide to Savvy Use of the Web.* Routledge, 2015.

Confessore, Nicholas and Gabriel J. X. Dance. "Battling fake accounts, Twitter to slash millions of followers." Last modified July 11, 2018. https://www.nytimes.com/2018/07/11/technology/twitter-fake-followers.html.

Constine, Josh. "Instagram launches "stories," a Snapchatty feature for imperfect sharing." *TechCrunch*. Last modified August 2, 2016. Accessed February 11, 2018. https://techcrunch.com/2016/08/02/instagram-stories/.

Cooke, Samantha. "Social teaching: Student perspectives on the inclusion of social media in higher education." *Education and Information Technologies* 22, no. 1 (2017): 255–269.

Cormode, Graham and Balachander Krishnamurthy. "Key differences between Web 1.0 and Web 2.0." *First Monday* 13, no. 6 (2008).

Crowston, Kevin and Barbara H. Kwasnik. "A framework for creating a facetted classification for genres: Addressing issues of multidimensionality." In *System Sciences, 2004. Proceedings of the 37th Annual Hawaii International Conference on*, 9pp. IEEE, 2004.

Culnan, Mary J., Patrick J. McHugh, and Jesus I. Zubillaga. "How large US companies can use Twitter and other social media to gain business value." *MIS Quarterly Executive* 9, no. 4 (2010): 243–259.

Deal, Walter F. "Making the connection: Technological literacy and technology assessment." *The Technology Teacher* 61, no. 7 (4, 2002): 16. http://molloy.idm.oclc.org/login?url=https://search.proquest.com/docview/235304206?accountid=28076.

Dillon, Andrew and Barbara A. Gushrowski. "Genres and the web: Is the personal home page the first uniquely digital genre?" *Journal of the Association for Information Science and Technology* 51, no. 2 (2000): 202–205.

Duke, Nell K. and Victoria Purcell-Gates. "Genres at home and at school: Bridging the known to the new." *The Reading Teacher* 57, no. 1 (2003): 30–37. http://www.jstor.org/stable/20205313.

Dunlap, Joanna C. and Patrick R. Lowenthal. "Tweeting the night away: Using Twitter to enhance social presence." *Journal of Information Systems Education* 20, no. 2 (2009): 129–135.

Evans, Chris. "Twitter for teaching: Can social media be used to enhance the process of learning?" *British Journal of Educational Technology* 45, no. 5 (2014): 902–915.

Forsgren, Emma and Katriina Byström. "Multiple social media in the workplace: Contradictions and congruencies." *Information Systems Journal* 28, no. 3 (2018): 442–464.

Fusi, Federica and Mary K. Feeney. "Social Media in the workplace: Information exchange, productivity, or waste?" *The American Review of Public Administration* 48, no. 5 (2018): 395–412.

Gannes, Liz. "The short and illustrious history of Twitter #hashtags." *GigaOM*. Accessed February 15, 2012. Available at http://gigaom.com/2010/04/30/the-short-and-illustrioushistory-of-twitter-hashtags/, 2010.

Giddens, Anthony. *The Constitution of Society: Outline of the Theory of Structuration*. University of California Press, 1984.

Gikas, Joanne and Michael M. Grant. "Mobile computing devices in higher education: Student perspectives on learning with cellphones, smartphones & social media." *The Internet and Higher Education* 19 (2013): 18–26.

Goff, David. "A history of the social media industries." *The Social Media Industries* 16 (2013): 16–45.

Gorman, Gary Eugene, Peter Robert Clayton, Sydney J. Shep, and Adela Clayton. *Qualitative Research for the Information Professional: A Practical Handbook*. Facet Publishing, 2005.

Greenhow, Christine. "Online social networks and learning." *On the Horizon* 19, no. 1 (2011): 4–12.

Hesel, R. A. "The influence of social media sites on the college search process." *StudentPoll* (2013).

Hesel, R. A. and R. C. Williams. "Social networking sites and college-bound students." *StudentPoll* 7, no. 2 (2009): 1–8.

Hinton, Sam and Larissa Hjorth. *Understanding Social Media*. Sage, 2013.

Huang, Jeff J. S., Stephen J. H. Yang, Huang Yueh-Min, and Indy Y. T. Hsiao. "Social learning networks: Build mobile learning networks based on collaborative services." *Journal of Educational Technology & Society* 13, no. 3 (2010): 78.

Hyatt, David F. "'Yes, a very good point!': A critical genre analysis of a corpus of feedback commentaries on Master of Education assignments." *Teaching in Higher Education* 10, no. 3 (2005): 339–353.

Im, Hyun-Gyung, JoAnne Yates, and Wanda Orlikowski. "Temporal coordination through communication: Using genres in a virtual start-up organization." *Information Technology & People* 18, no. 2 (2005): 89–119.

Jensen, Jakob Linaa and Anne Scott Sørensen. "Nobody has 257 friends." *Nordicom Review* 34, no. 1 (2013): 49–62.

Jones, Christopher and Binhui Shao. *The Net Generation and Digital Natives: Implications for Higher Education*. York: Higher Education Academy, 2011.

Junco, Reynol, Greg Heiberger, and Eric Loken. "The effect of Twitter on college student engagement and grades." *Journal of Computer Assisted Learning* 27, no. 2 (2011): 119–132.

Kaplan, Andreas M. and Michael Haenlein. "Users of the world, unite! The challenges and opportunities of social media." *Business Horizons* 53, no. 1 (2010): 59–68.

Kent, Michael L. "Directions in social media for professionals and scholars." *The Sage Handbook of Public Relations* 2 (2010): 643–656.

Kent, Michael L. "Using social media dialogically: Public relations role in reviving democracy." *Public Relations Review* 39, no. 4 (2013): 337–345.

Khan, Tehmina, Michael Kend, and Susan Robertson. "Use of social media by university accounting students and its impact on learning outcomes." *Accounting Education* 25, no. 6 (2016): 534–567.

Knight, Charles G. and Linda K. Kaye. "'To tweet or not to tweet? A comparison of academics' and students' usage of Twitter in academic contexts." *Innovations in Education and Teaching International* 53, no. 2 (2016): 145–155.

Kwaśnik, Barbara H. and Kevin Crowston. "Introduction to the special issue: Genres of digital documents." *Information Technology & People* 18, no. 2 (2005): 76–88.

Lehtinen, Esa and Pekka Palli. "Conversational use of genres in managerial meetings." *Scandinavian Journal of Management* 27, no. 3 (2011): 287–296.

Leidner, Dorothy, Hope Koch, and Ester Gonzalez. "Assimilating generation Y IT new hires into USAA's workforce: The role of an enterprise 2.0 system." *MIS Quarterly Executive* 9, no. 4 (2010): 229–242.

Leonardi, Paul M., Marleen Huysman, and Charles Steinfield. "Enterprise social media: Definition, history, and prospects for the study of social technologies in organizations." *Journal of Computer-Mediated Communication* 19, no. 1 (2013): 1–19.

Lincoln, Yvonna S. and Egon G. Guba. *Naturalistic Inquiry*. Vol. 75. Sage, 1985.

Likert, Rensis. "A technique for the measurement of attitudes." *Archives of Psychology 140* (1932): 5–55.

Lüders, Marika, Lin Prøitz, and Terje Rasmussen. "Emerging personal media genres." *New Media & Society* 12, no. 6 (2010): 947–963.

Mancillas, Linda K. and Peter W. Brusoe. "Born digital: Integrating media technology in the political science classroom." *Journal of Political Science Education* 12, no. 4 (2016): 375–386.

Mäntymäki, Matti and Kai Riemer. "Enterprise social networking: A knowledge management perspective." *International Journal of Information Management* 36, no. 6 (2016): 1042–1052.

Marczyk, Geoffrey, David DeMatteo, and David Festinger. *Essentials of Research Design and Methodology*. John Wiley, 2017.

McAfee, Andrew P. "Enterprise 2.0: The dawn of emergent collaboration." *MIT Sloan Management Review* 47, no. 3 (2006): 21.

Meikle, Graham. *Social Media: Communication, Sharing and Visibility*. Routledge, 2016.

Miller, C. R. "Genre as social action." *Quarterly Journal of Speech* 70, no. 2 (1984): 151–167.

Minot, Stephen. *Three Genres: The Writing of Fiction, Poetry, and Drama*. Englewood Cliffs, NJ: Prentice-Hall, 1965.

Moore, Andrew. "Facebook and the liberal arts." *The Journal of General Education* 61, no. 3 (2012): 264–276.

Moran, Mike, Jeff Seaman, and Hester Tinti-Kane. "Teaching, learning, and sharing: How today's higher education faculty use social media." *Babson Survey Research Group* (2011).

Morse, Robert, Eric Brooks, and Matt Mason. "How U.S. news calculated the 2010 best colleges rankings." Last modified September 9, 2018. https://www.usnews.com/education/best-colleges/articles/how-us-news-calculated-the-rankings.

Murthy, Dhiraj. *Twitter: Social Communication in the Twitter Age*. Polity Press, 2013.

Nevzat, Raziye, Yilmaz Amca, Cem Tanova, and Hasan Amca. "Role of social media community in strengthening trust and loyalty for a university." *Computers in Human Behavior* 65 (2016): 550–559.

Orlikowski, W. J. and J. Yates. "Genre repertoire: The structuring of communicative practices in organizations." *Administrative Science Quarterly* 39, no. 4 (1994): 541–574.

Paine, Katie Delahaye. *Measure What Matters: Online Tools for Understanding Customers, Social Media, Engagement, and Key Relationships*. John Wiley & Sons, 2011.

Pang, Bo and Lillian Lee. "Opinion mining and sentiment analysis." *Foundations and Trends in Information Retrieval* 2, no. 1–2 (2008): 1–135.

Payant, Caroline and Eliana Hirano. "Recurring topics in English language teachers' written teaching philosophy statements." *TESL Canada Journal* 35, no. 1 (2018): 29–51.

Peruta, Adam, William Ryan, and Robertson Engelsman. "Social media branding strategies for higher education: Comparing Facebook pages and web sites." *International Journal of Technology, Knowledge & Society* 9, no. 1 (2013): 11–23.

Peruta, Adam and Alison B. Shields. "Social media in higher education: Understanding how colleges and universities use Facebook." *Journal of Marketing for Higher Education* 27, no. 1 (2017): 131–143.

Russo, Angelina, Jerry Watkins, Lynda Kelly, and Sebastian Chan. "Participatory communication with social media." *Curator: The Museum Journal* 51, no. 1 (2008): 21–31.

Samuels, Helen Willa. *Varsity Letters: Documenting Modern Colleges and Universities*. Scarecrow Press, 1998.

Sandlin, Jean Kelso and Edlyn Vallejo Peña. "Building authenticity in social media tools to recruit postsecondary students." *Innovative Higher Education* 39, no. 4 (2014): 333–346.

Santini, Marina. "Characterizing genres of web pages: Genre hybridism and individualization." In *System Sciences, 2007. HICSS 2007. 40th Annual Hawaii International Conference on Waikoloa, HI*, 71–71. IEEE, 2007.

Schroeder, Harold M. "Social media in business strategy: The learning and development implications." *Development and Learning in Organizations: An International Journal* 28, no. 6 (2014): 12–15.

Sessa, Whitney L. "Targeting millennials social media strategies within higher education." *College and University* 90, no. 1 (2014): 2–11.

Shepherd, Michael and Carolyn Watters. "The evolution of cybergenres." In *System Sciences, 1998, Proceedings of the Thirty-First Hawaii International Conference on Kohala Coast, HI*, vol. 2, 97–109. IEEE, 1998.

Shepherd, M. and C. Watters. "The functionality attribute of cybergenres." In *Systems Sciences, 1999. HICSS-32. Proceedings of the 32nd Annual Hawaii International Conference on*, Maui, HI, 9pp. IEEE, 1999, January.

Smith, Aaron and Monica Anderson. "Social media use in 2018." Last modified March 1, 2018. http://www.pewinternet.org/2018/03/01/social-media-use-in-2018/.

Smith, Dorothy E. "The social construction of documentary reality." *Sociological Inquiry* 44, no. 4 (1974): 257–268.

Smith, Dorothy E. "Textually mediated social-organization." *International Social Science Journal* 36, no. 1 (1984): 59–75.

Swales, John. *Genre Analysis: English in Academic and Research Settings*. Cambridge University Press, 1990.

Tereszkiewicz, Anna. *Genre Analysis of Online Encyclopedias: The Case of Wikipedia*. Wydawnictwo UJ, 2013.

Thomas, Kristopher J. and Mesut Akdere. "Social media as collaborative media in workplace learning." *Human Resource Development Review* 12, no. 3 (2013): 329–344.

U.S. News & World Report. "Best colleges rankings: National liberal arts colleges." *usnews.com*. Accessed September 14, 2018. https://www.usnews.com/best-colleges/rankings/national-liberal-arts-colleges.

Veletsianos, George and Royce Kimmons. "Scholars and faculty members' lived experiences in online social networks." *The Internet and Higher Education* 16 (2013): 43–50.

Wenger, Etienne. *Communities of Practice: Learning, Meaning, and Identity*. Cambridge University Press, 1998.

Williams Marie and Kevin Crowston. "Reproduced and emergent genres of communication on the World Wide Web." *The Information Society* 16, no. 3 (2000): 201–215.

Yates, JoAnne. *Control through Communication: The Rise of System in American Management*. Baltimore, MD: Johns Hopkins University Press, 1989.

Yates, JoAnne, Wanda J. Orlikowski, and Kazuo Okamura. "Explicit and implicit structuring of genres in electronic communication: Reinforcement and change of social interaction." *Organization Science* 10, no. 1 (1999): 83–103.

Yates, JoAnne and Wanda Orlikowski. "Genre systems: Chronos and Kairos in communicative interaction." *The Rhetoric and Ideology of Genre* (2002): 103–121.

Yates, J. and W. J. Orlikowski. "Genres of organizational communication: A structurational approach to studying communication and media." *Academy of Management Review* 17, no. 2 (1992): 299–326.

Yates, JoAnne, Wanda J. Orlikowski, and Anne Jackson. "The six key dimensions of understanding media." *MIT Sloan Management Review* 49, no. 2 (2008): 63–69.

Yoshioka, Takeshi, George Herman, JoAnne Yates, and Wanda Orlikowski. "Genre taxonomy: A knowledge repository of communicative actions." *ACM Transactions on Information Systems (TOIS)* 19, no. 4 (2001): 431–456.

Index

About the Author

Dr. Thomas Kenny is an assistant professor, chairperson, and director of the TV Studio for the Communications Department at Molloy University. He teaches courses in television production and studies, screenwriting, social media, journalism, and video editing. His research interests include serial television, media literacy, and emerging technologies. He holds a PhD in information studies from Long Island University.